I0800219

IMAGES
of America

KENT COUNTY

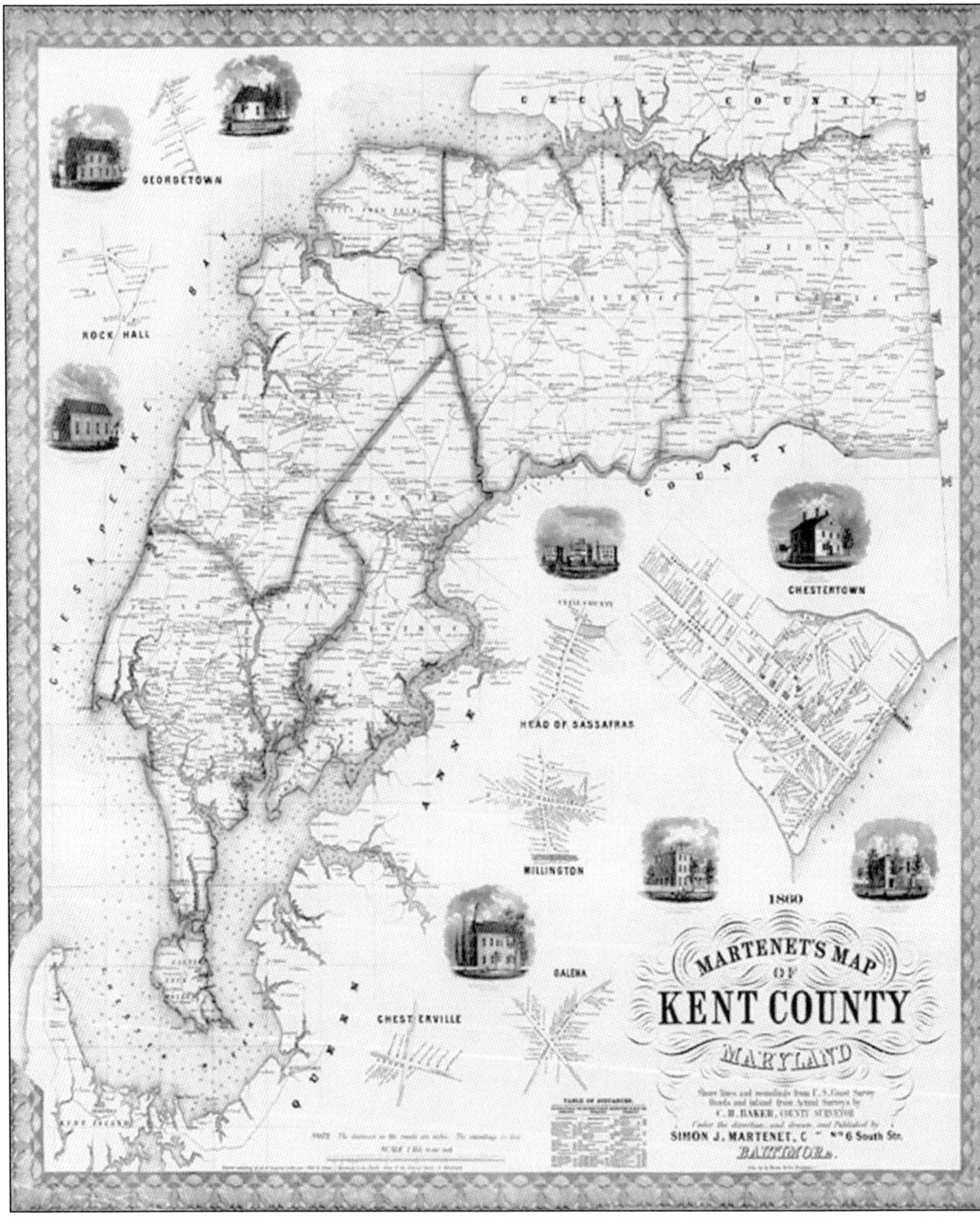

This cartographic image, entitled "Martenet's Map of Kent County, Maryland," was published in 1860. It provides a rare glimpse into the cultural and geographic landscapes of antebellum Kent County, as it is one of the last maps Simon Martenet made before the outbreak of the Civil War. The map was compiled from the original surveys of county surveyor Simon Martenet, and it is hand-colored with seven inset engravings of the following: A. Hoen, Amory and Market House, Protestant Episcopal Church, George Vickers House, Washington College, the county jail, Methodist Protestant Church, Methodist Episcopal Church, and the courthouse. These are some of the earliest surviving images of these Kent County landmarks.

IMAGES
of America

KENT COUNTY

Patricia Joan O. Horsey
and R. Jerry Keiser

ARCADIA
PUBLISHING

ISBN 978-0-7385-1839-8

Published by Arcadia Publishing
Charleston, South Carolina

Printed in the United States of America

Library of Congress Catalog Card Number: 2005923835

For all general information contact Arcadia Publishing at:
Telephone 843-853-2070
Fax 843-853-0044
E-mail sales@arcadiapublishing.com
For customer service and orders:
Toll-Free 1-888-313-2665

Visit us on the Internet at www.arcadiapublishing.com

Contents

ACKNOWLEDGMENTS

The authors are indebted to many people for sharing their information, family photographs, and personal collections to make this book possible. We also want to acknowledge the many who shared photographs and may not find them in this book. Space was limited, and many of the wonderful images had to be eliminated for this book. There may be a second volume, however, and we invite any readers to submit additional pictures.

Among those who made significant contributions are the following: Mary Kate O'Donnell, executive director of the Historical Society of Kent County, Inc., who so generously shared the society's collection for use in this book; the Historic American Buildings Survey (Library of Congress); Mr. and Mrs. Garfield Ashley; William F. (Bill) Bennett; William Betts and the Tolchester Beach Revisited Museum; William A. (Pat) Biddle; Jackie Bonwill Conley; Carolyn E. Cooper; Larry Crew, who was most generous with his Betterton collection; Ethel H. Cunningham; Judy J. Dagenais; John Eliason, who shared his personal collection of Eliason family photographs; Mr. and Mrs. Charles H. Gill, who shared their memorabilia; Mrs. James F. Greenwood; Kevin Hemstock, editor of the *Kent County News*; Catharine Wroth Hepbron Harris; Heidi Brown Hollomon; Hilda G. Hopkins; Elmer E. Horsey; Curtis Jacquette Sr.; Francis Lamb; Tracye Smith Landon; Maryland Massey; Robert R. Ramsey and the Finishing Touch; Carrie E. Schreiber and the Schreiber family; Louise Bonwill Skinner; Karen Somerville, who shared images from the collection of the African American Schoolhouse Museum; Scott O. Smith; Todd B. Smith; the Howard and Marion Strong families; Mrs. Robert H. Strong Sr.; Doris Jacquette Tyranski; Gloria Urban, director of the Kent County Public Library; Mrs. William B. Usilton; Anne B. Vansant; Austin Walmsley; the Maynard P. White family; Francis P. (Skip) Willits; the staff of the Kent County Public Library, including Beverley Blakeney, Karin Cowperthwait, Babs Danneberg, Liz Darrah, Joy Eliassen, Jeanne Geibel, Marianne Hickman, Sue Hughes Lindsay Lusby, Linda Nitsche, Jeffrey Phillips, Susan Reihl, Chris Roseberry, and Debe Voshell; mapsofthepast.com for use of the map of Kent County; librarians Robert Horvath, Robert Long, and Scotti Oliver of the Talbot County Free Library for the 1877 engravings of Kent County; and librarian David Dudek of Washington College's Miller Library. We would especially like to thank Jennifer, Jacob, and Evelyn Keiser for their enduring support during this project.

INTRODUCTION

On July 24, 1608, Capt. John Smith and 12 of his men boarded a shallop and started their second voyage of the summer into the Chesapeake Bay. Weather soon carried their boat past the Potomac River to its headwaters, where Captain Smith and his crew discovered the four tributary rivers that fed into the bay. Captain Smith entered one of those tributaries on what his men called the "Easterne Shore" of the bay. The tributary that Smith and his men entered was the Sassafras River, which Captain Smith named "Tockwough" after the Native Americans who lived in towns on the banks of the river. Capt. John Smith's 1612 *Map of Virginia* clearly shows Tockwough in what is today Kent County, Maryland.

Kent County, named for Kent County in England, was officially founded in the year 1642, about 34 years after John Smith discovered and explored its northern boundary. On Kent's southern boundary is the Chester River, a river that also meanders its way to the bay. On the banks of this river, the town of Newtown (later named Chestertown) was founded.

Chestertown was designated as the port of entry for the northern counties of Cecil, Kent, and Queen Anne's Counties. Founded in 1706, Chestertown is the largest town in Kent County and is the county seat of government. Chestertown is a quiet, quaint Colonial town that has maintained most of its 18th-century architecture and history, both of which are on display every Memorial Day weekend for the Chestertown Tea Party. This annual event commemorates the boarding of the brigantine *Geddes*, anchored in the Chester River, on May 23, 1774. A group of citizens tossed the *Geddes* cargo of tea into the Chester River in response to the closing of the Port of Boston.

In addition to dissenting against Great Britain's Colonial policies, Chestertown and Kent County contributed men, arms, and food to the Revolutionary War. Kent County was the most vital source on the Eastern Shore for armaments, and the county's farmers' and millers' war contributions are reasons the Eastern Shore has been referred as the "Bread Basket of the Revolution." Finally, Col. Tench Tilghman, George Washington's aide-de-camp, carried the news of Gen. Charles Cornwallis's surrender at Yorktown to end the Revolutionary War. Tilghman crossed the Chesapeake Bay by ferry, landing at Rock Hall, then galloped through Kent County toward the Congress at Philadelphia.

With the war finally over, the citizens of Kent County returned to their farms, mercantile affairs, and to the proper education of their young men. It was in Kent County, in the town of Chestertown, that Washington College was founded in the year 1782. Washington College has been a significant part of Kent County and the nation's history, as it was the first college founded in the United States of America. It was named for Pres. George Washington and was the only college to receive his "expressed consent" and monies donated to its founding. Throughout his life, Washington's connection with the school became a source of historical pride for county residents.

However, it did not take Britain long to forget its experiences with her former colonies and especially those colonists located in Kent County. After the British invaded and burned down the town of Georgetown in May 1813, except for the house belonging to Miss Kitty Knight, the Kent County militia quickly dispersed the British Regulars back into the Chesapeake Bay.

Kent County, its town, and its villages continued to play an important role in Maryland and United States history. Mason and Dixon would spend time surveying the boundary line between Maryland and Delaware, the Civil War would claim 400 of our citizens, thousands would come and play at our beaches at Betterton and Tolchester, and women would vote before the 19th Amendment even made it legal. It is our hope that this photographic narrative will provide a glimpse into the cultural landscape of Kent County and that you will discover, as did John Smith and others after him, that Kent County is a great place to visit and even a greater place to live and experience history in the making.

One

EARLY DAYS

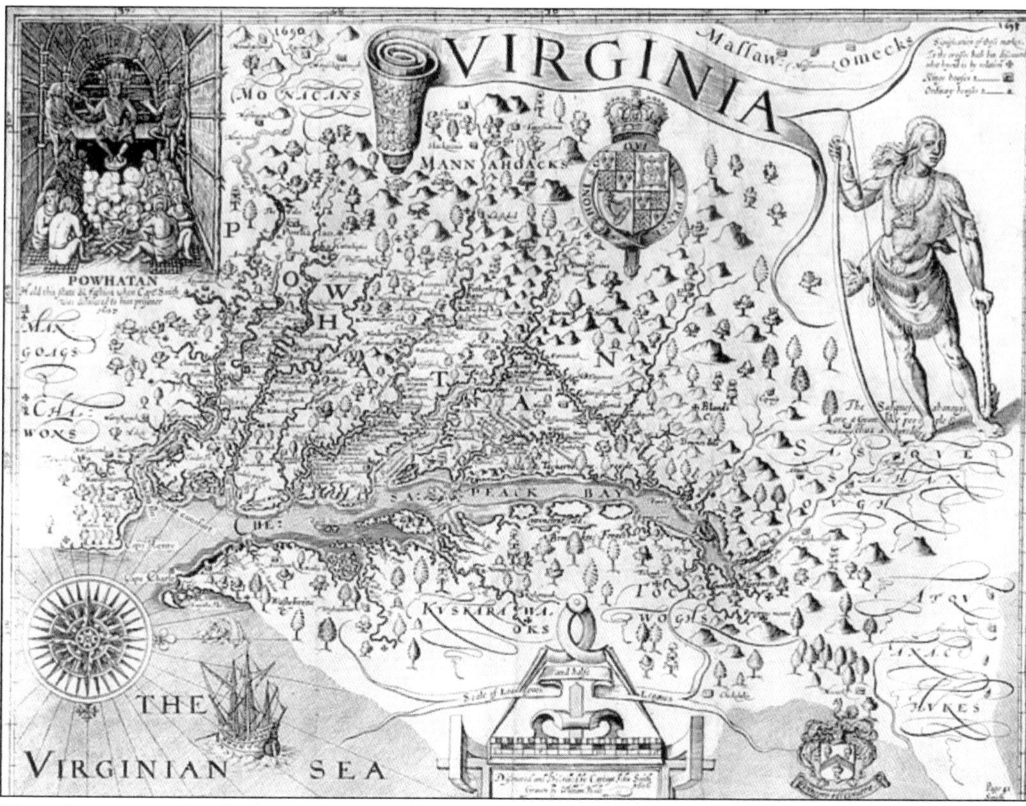

Kent County is clearly shown here in this image of Capt. John Smith's *Map of Virginia* from 1612. Smith mapped the Chesapeake Bay during the summer of 1608. He entered Kent County on the river named Tockwough, known today as the Sassafras. The Tockwough is clearly marked on this map.

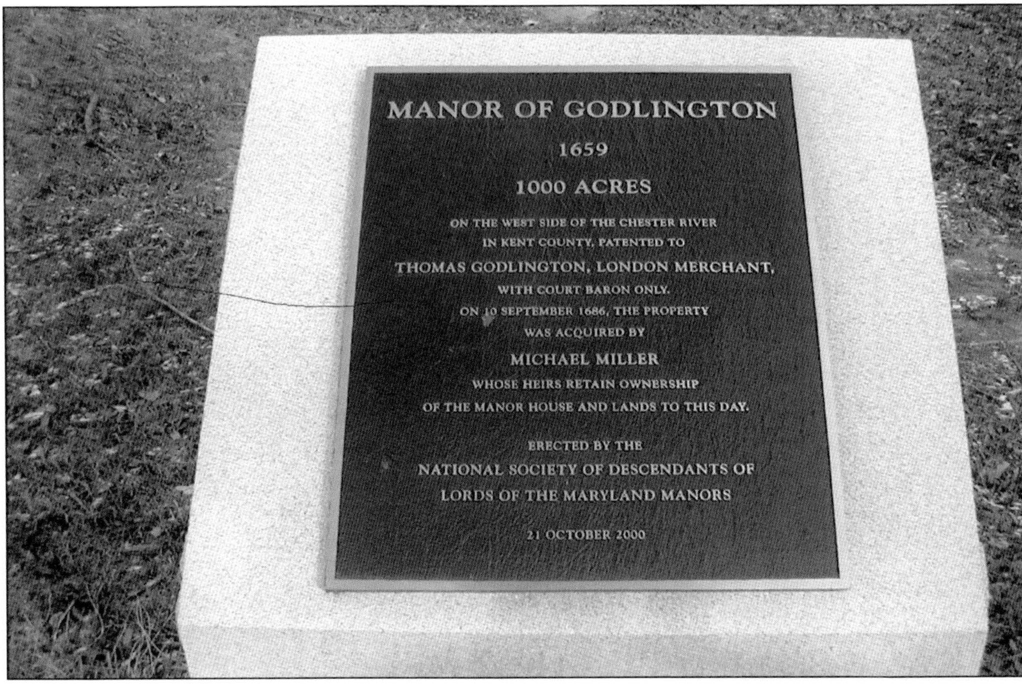

The 1,000-acre Manor of Godlington was patented with Court Baron Only (meaning the owner had only partial authority over his inhabitants) to Thomas Godlington, a London merchant, in 1659. On September 10, 1686, the property was acquired by Michael Miller, whose heirs retain ownership of the manor house and lands to this day. The National Society of the Descendants of Lords of the Maryland Manors erected a plaque on the property in 2000.

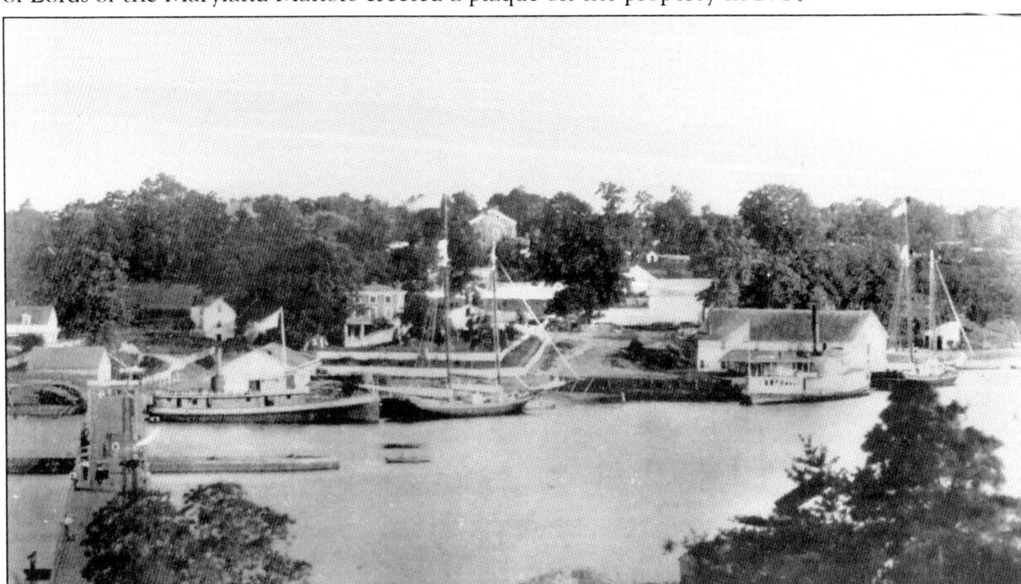

Unscathed by the British burning of Georgetown in 1814, the Kitty Knight House (top center) sits atop the Sassafras River bank overlooking the port of Georgetown. This 1877 photograph of Georgetown highlights the various types of ships that visited the harbor in the later part of the 19th century.

This photograph shows the large stone monument dedicated to the naming of the Sassafras River by Capt. John Smith. The Sassafras River was first called the Tockwough River by Captain Smith, who discovered and explored it between 1607 and 1609. He named it Tockwough after the tribe of Native Americans who inhabited its banks. The river's name was later changed to Sassafras, as Tockwough is the original Native Americans name for Sassafras, a root from which they made a form of bread.

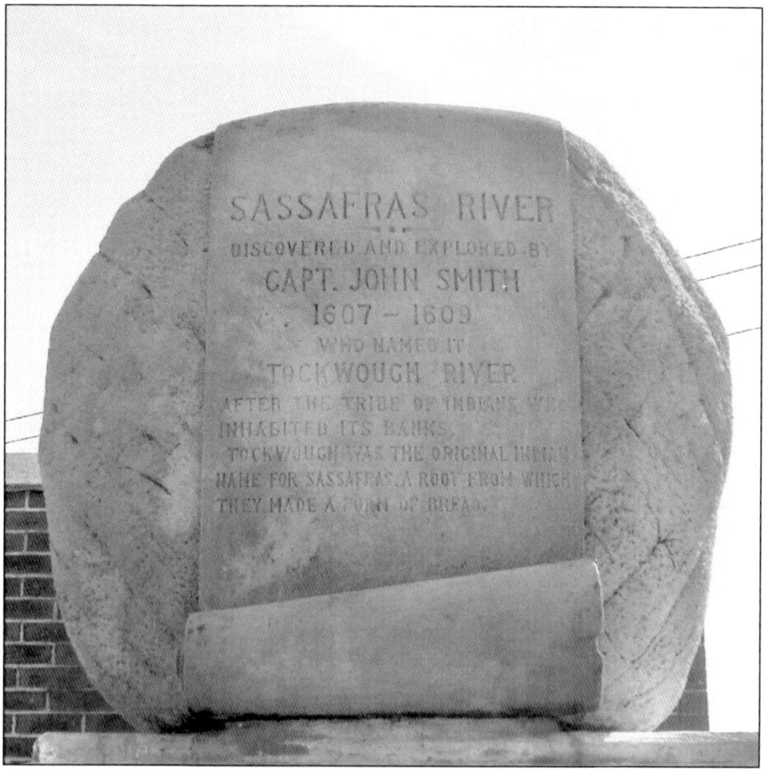

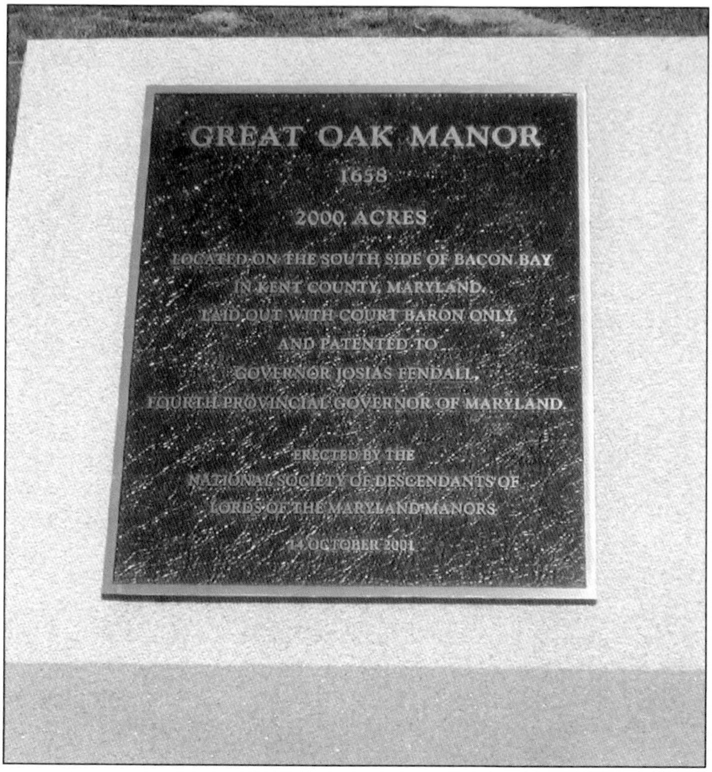

The Great Oak Manor plaque, shown here, was placed by the National Society of the Descendants of Lords of the Maryland Manors in 2001. It commemorates the 1658 patent of Great Oak Manor, which was situated on 2,000 acres on the south side of Bacon Bay. The patent was laid out with Court Baron Only and patented to Gov. Josias Fendall, the fourth provincial governor of Maryland.

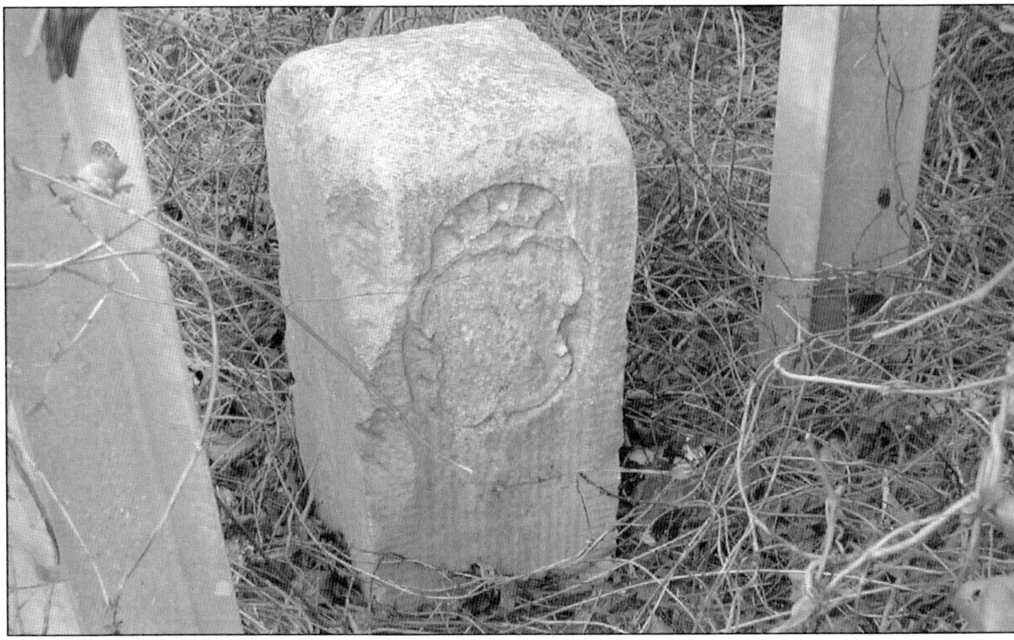

Renowned as the dividing line between free and slave states before the Civil War, the Mason-Dixon Line is arguably the most famous border in America. Charles Mason and Jeremiah Dixon started their survey, which created the Maryland-Delaware boundary, in 1763. The French and Indian War interrupted the survey, and they did not complete it until 1784. This weathered stone crown stone marker, shown here in a contemporary photograph, divides what is known as the "Tangent Line" that divides Kent County from Delaware.

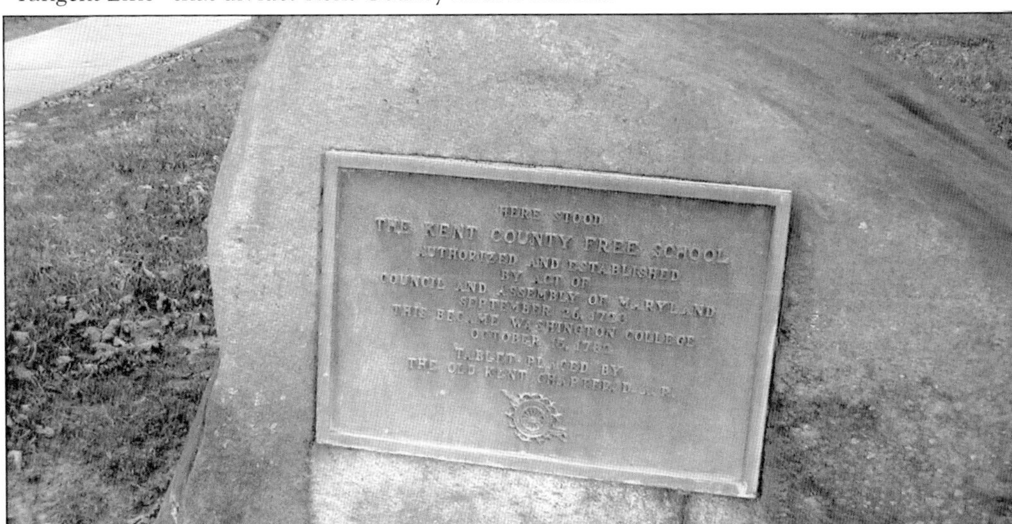

The Provincial Assembly of Maryland passed a bill authorizing the establishment of a free school in each Maryland county in 1723. This stone placard marks the location of the Kenty County Free School on Washington Avenue in Chestertown. In 1782, the Maryland General Assembly granted the school a charter, upgrading the school to college level, naming it Washington College, and making it the first chartered college in Maryland. The Old Kent Chapter of the Daughters of the American Revolution placed the placard to commemorate Kent County's educational heritage.

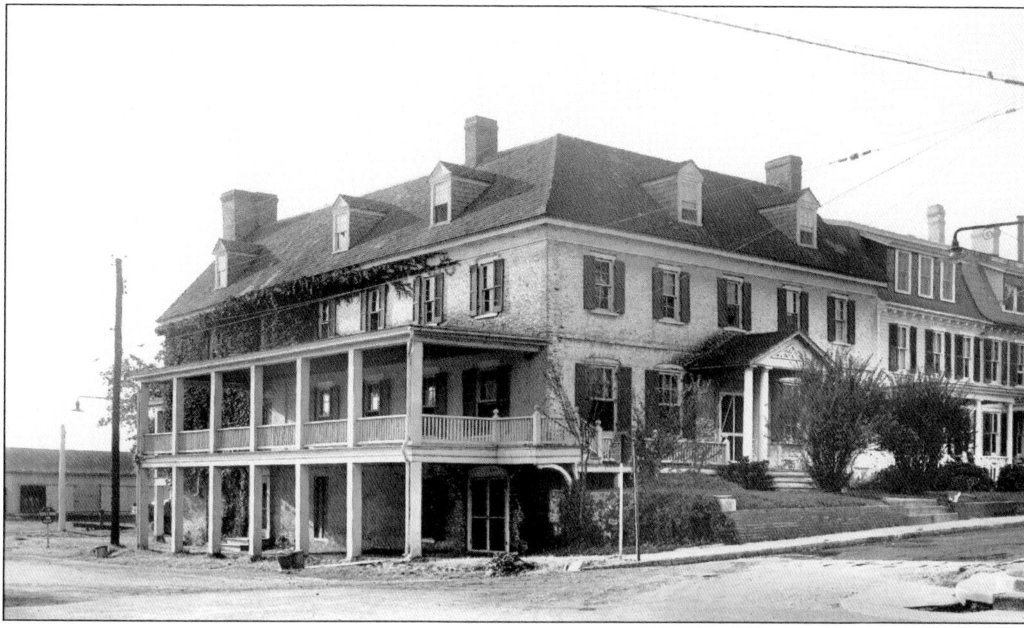

Merchant Samuel Massey constructed the Custom House, located along Chester Riverfront in Chestertown, in 1745. Thomas Ringgold IV acquired the property in 1749. Mr. Ringgold was an attorney with a variety of mercantile concerns and interests. He ran his business from the Custom House and earned five pounds per year from office space he rented to the district custom collector. In the late 19th century, Chestertown declined in trade and industry, and the Custom House was converted into contemporary apartments in 1923. The photograph here shows the Custom House in the 1930s when it was apartments. The building is now recognized on the National Register of Historic Places and is currently home to Washington College's C. V. Starr Center for the American Experience.

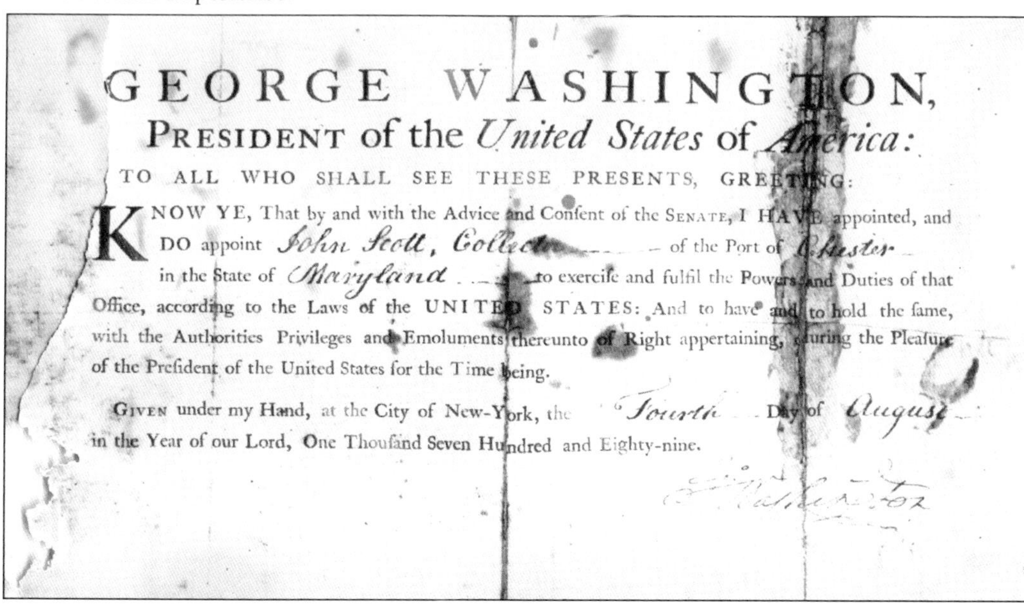

GEORGE WASHINGTON,

PRESIDENT of the *United States* of *America*:

TO ALL WHO SHALL SEE THESE PRESENTS, GREETING:

KNOW YE, That by and with the Advice and Confent of the SENATE, I HAVE appointed, and DO appoint *John Scott, Collector* of the Port of *Chester* in the State of *Maryland* to exercife and fulfil the Powers and Duties of that Office, according to the Laws of the UNITED STATES: And to have and to hold the fame, with the Authorities Privileges and Emoluments thereunto of Right appertaining, during the Pleafure of the Prefident of the United States for the Time being.

GIVEN under my Hand, at the City of New-York, the *Fourth* Day of *August* in the Year of our Lord, One Thoufand Seven Hundred and Eighty-nine.

GWashington

On August 4, 1789, Pres. George Washington, with the advice and consent of the United States Senate, appointed John Scott to the tax collector post for the port of Chester.

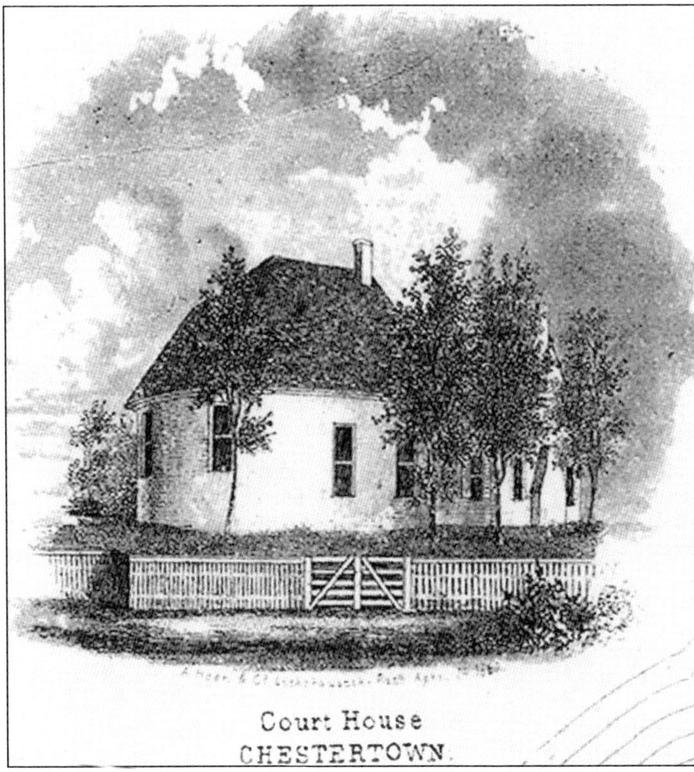

The original Kent County courthouse was built in Chestertown around the year 1707. An early plat of Chestertown shows an 18th-century apsidal-ended courthouse in the center of a large area of public ground, with Emmanuel Church in one corner and the churchyard cemetery using much of the rest. This image is from the April 24, 1860, engraving by A. Hoen of Baltimore. It originally appeared on Simon J. Martenet's 1860 *Map of Kent County*. Remains in the cemetery were moved to the Chester Cemetery and a Colonial Revival addition was attached to the rear in 1969. Ghosts have been reported in the local and national press ever since.

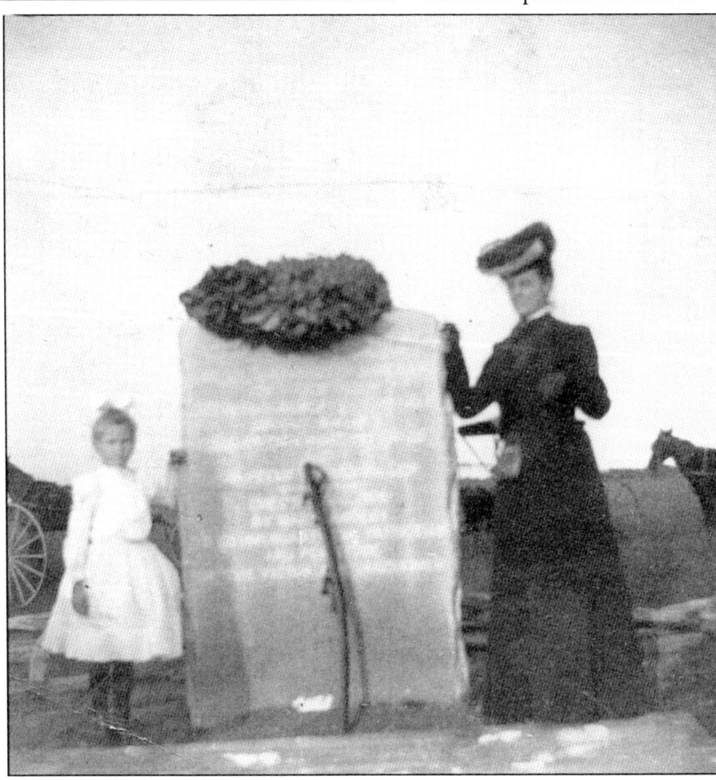

On October 18, 1902, ceremonies were held to unveil a granite monument commemorating the Battle of Caulk's Field near Tolchester in Kent County, Maryland. The monument was "Erected to commemorate the Patriotism and Fortitude of the Victor and the Vanquished." The notable battle took place near the farmhouse owned by Isaac Caulk. The British, commanded by Sir Peter Parker Baronet, and the Americans, commanded by Col. Philip Reed, met in engagement on this field on August 14, 1814. The British were defeated, and Sir Peter Parker was killed.

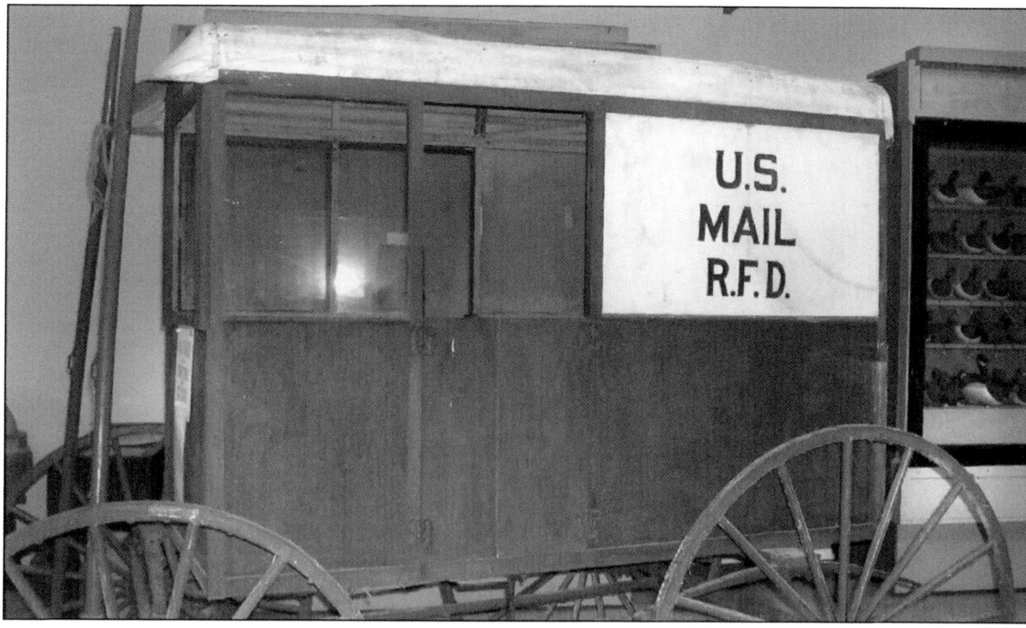

Kent Museum was organized in the 1960s to preserve Kent County's rural heritage. Local farming families have donated agricultural equipment and household items from the past. Over 200 items depict the life and livelihood of rural living. On display are antique tractors, horse-drawn wagons and sleds, and household gadgets that helped the farm wife with her chores. Shown above is the old Kent County Postal Wagon.

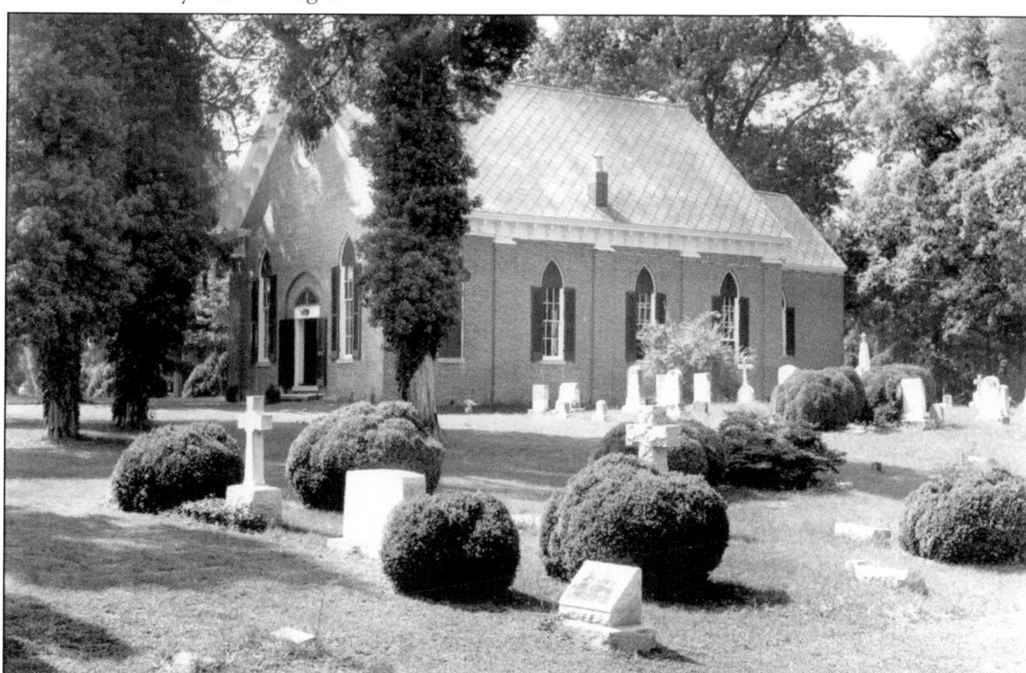

This photograph is of I. U. Christ Church, located in the village of Worton. The church is a 1860s Gothic Revival building. It is one of the many properties Kent County has listed on the National Register of Historic Places.

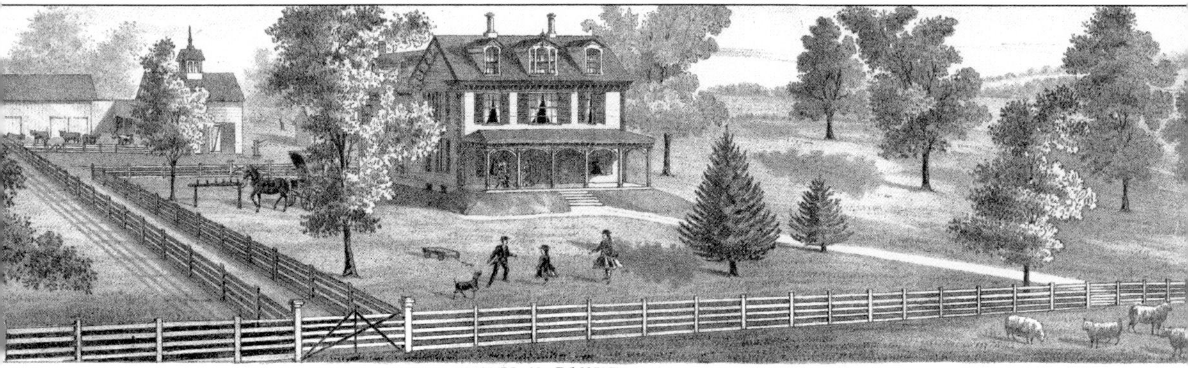

RESIDENCE OF JAMES H. BAKER, BAKERVILLE KENT CO. MD.

This 1877 engraving of the James H. Baker residence in the village of Bakerville was inset in the Kent County map of the time. It shows an aspect of the life of a mid-19th-century well-to-do farmer.

Two

CHESTERTOWN, SEAT OF GOVERNMENT

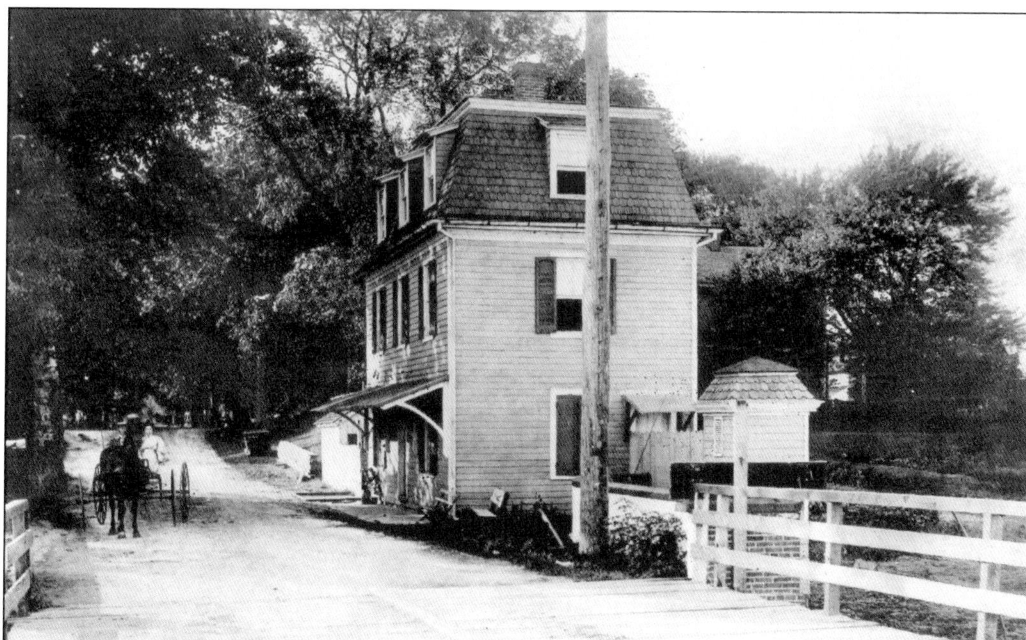

The Chester River Bridge was reportedly begun in 1802 by a committee of citizens from both Kent and Queen Anne's Counties. By 1821, the bridge was actually built, a toll was imposed, and a lottery was authorized to reimburse those who erected it by private subscriptions. The bridge burned and was rebuilt by lottery. In 1890, it was purchased by the two counties for $11,400, and the toll was lifted. The Maryland State Roads Commission took over the bridge in 1914. The old wooden bridge was replaced by a concrete bridge in 1929. The home at the end of the bridge on the Chestertown side is said to be that of author Gilbert Byron.

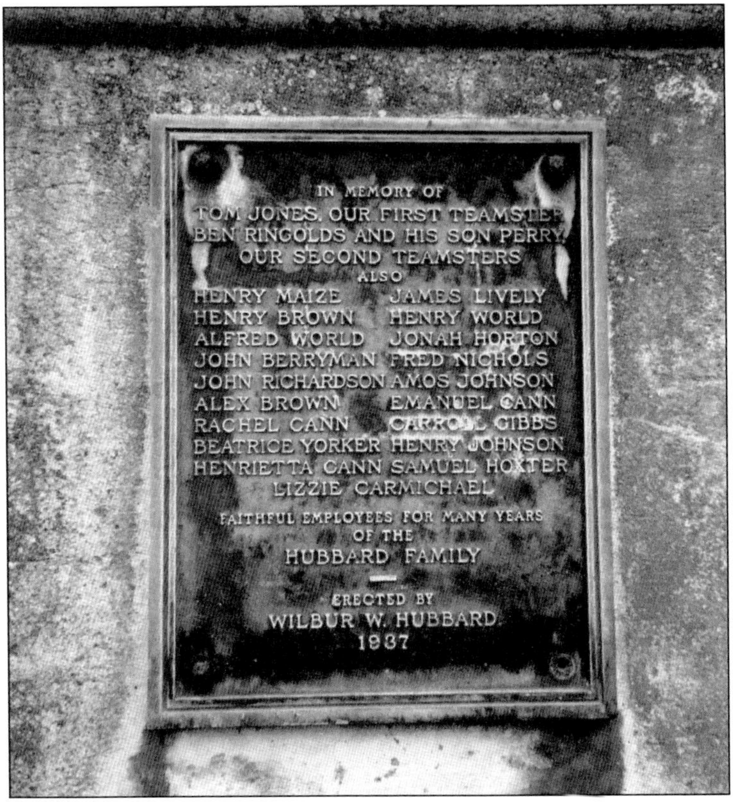

This monument reads: "In memory of Tom Jones, our first teamster; Ben Ringolds and his son Perry, our second teamsters. Also, Henry Maize, James Lively, Henry Brown, Henry World, Alfred World, Jonah Horton, John Berryman, Fred Nichols, John Richardson, Amos Johnson, Alex Brown, Emanuel Cann, Rachel Cann, Carroll Gibbs, Beatrice Yorker, Henry Johnson, Henrietta Cann, Samuel Hoxter, Lizzie Carmichael, faithful employees for many years of the Hubbard Family." It was erected in Chestertown by Wilbur W. Hubbard in 1937.

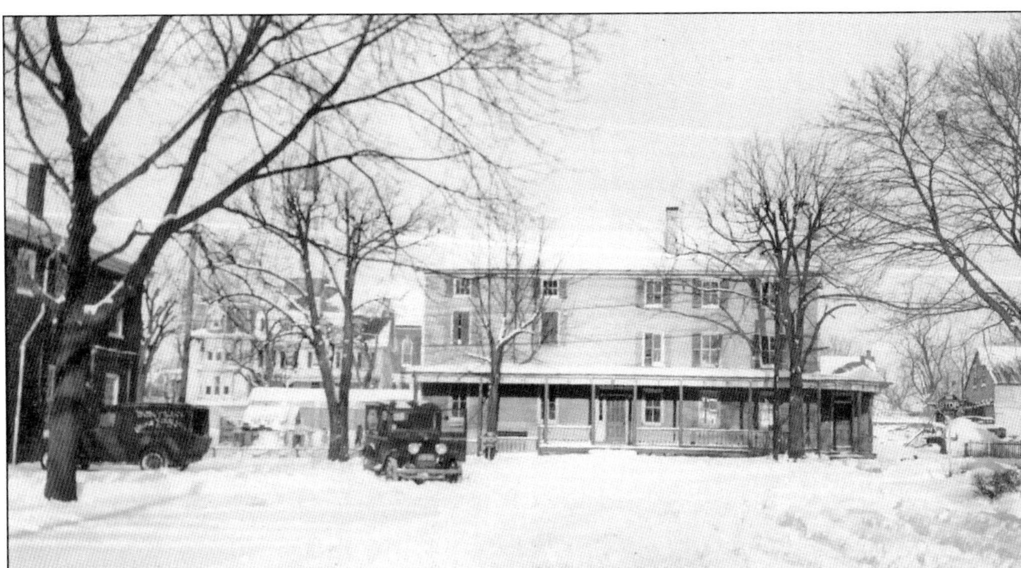

The Bibb's Inn was located on Spring Avenue in downtown Chestertown, where the present post office is now located. It was owned by Thomas W. Eliason and rented to Mr. and Mrs. Bibb, who ran it as an inn. It later became the residence of their son, John Bibb. Mr. Eliason sold it in the mid-1930s to the federal government for the site of a new post office.

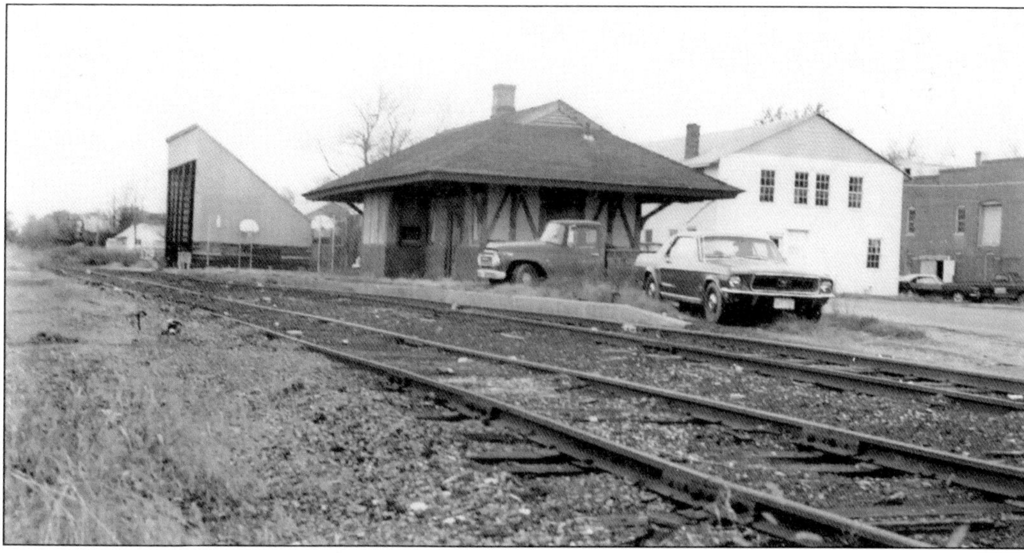

Construction on the Chestertown rail line began in 1869. It was originally called the Kent County Railroad. The Chestertown Railroad Station was built by the Pennsylvania Railroad between 1902 and 1903. From the late 19th century through World War I, much of Kent County's major crops of peaches, apples, and tomatoes were shipped through the Chestertown train station to the north. Coal, fertilizer, and raw materials for the basket factory located near the station in Chestertown were transported over this line. The Chestertown Railroad Station was moved about 44 feet to the north in 1981, parallel to and the same distance from the railroad tracks, so that Cross Street could be extended to Route 289.

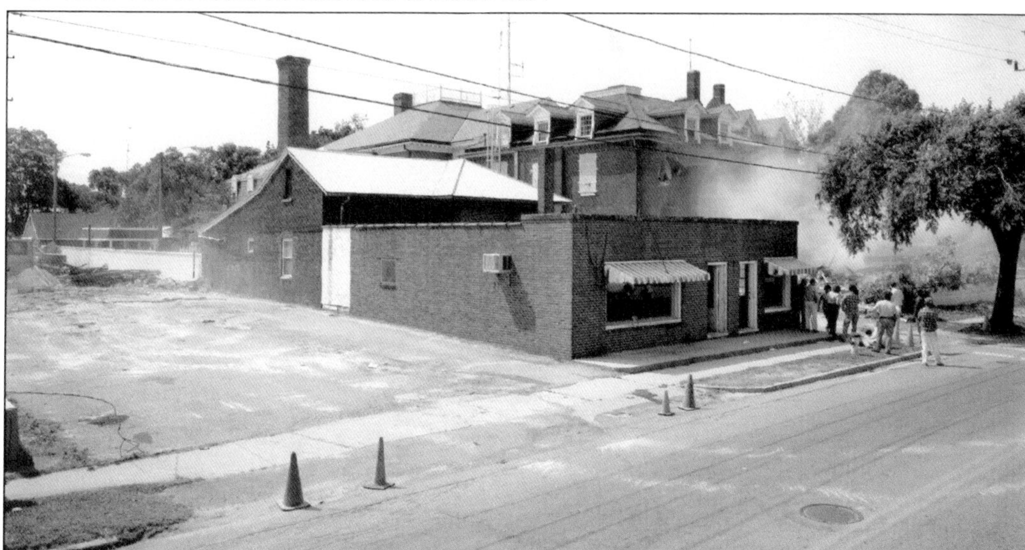

The former Kent County Liquor Dispensary building (now the parking lot for the Kent County courthouse) is shown facing Cross Street in downtown Chestertown. Beside it to the left is the rear of the old sheriff's stable, which was being used as the Kent County magistrate's court. The former Kent County jail can be seen as well as the current courthouse. The old sheriff's stable was moved in 1988 from this location to South Cross Street, where it was restored. It is now used as the headquarters for the Chestertown Police Department.

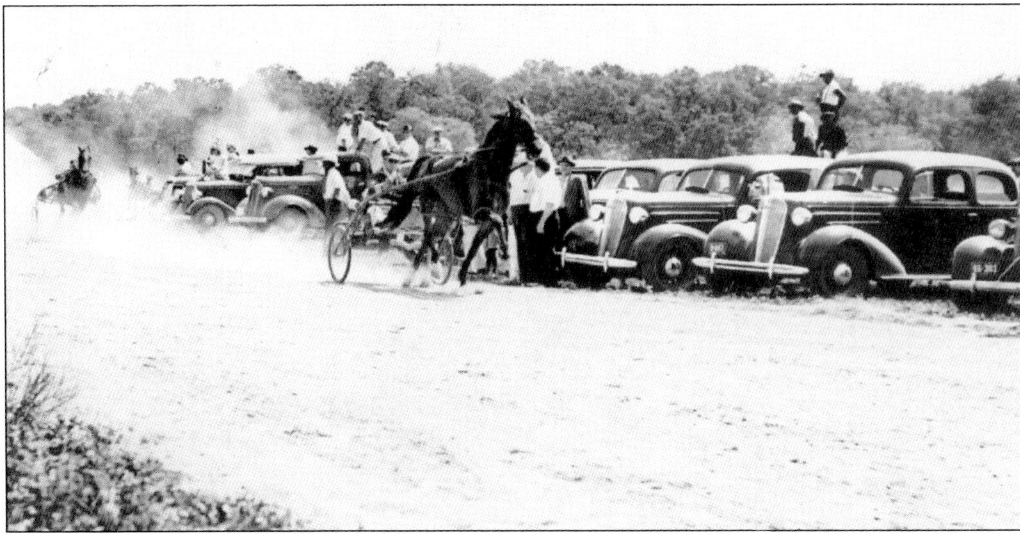

Chestertown Driving Park was the site of horse racing at the turn of the century. In later years it became known as Stepney Race Track, where harness horses trained on the half-mile track. The property is part of a 1,000-acre land grant known as Stepney Manor. The manor house and 85 acres of the original 1,000 acres were purchased in 1953 by Mr. and Mrs. Arthur Lusby, who improved the track and restored the manor house.

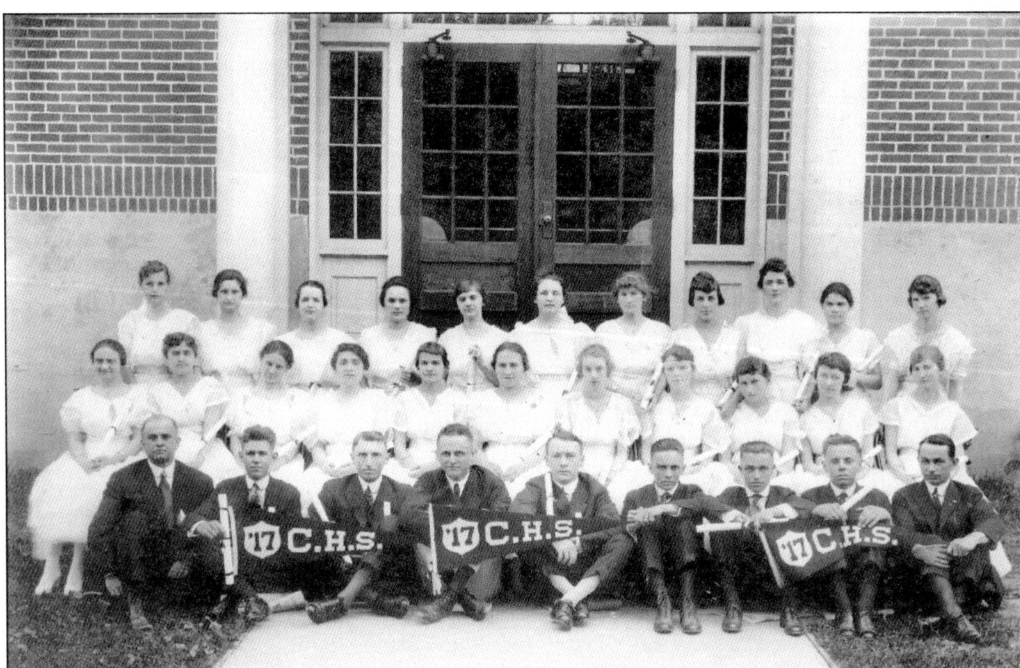

The Chestertown High School class of 1917 is shown on the front steps of the new high school, which was built in 1915. The cost was $3,700 for the lot and $16,800 for the building. A. M. Culp was the contractor and builder. Prof. Mark Creasy was the principal.

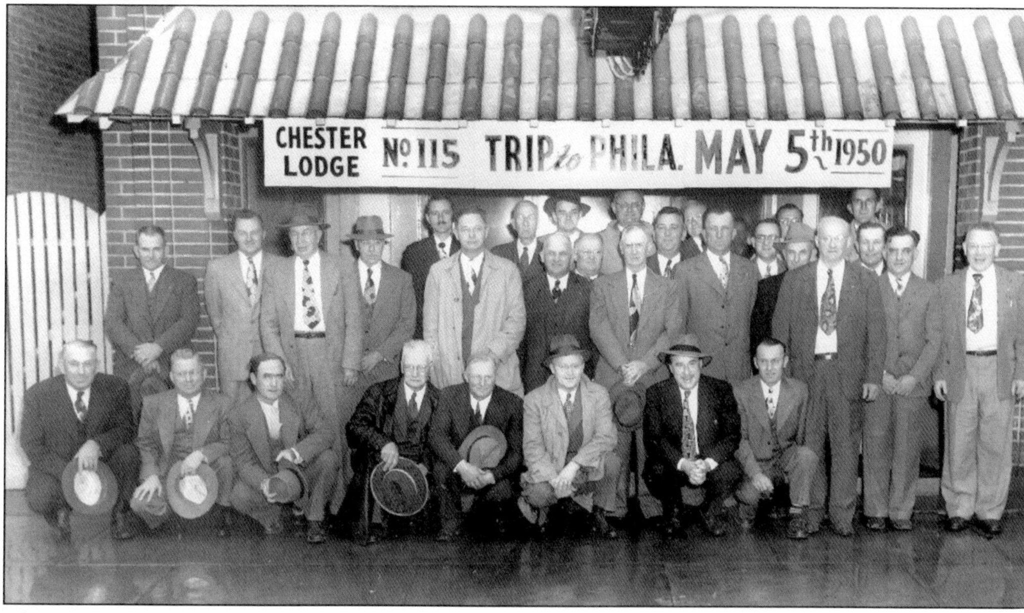

This image is of Chester Lodge No. 115 in 1950. Pictured, from left to right, are the following: (first row) John Crouch, Bruce Dukes, J. W. Ivens, O. C. Steinert, Thomas McGinnis, Spencer Smith, J. St. Clair Martinet, and Elwood R. Burgess; (second row) C. Burton Vansant, Kenneth Trumbauer, George E. Clark, J. W. Higman, Clarence B. Minner, W. M. Stewart Price, Clarence M. Melvin Jr., Poe Hartley, Hilton Crouch, Harvey Mentzer, V. Kennard Ross, and Henry Gill; (third row) Jack Kieffer, William G. Smith, A. Parks Rasin, Rolph Townshend, Cecil Crouch, Harry Higman, Dr. Sylvester Smith, V. Melvin Kendall, W. Melvin Warner, R. Weldon Joiner, and (extreme rear) James Hearn.

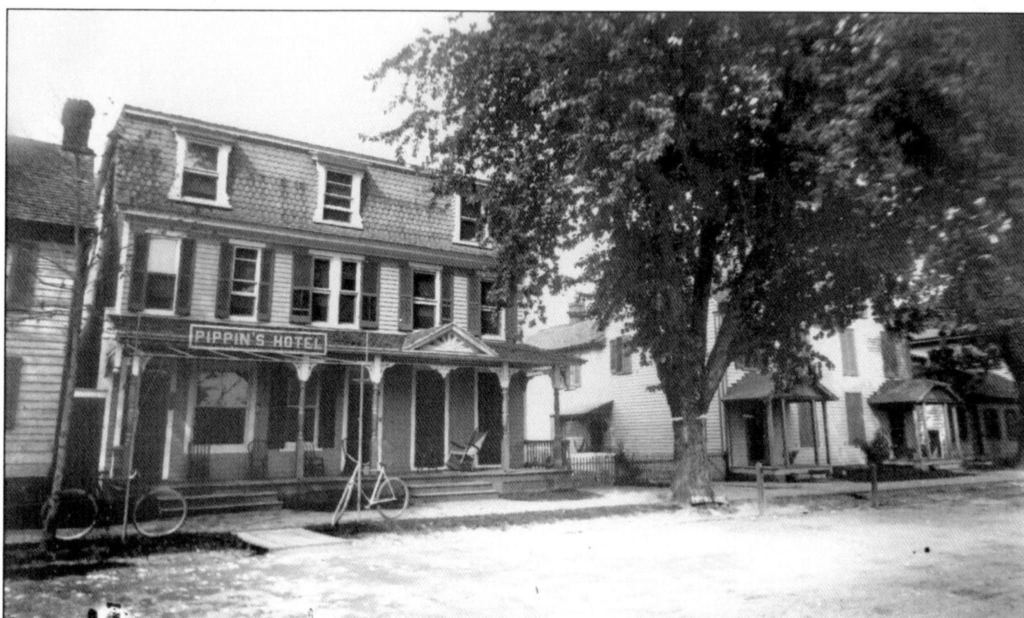

Pippin's Hotel was located on Park Row in Chestertown, as shown in this early-19th-century photograph. This building exists today as a rooming house and is located in the same place.

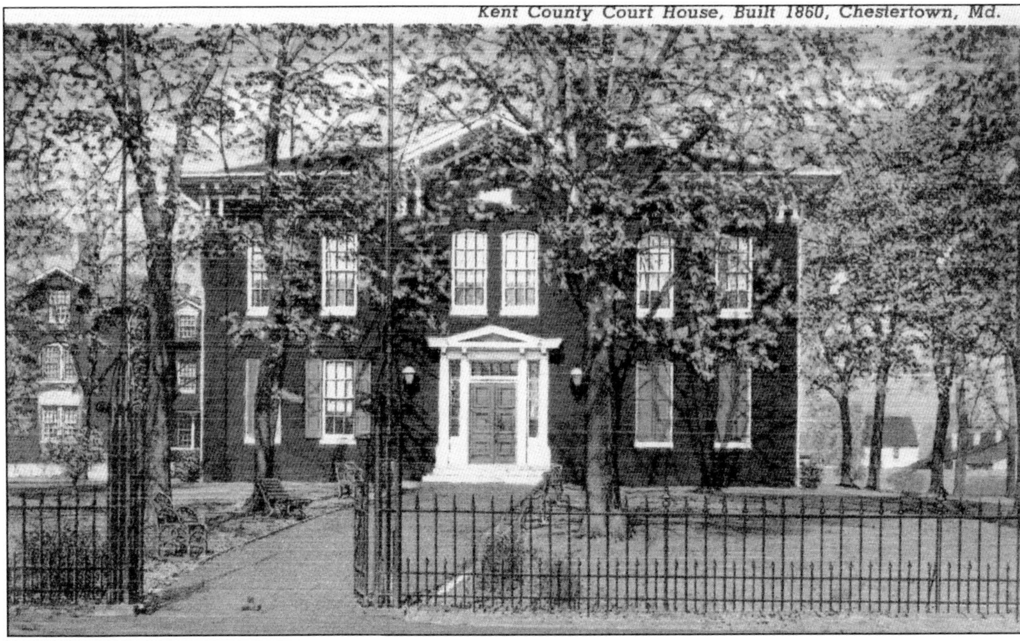

This picture shows the oldest section of the Kent County courthouse, which was built in 1860. It is reportedly of the Victorian Italianate style. A Colonial addition was added in 1969 that faces Cross Street in Chestertown.

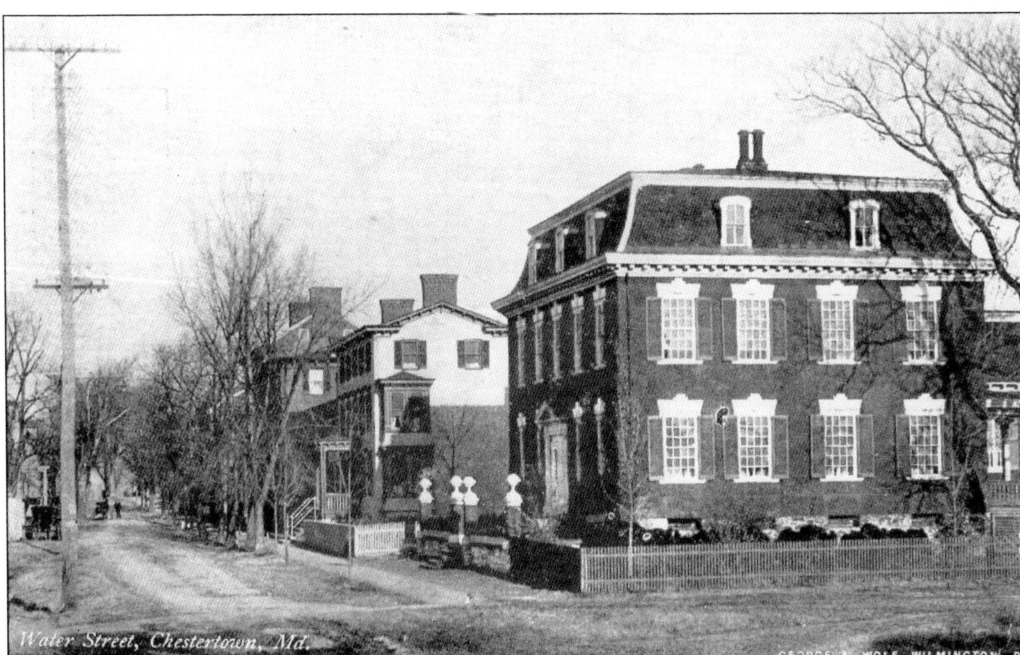

Widehall sits on the corner of Water and High Streets. It was built c. 1770 by Thomas Smythe, a wealthy merchant and shipbuilder. It is one of the largest classic brick Georgian mansions in Chestertown.

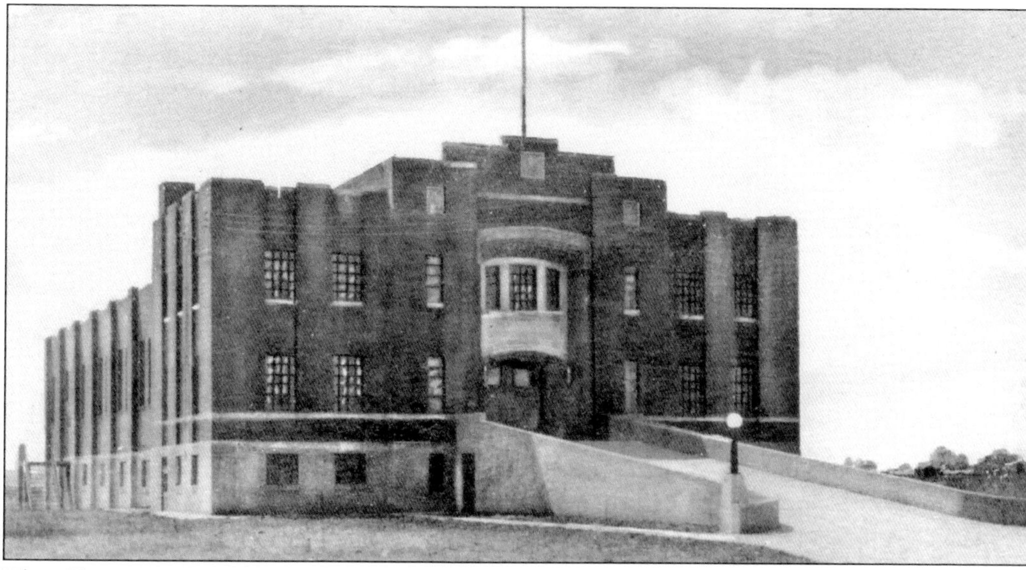

The Chestertown Armory, located on Quaker Neck Road, was constructed in 1931. It was added to the National Register of Historic Places in 1985. An addition and major renovation were completed in 1993. After renovations were completed, the armory was named in honor of longtime member SFC John H. Newnam. The addition of the rear of the armory was further named in honor of 1st Sgt. Edward R. Elburn. Historically the armory has been home to infantry units of the Maryland Army National Guard. Most of its history and lineage is tied to the 29th Infantry Division (Light). The 29th Infantry Division (Light) made history as being one of the first divisions of the U.S. Army to land at Normandy during World War II.

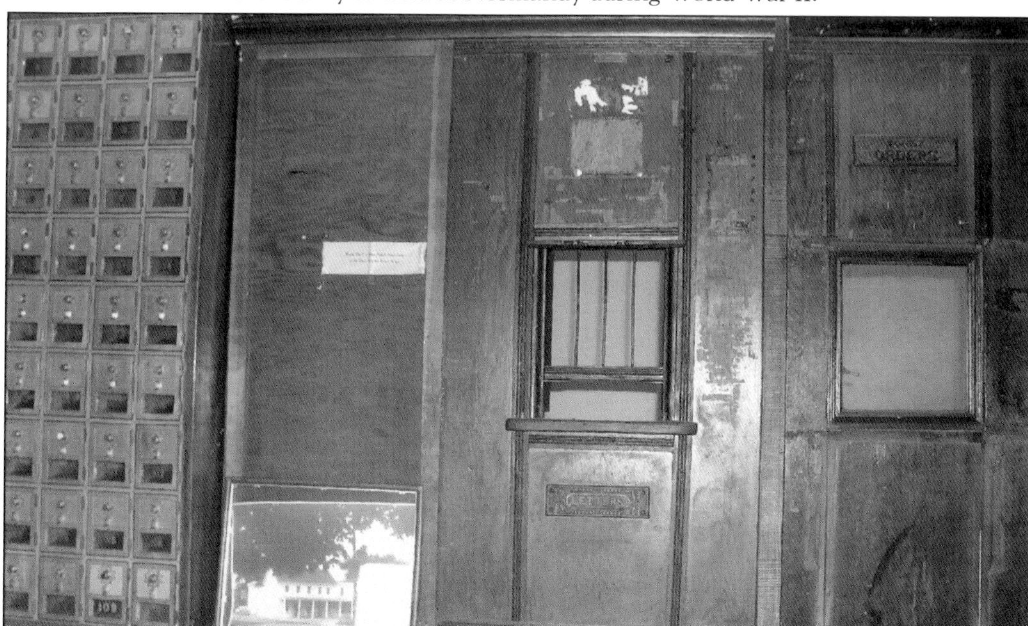

Kent Museum has preserved many items of Kent County agricultural and cultural history. Shown above is the inside remains of one of Kent County's post offices from the turn of the 20th century.

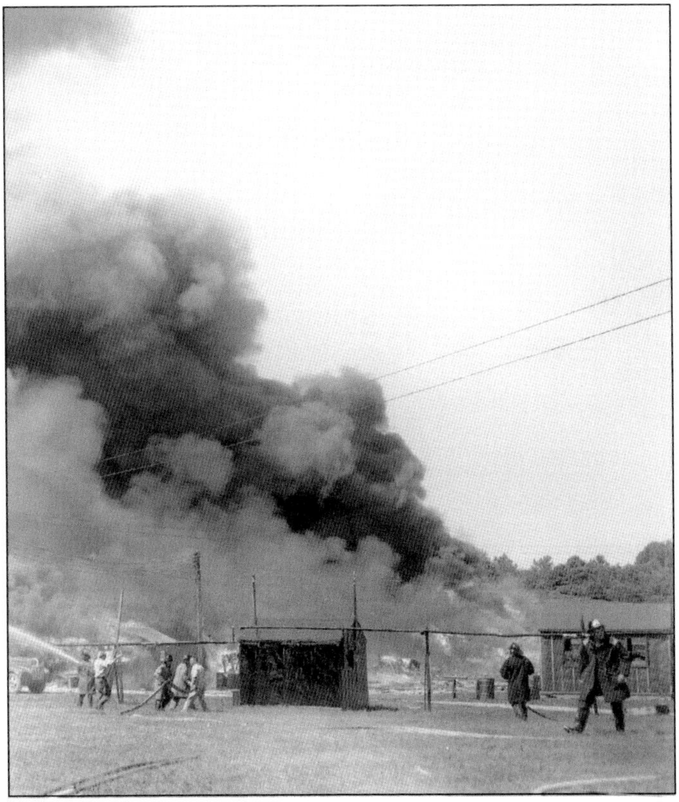

The Kent Defense and Fireworks Manufacturing Plant in Chestertown (now occupied by KRM Development) exploded on July 16, 1954. Firefighters fought in vain to bring the area under control.

The photograph below shows the devastation of the blast at the Kent Defense and Fireworks Manufacturing Plant in 1954. Eleven people were killed, and many more were injured. It destroyed over half of the five-acre plant. One of the owners of the plant was Chestertown mayor Philip G. Wilmer.

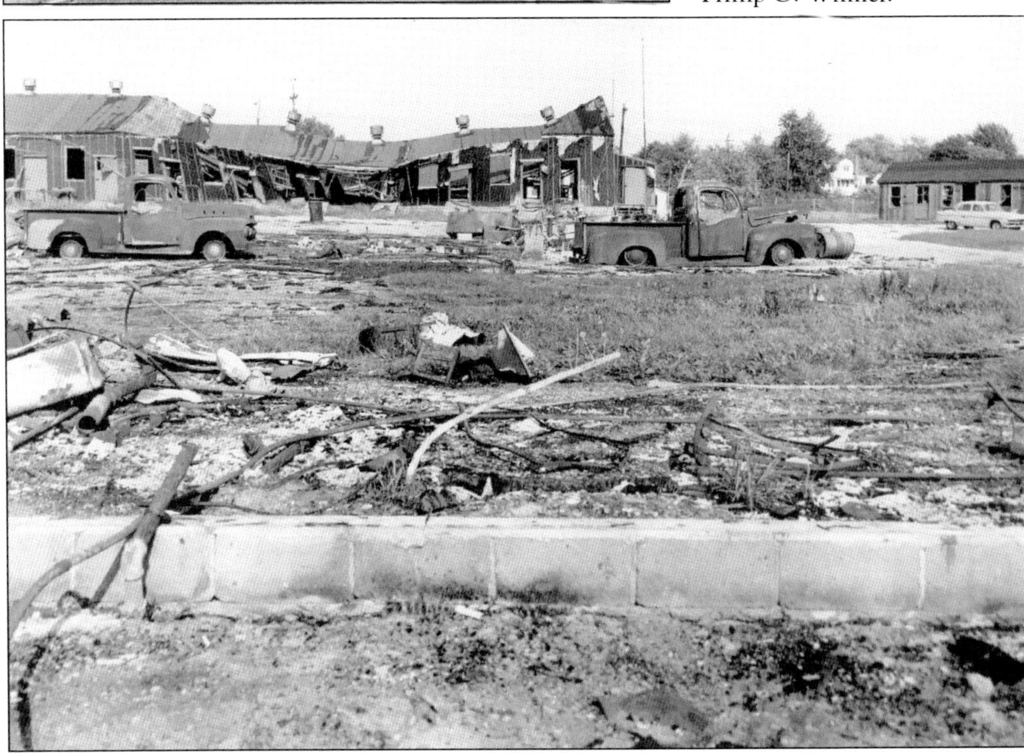

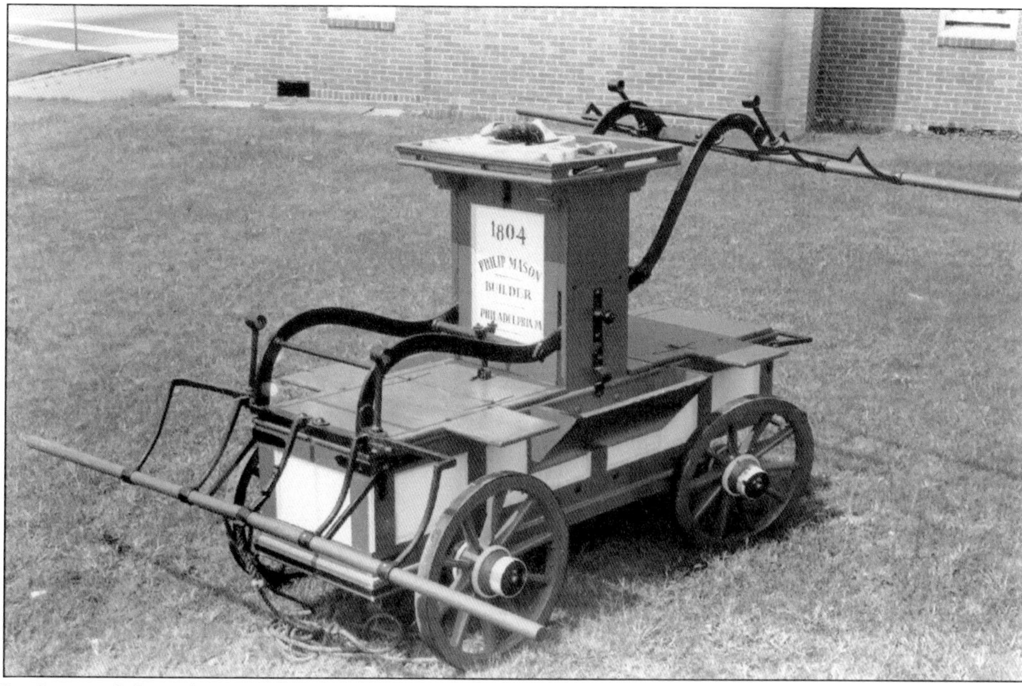

In front of the Chestertown Volunteer Fire Department on Maple Avenue is the 1804 Philip Mason fire pump that was originally used to put out fires in Chestertown in the early part of the 19th century.

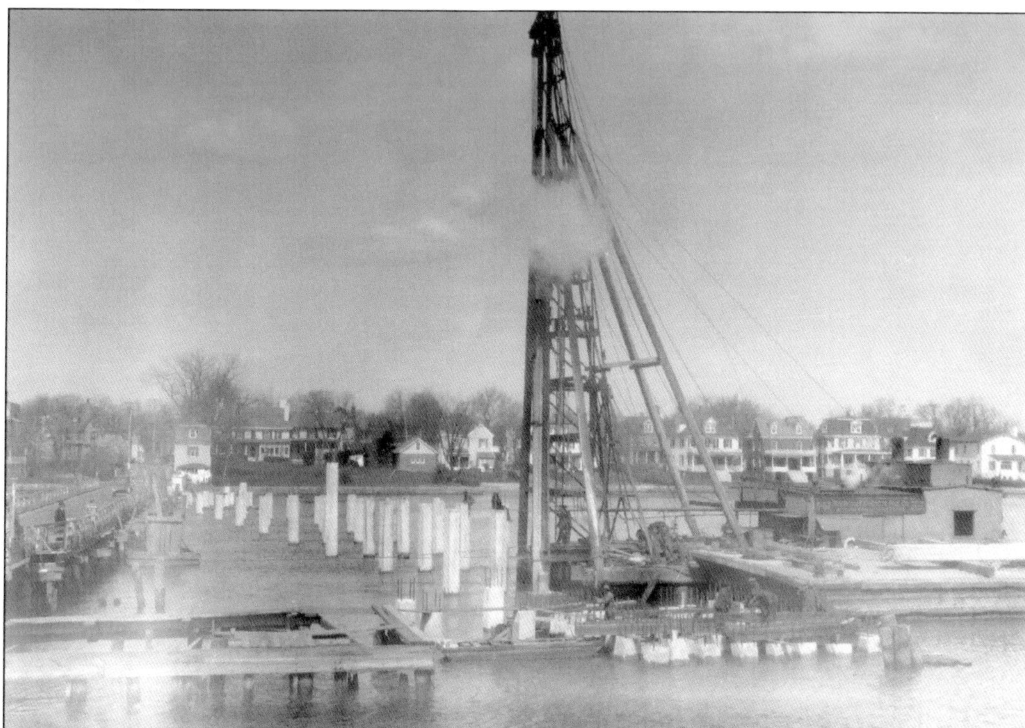
Pilings being put in the Chester River for the new Chester River Bridge are shown here.

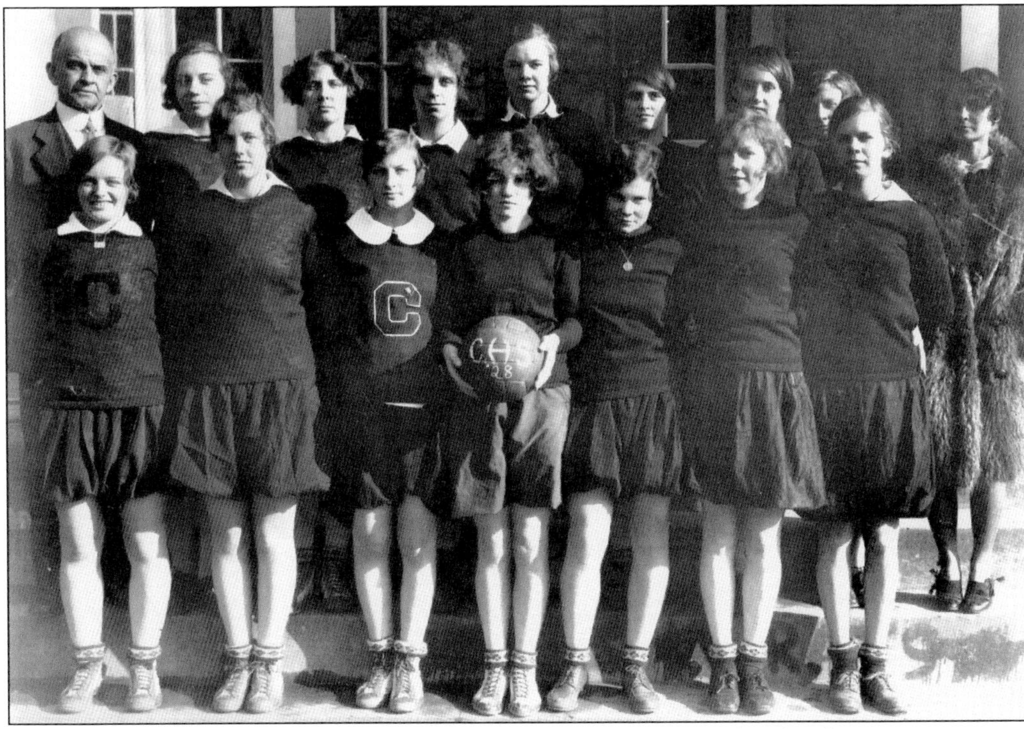

This image shows the women's basketball team at Chestertown High School in 1928.

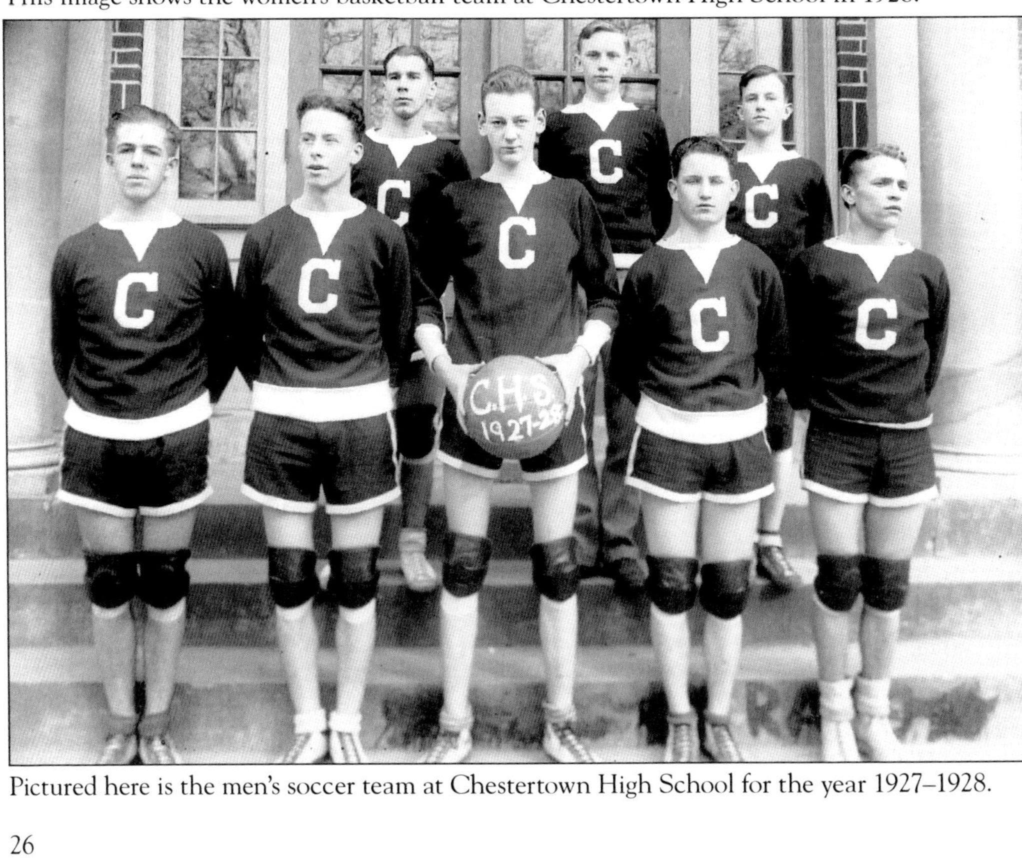

Pictured here is the men's soccer team at Chestertown High School for the year 1927–1928.

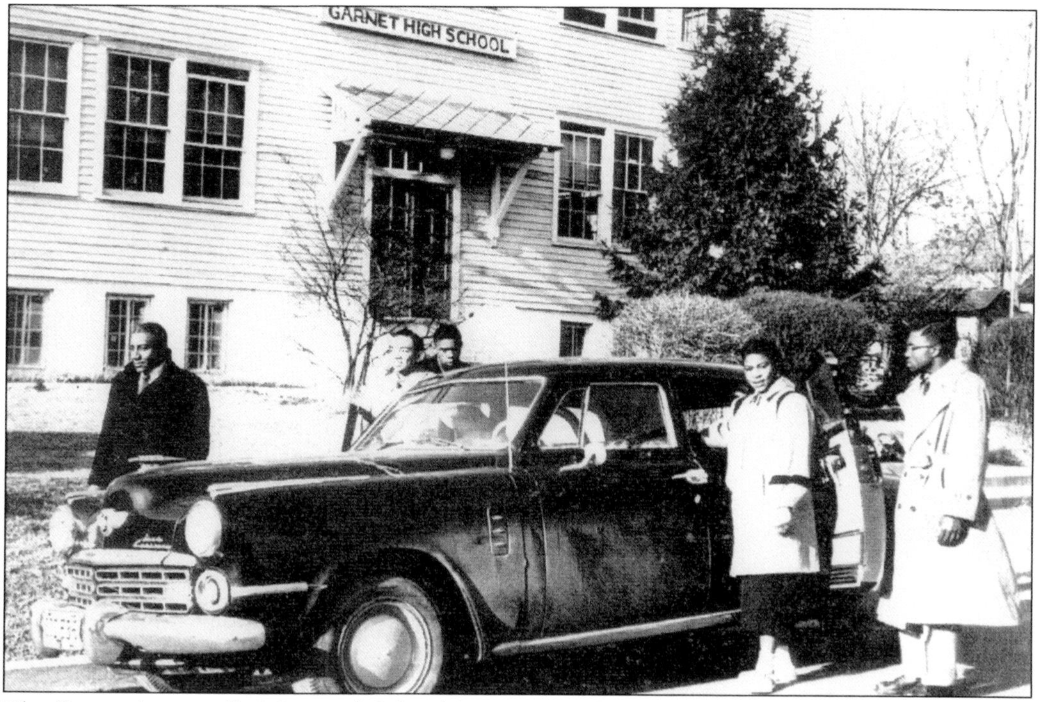

The Garnet (now spelled Garnett) School Quintette included Margaret Briscoe (soprano), George Wicks (tenor), Elbert Wilson (bass), Roy F. Knight (director), and principal Elmer T. Hawkins. They are shown here in 1949 getting ready for a trip to Poughkeepsie, New York, to perform in a concert at Oakwood School. Garnet High School was then located on College Avenue in Chestertown. It opened its doors in 1916 solely as an African American elementary school. Seven years later, it was granted use as a high school. The first class graduated from Garnet High School in 1925. The school was named for Henry Highland Garnet, a scholar, lecturer, and minister, who was born as an enslaved person in New Market in Kent County (near Golts). This school was razed in 1964.

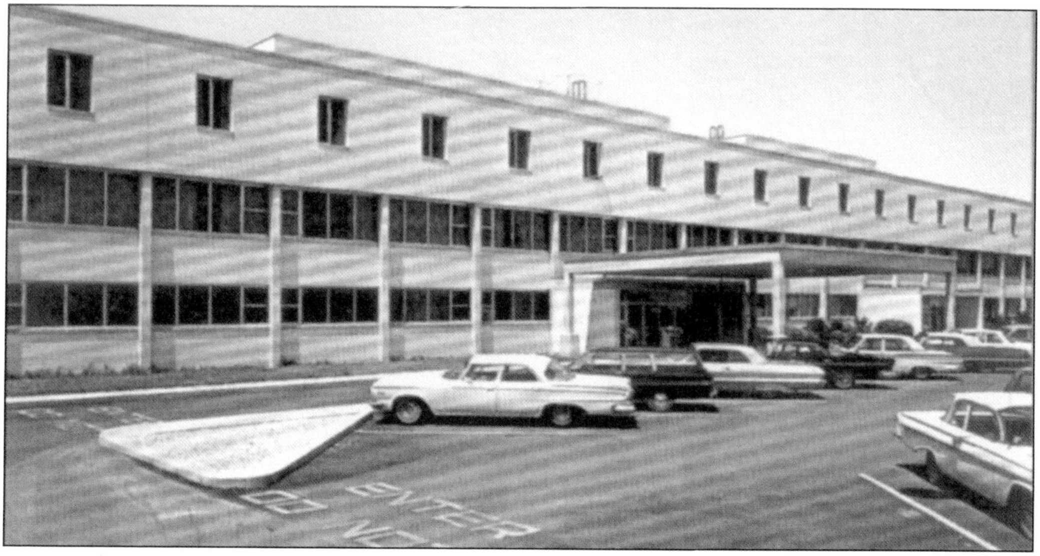

Kent and Queen Anne's Hospital had its beginnings in 1928. Shown here in the early 1970s, it has come a long way from four rented rooms on the second floor of William Rodney's home.

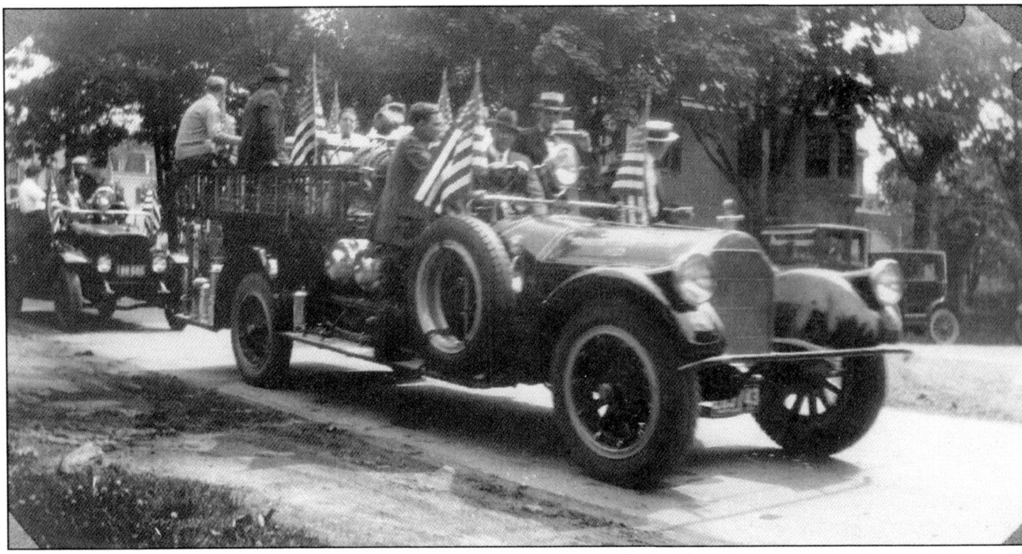

Chestertown Fire Company's new Pierce Arrow hook-and-ladder fire engine along the parade route in Chestertown on July 4, 1925.

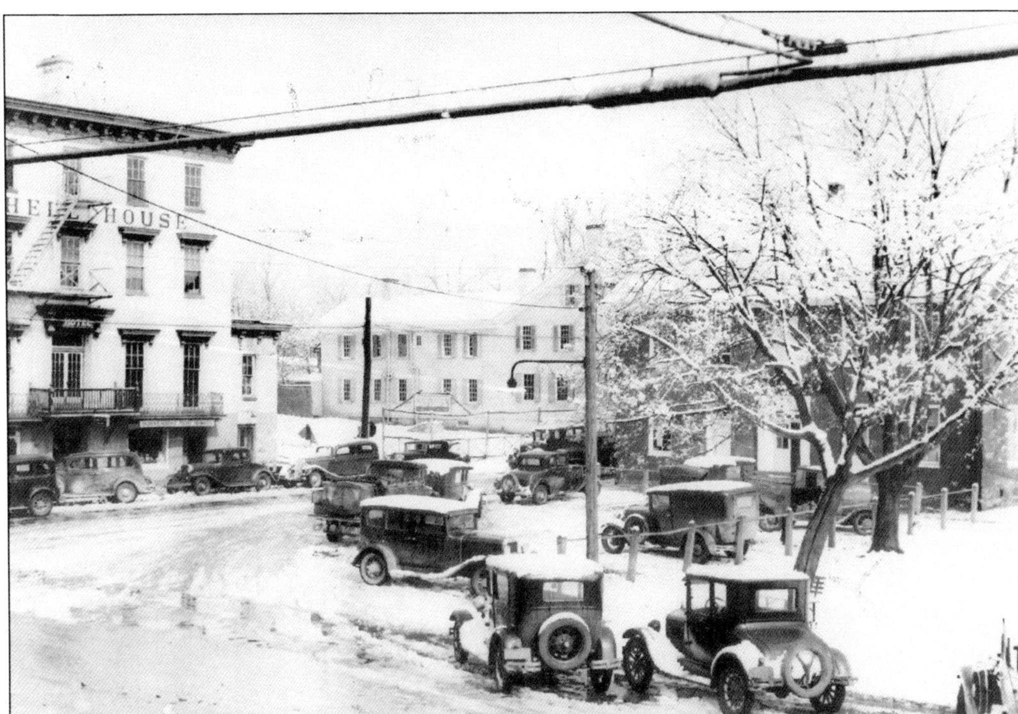

The Voshell House (now the Peoples Bank building) is shown on the left across from the Market House and next to Bibb's Inn on Spring Avenue in downtown Chestertown. It was opened in 1864 and cost $28,000 to build.

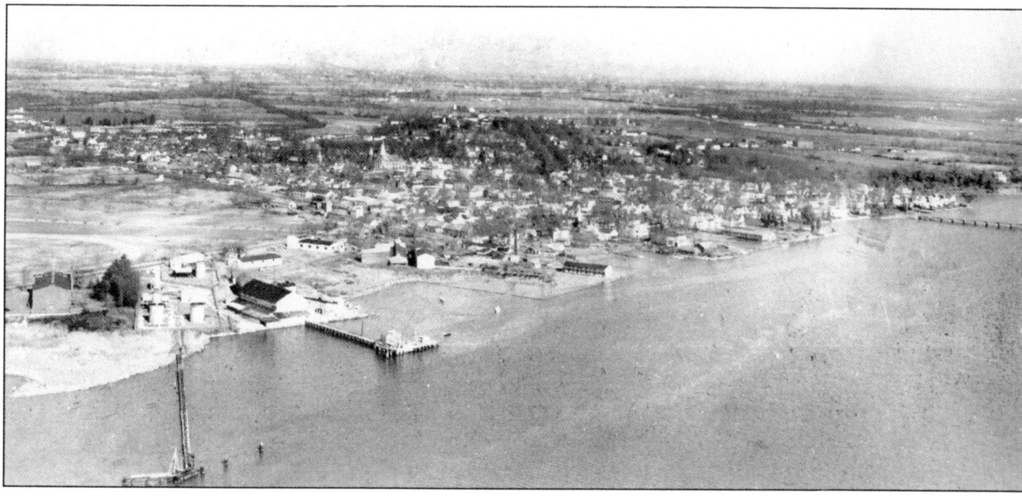

In this image, one can see Chestertown's waterfront as it once was.

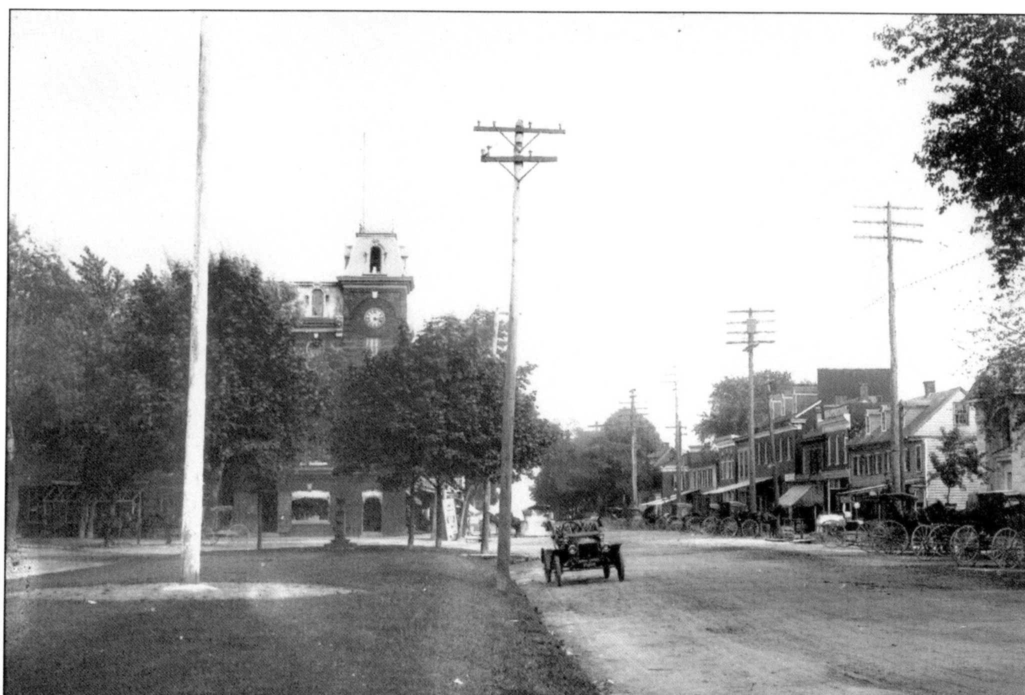

Chestertown's High Street businesses (looking east) are shown in this picture along with Memorial Park, in front of Stam's Hall, and the town clock. Stam's Hall was built in 1886 and has been used over the years for town meetings and as a playhouse, movie hall, post office, and at one time as Stam's Drug Store. The clock was installed at a cost of $800; the tower was erected as a part of Stam's Hall. An inscription on the bell, which is located in the tower above the clock, reads, "Town bell and clock donated by citizens to adorn the tower and endorse the enterprise of our fellow townsman in the erection of Stam's Hall; and to warn us by its solemn strokes of the flight of time and our approaching end."

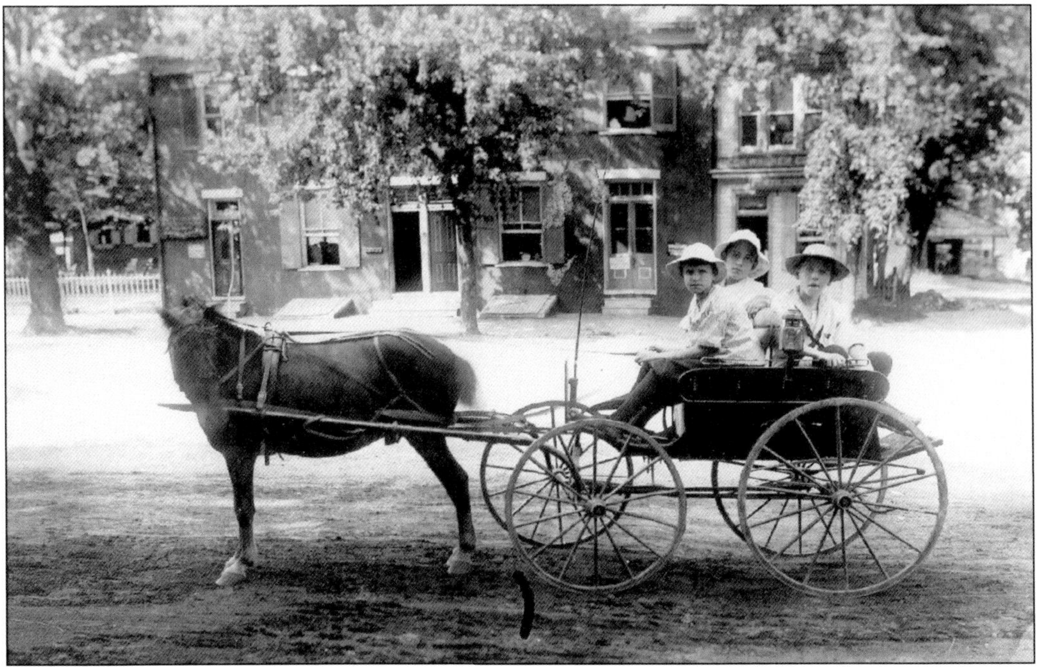

Three unidentified children sit in front of the Masonic Temple Building, which faces High Street in downtown Chestertown c. 1900. The building exists today as an office building.

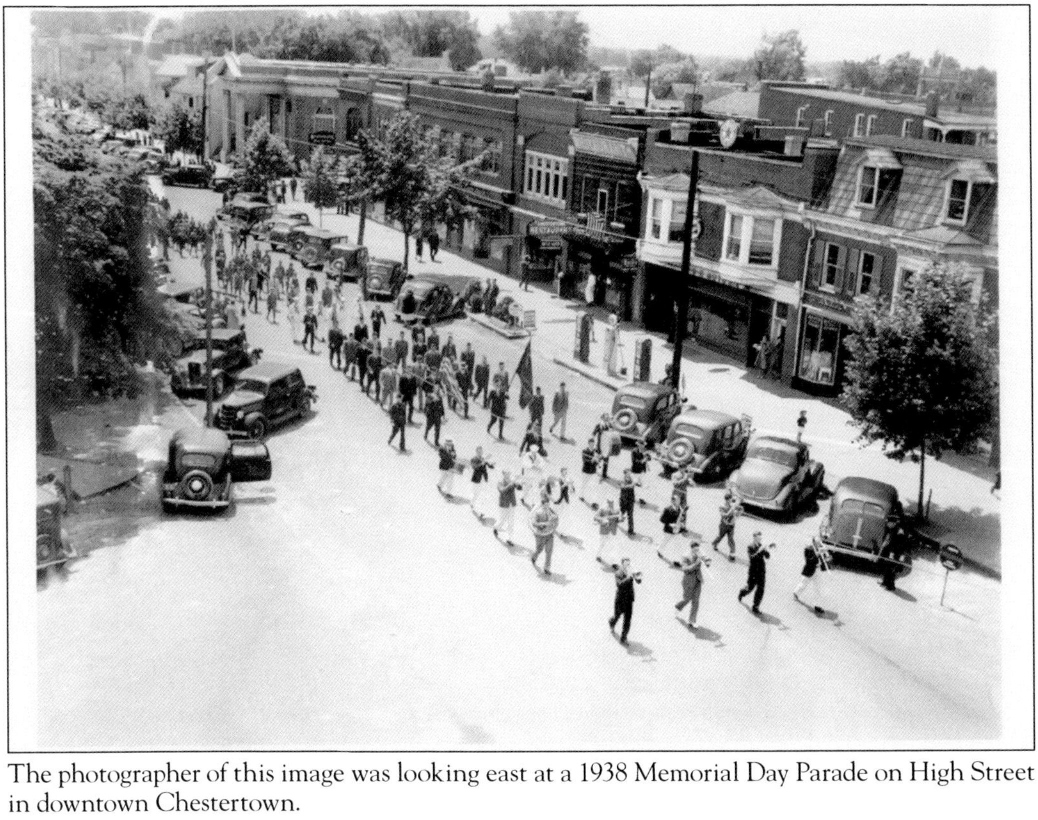

The photographer of this image was looking east at a 1938 Memorial Day Parade on High Street in downtown Chestertown.

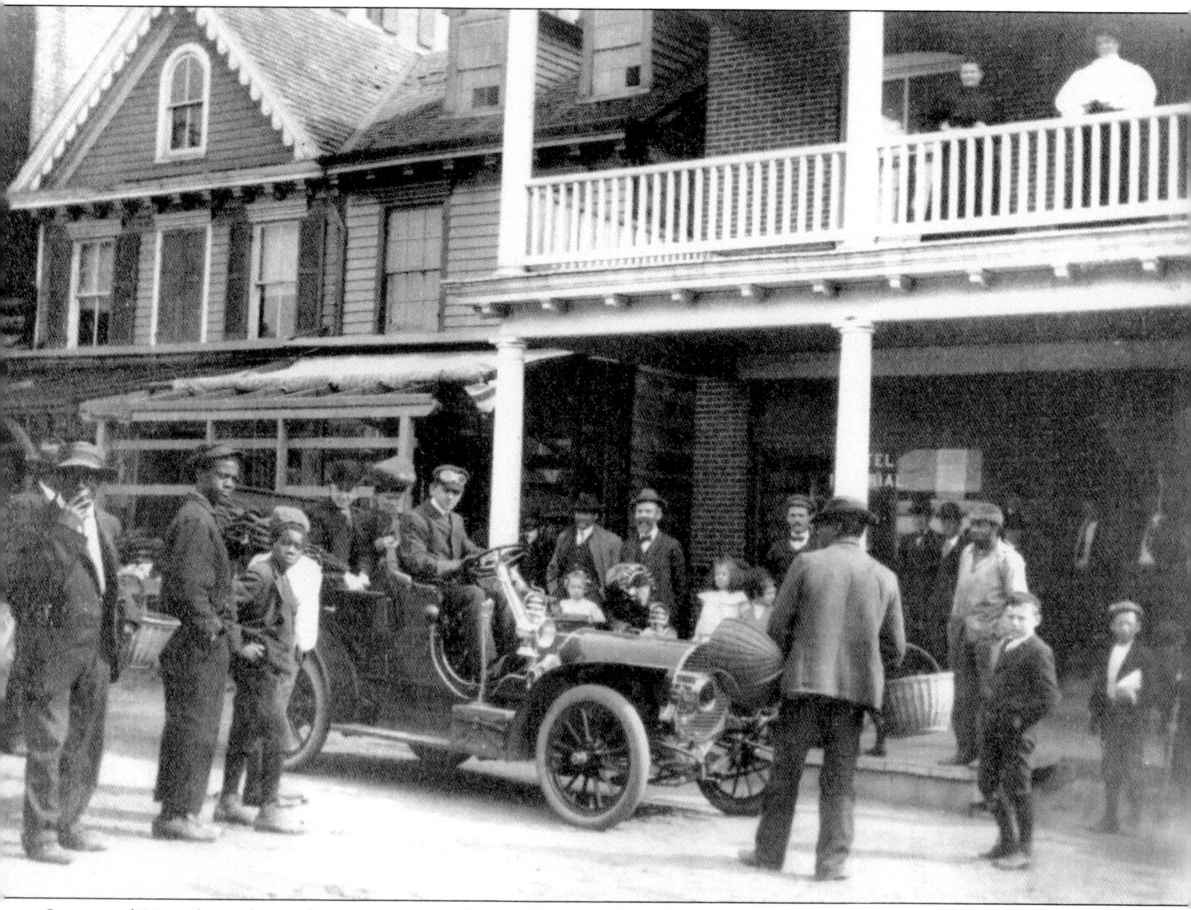

Imperial Hotel, to the right, appears in the background in this photograph depicting when Charles Quincy Tirrell, congressman from Massachusetts, visited Chestertown in 1907 in the first gas-propelled car ever seen in Chestertown.

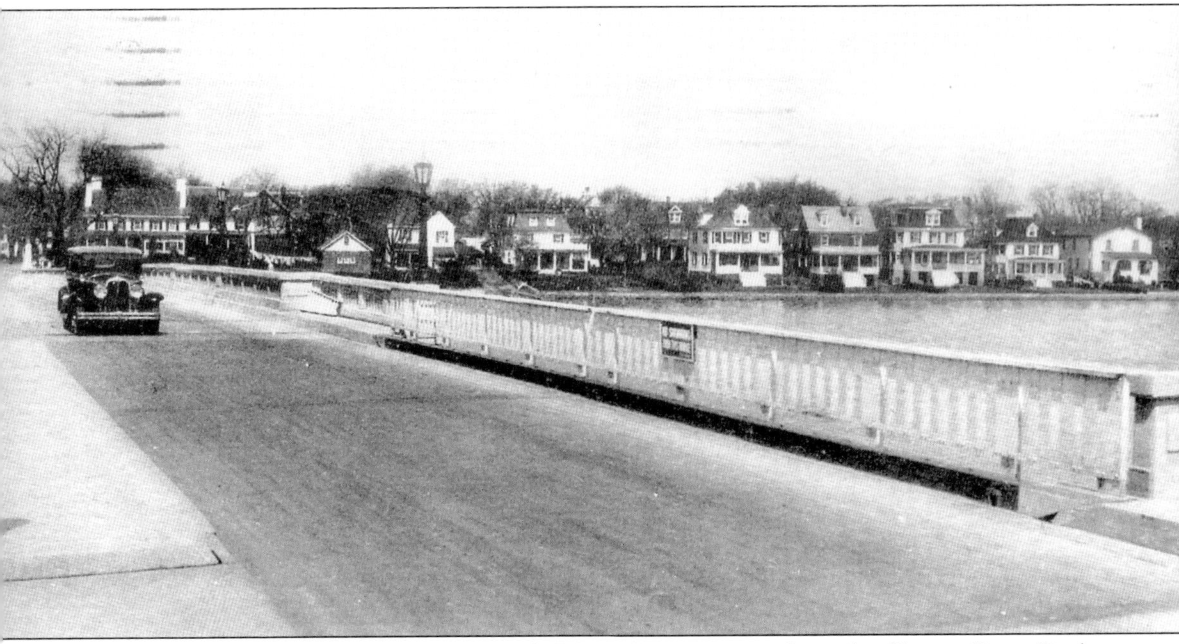

This is an image of Chestertown's North Water Street as seen from the Chester River Bridge.

Three

WASHINGTON COLLEGE

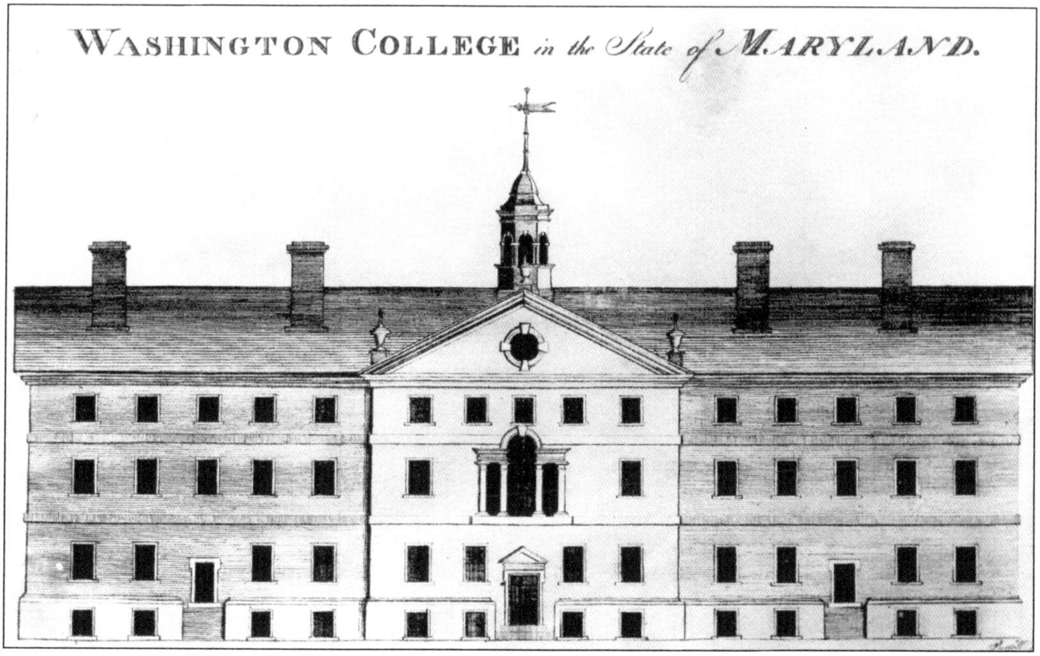

This image is an artist's conception of the original Washington College building in Chestertown. The plans were prepared by the firm of Rakestraw and Hicks of Philadelphia. The building was four stories and 160 feet long by 100 feet deep. The estimated cost of construction was $28,000.

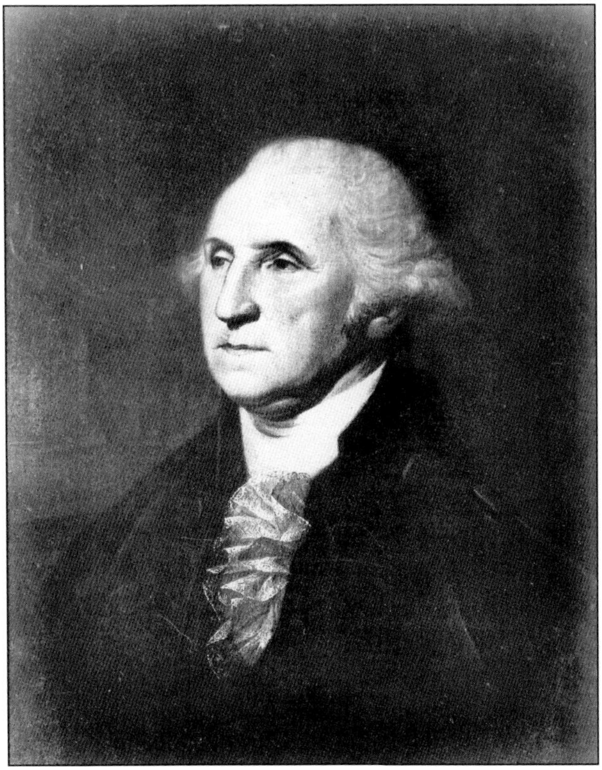

In a letter dated August 18, 1782, Pres. George Washington gave his consent to "giving my name to the College at Chester." In addition to his name, President Washington also gave money in November 1782. The college continues to pursue ways to honor their namesake. In 2005, the college will give the George Washington Book Prize, which is $50,000 to be awarded annually to a published author who contributes to a greater understanding of the life and career of George Washington. It is the largest book prize for early American history.

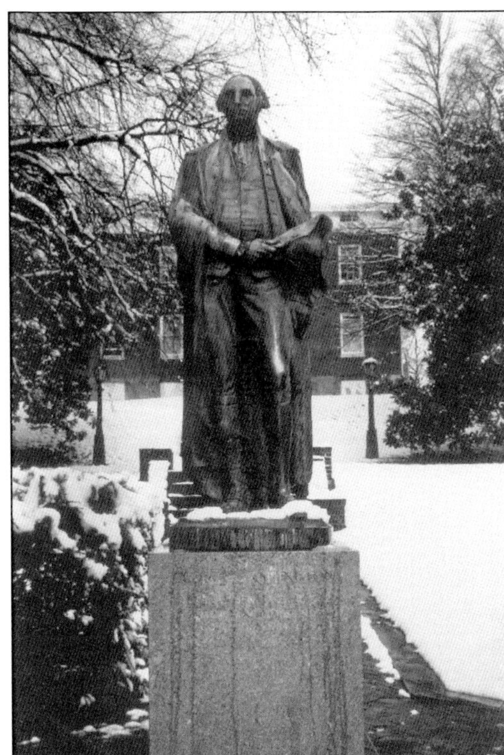

In 1975, on the 175th anniversary of the founding of Washington College, this statue of George Washington was dedicated. The statue was designed and sculpted by Lee Lawrie, whose other contributions include the relief design of Roosevelt on the dime.

This picture is of one of the original subscriptions lists outlining the founding of Washington College. The document currently is property of the Talbot Country Free Library Maryland Room.

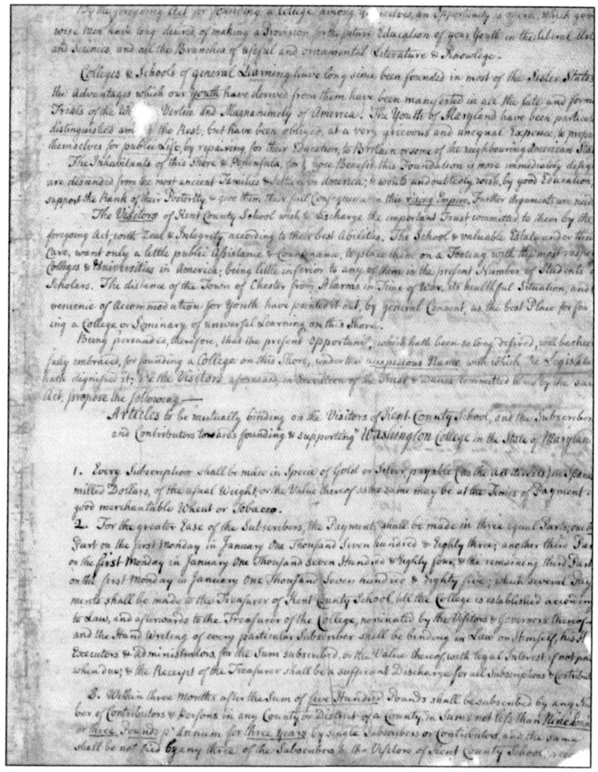

By the foregoing Act for founding a College among [illegible] an Opportunity is [illegible] which [illegible] wise Men have long desired of making a Provision for the future Education of your Youth in the liberal [illegible] and Sciences and all the Branches of useful and ornamental Literature & Knowledge.

Colleges & Schools of general Learning have long since been founded in most of the Sister States [illegible] the Advantages which our Youth have derived from them have been manifested in all the late and [illegible] Trials of the [illegible] Virtue and Magnanimity of America. The Youth of Maryland have been [illegible] distinguished am[illegible] the Rest, but have been obliged, at a very grievous and unequal Expence, to [illegible] themselves for public Life, by repairing for their Education, to Britain or some of the neighbouring American [illegible]

The Inhabitants of this Shore & Peninsula, for [illegible] Benefit this Foundation is more immediately [illegible] are descended from the most ancient Families & Settlers in America; & would undoubtedly wish, by good Education, [illegible] support the Rank of their Posterity & give them their full Consequence in this rising Empire. Further Arguments are [illegible]

The Visitors of Kent County School wish to discharge the important Trust committed to them by the foregoing Act, with Zeal & Integrity according to their best Abilities. The School & valuable Estate under their Care, want only a little public Assistance & Countenance, to place them on a Footing with the most [illegible] Colleges & Universities in America; being little inferior to any of them in the present Number of Students [illegible] Scholars. The distance of the Town of Chester from Alarms in Time of War, its healthful Situation, and [illegible]venience of Accommodation for Youth have pointed it out, by general Consent, as the best Place for [illegible]ing a College or Seminary of universal Learning on this Shore.

Being persuaded, therefore, that the present Opportunity, which hath been so long desired, will be [illegible] fully embraced, for founding a College on this Shore, under the auspicious Name with which the Legisla[illegible] hath dignified it; We the Visitors aforesaid, in Execution of the Trust & Duties committed to us by the [illegible] Act, propose the following —

Articles to be mutually binding on the Visitors of Kent County School, and the Subscribe[illegible] and Contributors towards founding & supporting "Washington College in the State of Marylan[illegible]

1. Every Subscription shall be made in Specie of Gold or Silver, payable (as the Act directs) in [illegible] milled Dollars, of the usual Weight, or the Value thereof as the same may be at the Times of Payment [illegible] good merchantable Wheat or Tobacco.

2. For the greater Ease of the Subscribers, the Payment shall be made in three equal Parts; one [illegible] Part on the first Monday in January One Thousand Seven hundred & Eighty three; another third Pa[illegible] on the first Monday in January One Thousand Seven Hundred & Eighty four, & the remaining third Par[illegible] on the first Monday in January One Thousand Seven hundred & Eighty five; which several Pay[illegible]ments shall be made to the Treasurer of Kent County School till the College is established accordin[illegible] to Law, and afterwards to the Treasurer of the College, nominated by the Visitors & Governors thereof [illegible] and the Hand Writing of every particular Subscriber shall be binding in Law on Himself, his H[illegible] Executors & Administrators, for the Sum subscribed, or the Value thereof, with legal Interest, if not pa[illegible] when due; & the Receipt of the Treasurer shall be a sufficient Discharge for all Subscriptions & Contribut[illegible]

3. Within three Months after the Sum of five Hundred Pounds shall be subscribed by any N[illegible]ber of Contributors & Persons in any County or District of a County, in Sums not less than Nine Pound[illegible] or three Pounds p^r Annum for three Years by single Subscribers or Contributors, and the same shall be notified by any three of the Subscribers to the Visitors of Kent County School [illegible]

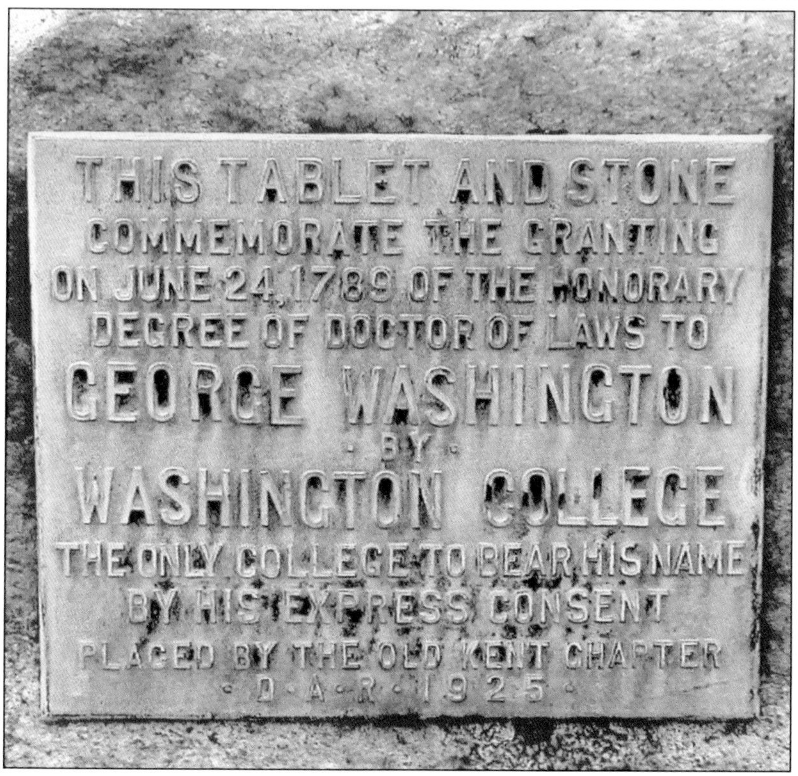

This image depicts the granting of the honorary Doctor of Laws degree to George Washington by Washington College on June 24, 1789. Washington College was the only college to bear the first president's name by his express consent. This monument was placed by the Old Kent Chapter of the Daughters of the American Revolution in 1925.

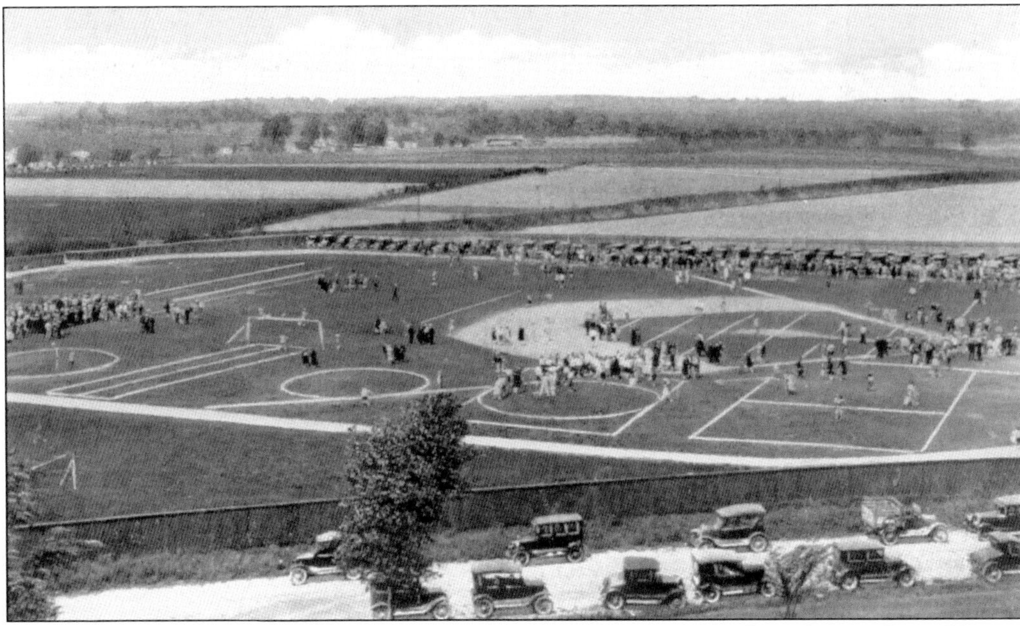

The postcard photograph shows the athletic field at Washington College during the 1930s.

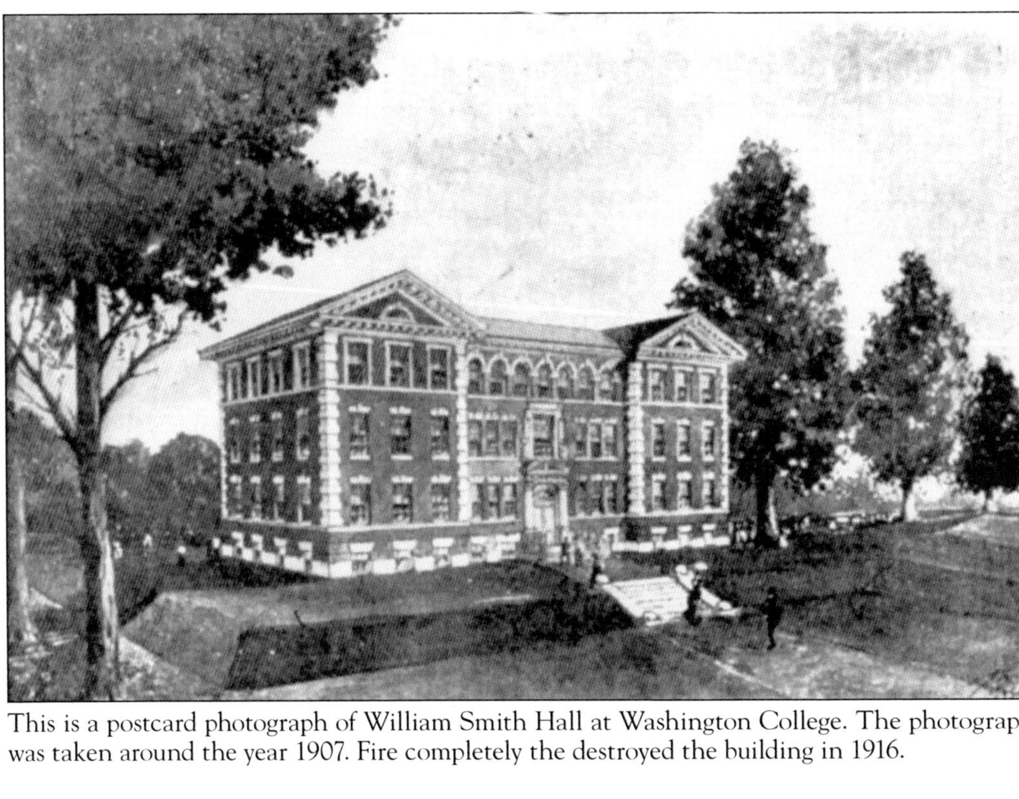

This is a postcard photograph of William Smith Hall at Washington College. The photograph was taken around the year 1907. Fire completely the destroyed the building in 1916.

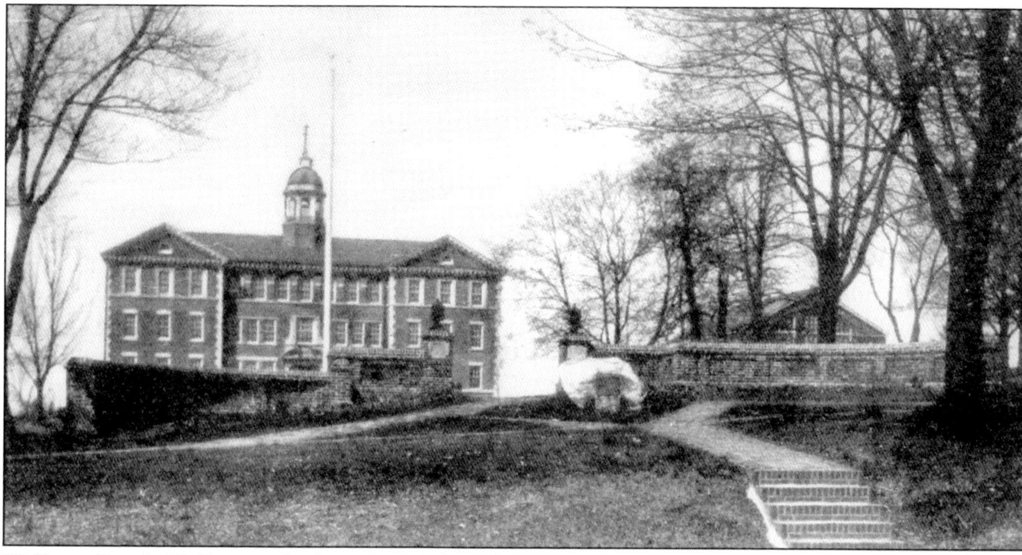

William Smith Hall was rebuilt in 1918. This photograph is from the late 1920s and shows William Smith Hall in the distance.

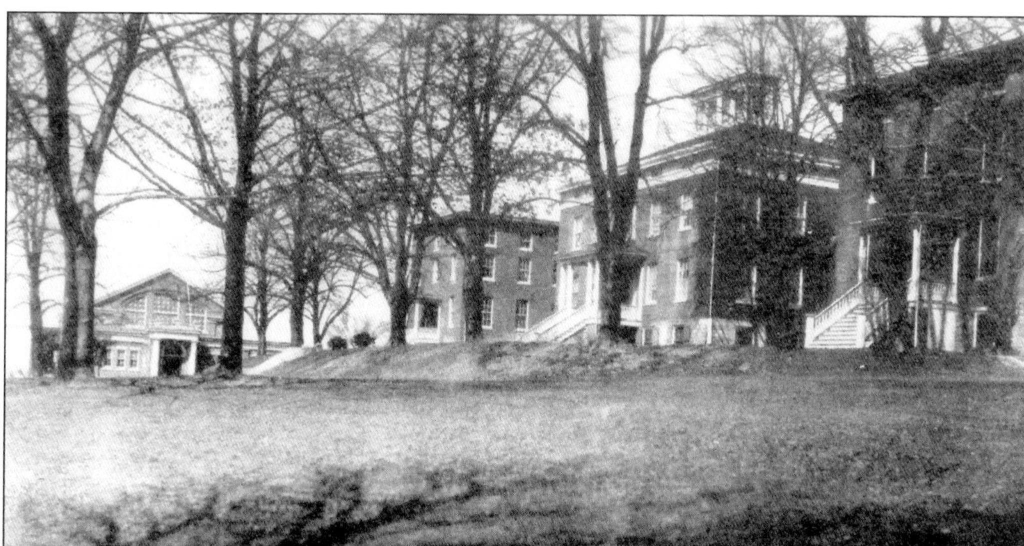

These three buildings, situated on the highest point in Kent County, were once called Middle, East, and West Colleges. Today they are referred to as Middle (second from right), East (far right), and West (second from left) Halls. The building on the left in the distance was the Cain Gymnasium, which is the current location of Miller Library.

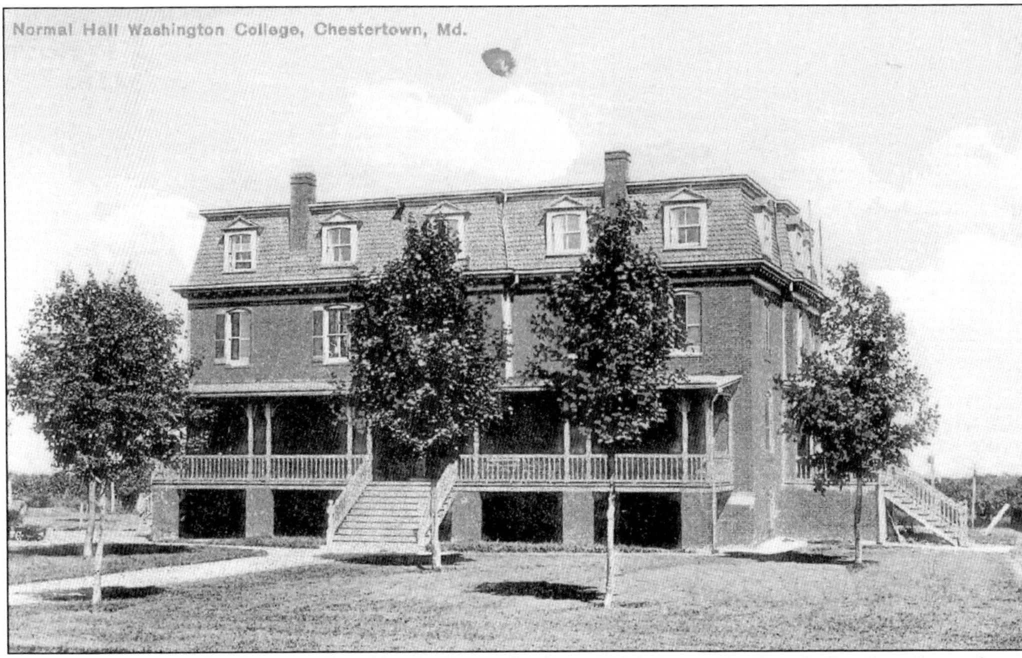

This is a photograph of Normal Hall, which was built in 1896. It was built to lodge female students. Miss May Matthews was the first woman to earn a degree from Washington College in 1895.

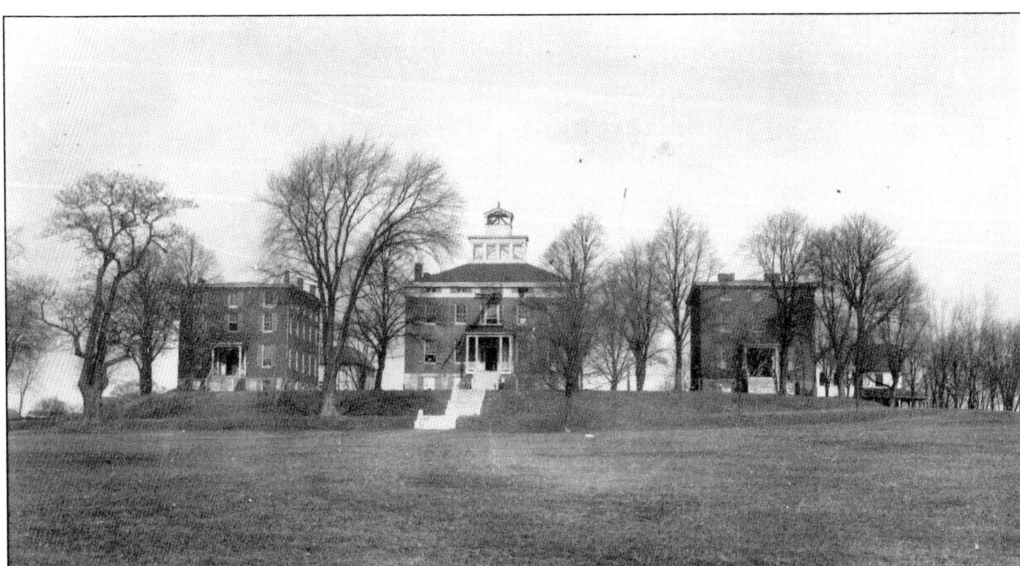

This early photograph shows the East, West, and Middle Colleges. Middle College, located in the center, was destroyed by fire in 1827 and rebuilt in 1845. East College is to the right of Middle College, and West College is to the left of Middle College.

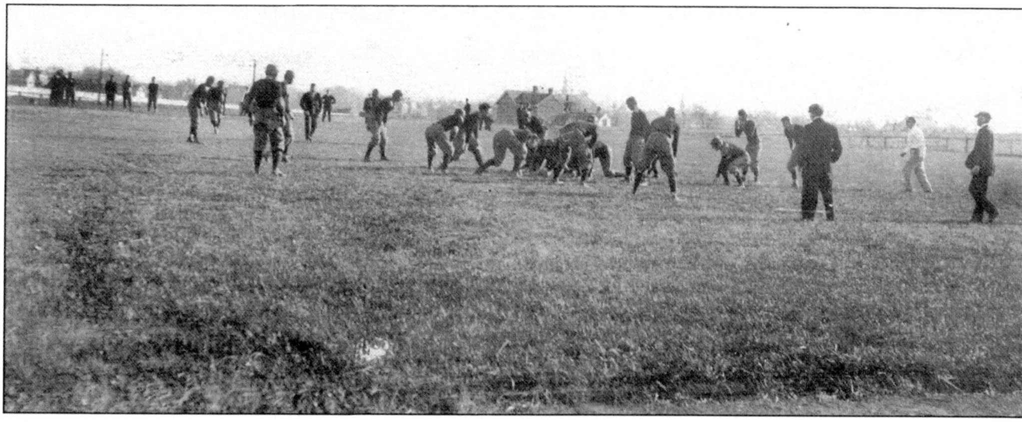

The Washington College football team played its first game at Chestertown against St. John's College in 1888. Washington College was defeated 119-0. This humiliating score did not discourage the college from continuing to play the sport, and this photograph shows the Washington College football team during a 1926 game. Football was permanently eliminated from Washington College in 1952 because of fiscal constraints.

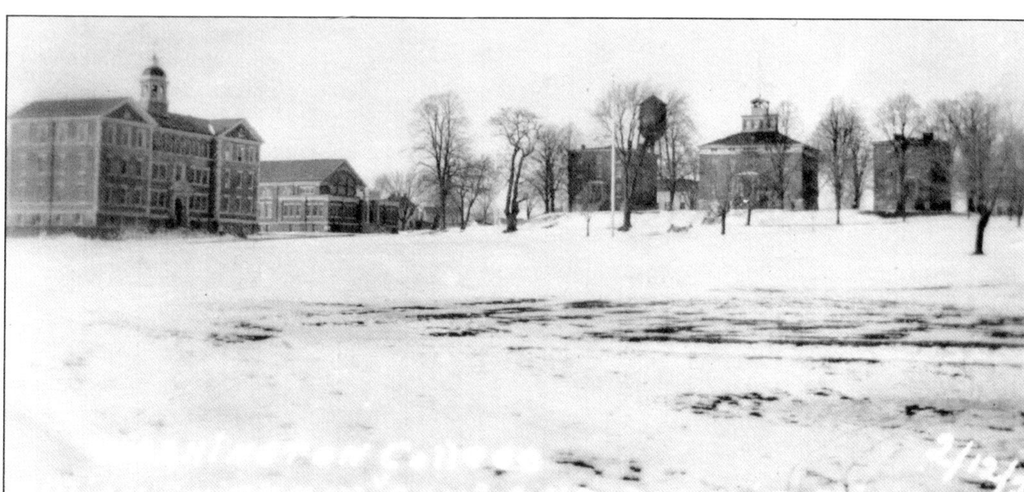

In this image, snow covers the Washington College campus. Taken in February 1926, this photograph shows William Smith Hall, on the left; the gym, next to William Smith Hall; and West, Middle, and East Hall dormitories on the right.

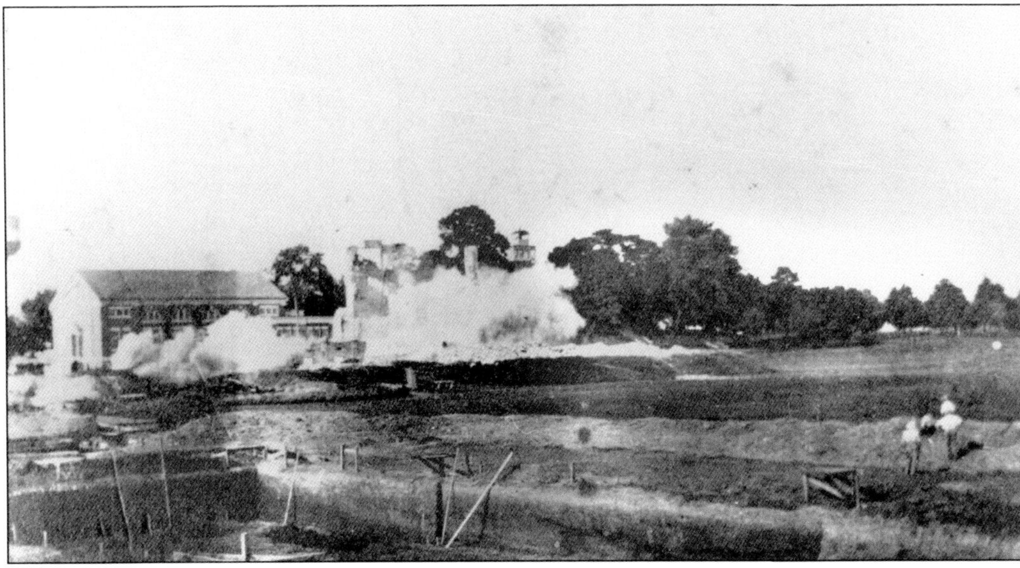

William Smith Hall was destroyed by fire shortly after midnight on January 16, 1916. The entire structure was lost thanks to coal storage in the basement. This photograph shows what was left of William Smith Hall as it was demolished.

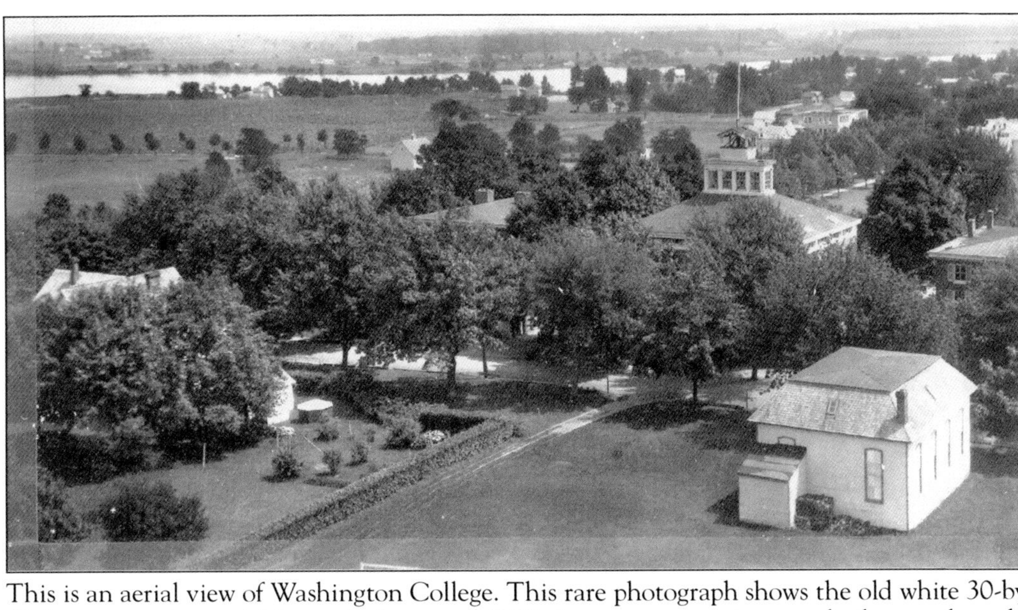

This is an aerial view of Washington College. This rare photograph shows the old white 30-by-40-foot gymnasium, which was built around 1890. A newer gymnasium was built to replace the old structure. Construction on the new facility started in the fall of 1912, and the new gym was open for use on January 31, 1931. It cost approximately $25,000.

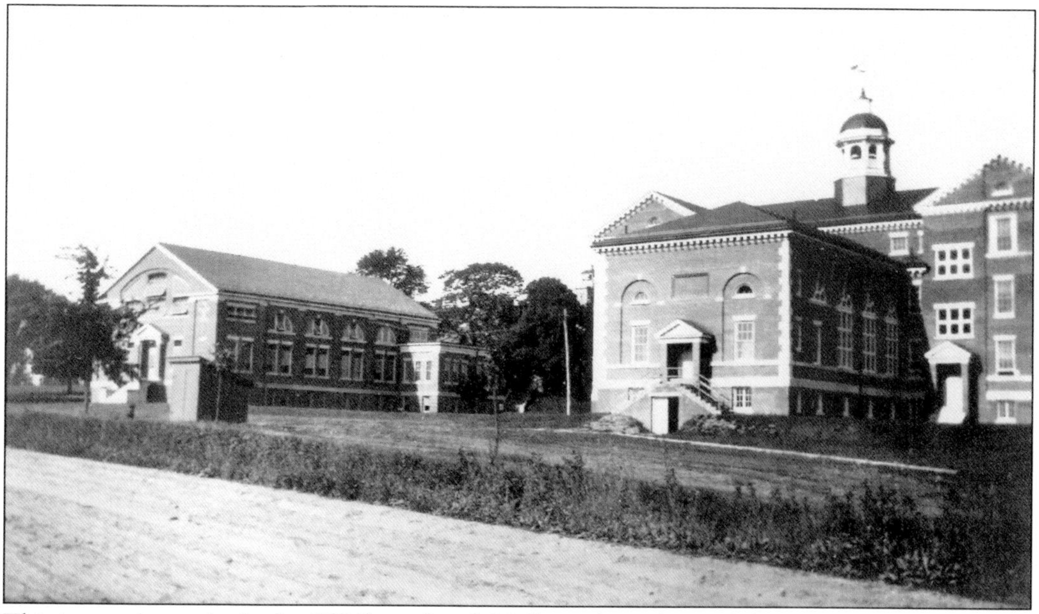

This image shows the back of William Smith Hall, on the right, and the new Cain Gymnasium, on the left, which was opened in January 1913. The Cain Gymnasium was named for Dr. James W. Cain. Dr. Cain was vice president of St. John's College when he was selected to become president of Washington College in 1903. He served until his resignation on June 18, 1918.

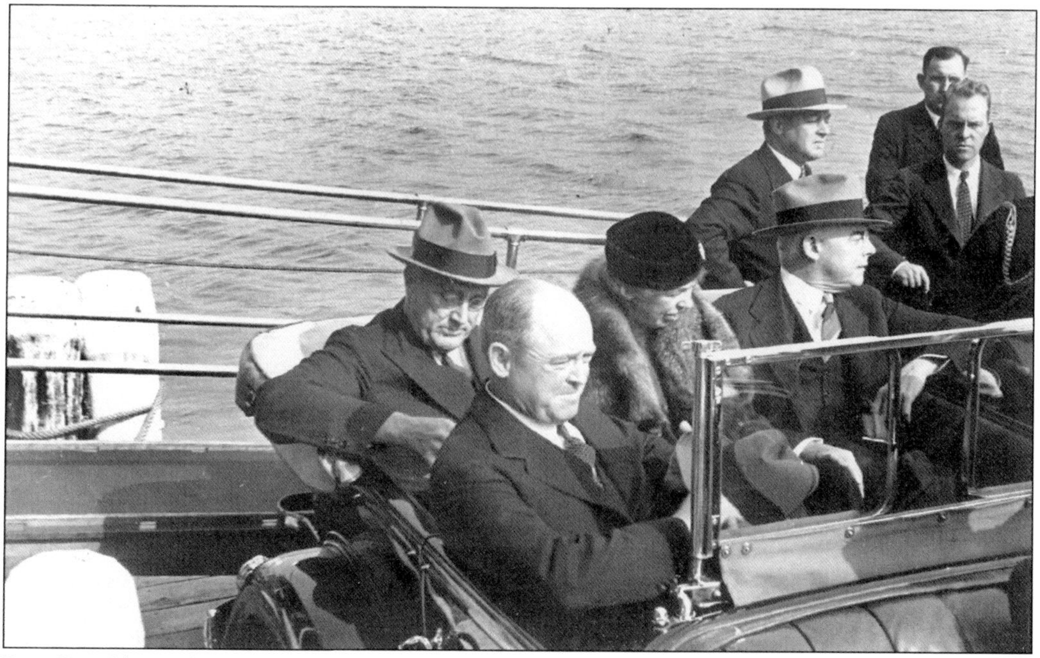

Pres. Franklin Delano Roosevelt and his wife, Eleanor, are pictured in the rear of the car that met them when the presidential yacht, *Sequoia*, docked at Godlington Manor on October 2, 1933. Col. Hiram S. Brown, chairman of the Board of Visitors and Governors at Washington College, is seated in front of the president. The president's arrival at Chestertown was marked by a 21-gun salute fired by a detachment off artillery from Fort Hoyle.

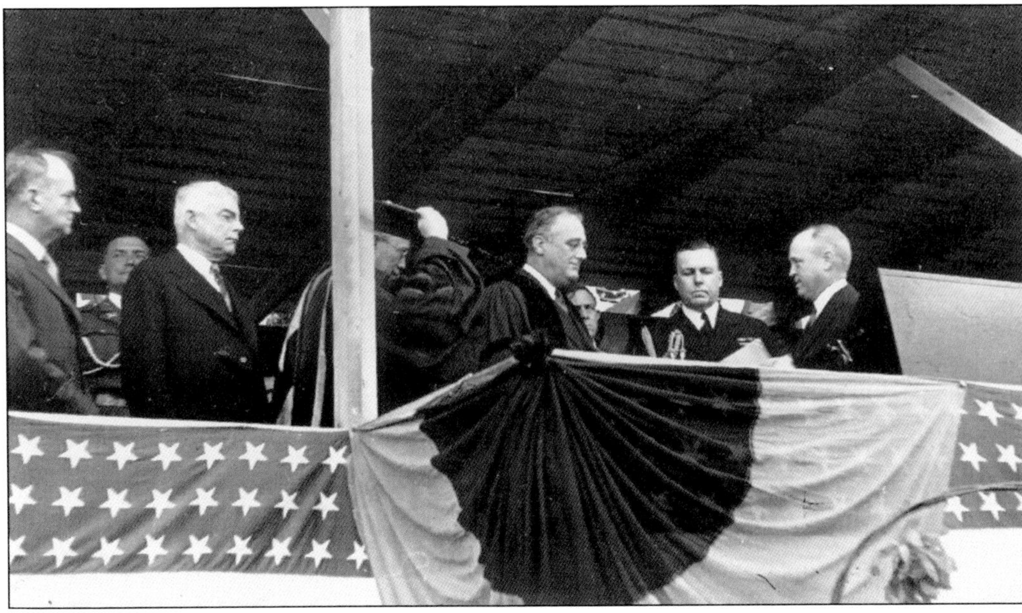

Here, President Roosevelt receives an honorary Doctorate of Laws from Washington College in front of a crowd of 1,500. President Roosevelt was the first president since George Washington to receive the honor. He would be followed by Pres. Harry S. Truman and Pres. Dwight D. Eisenhower.

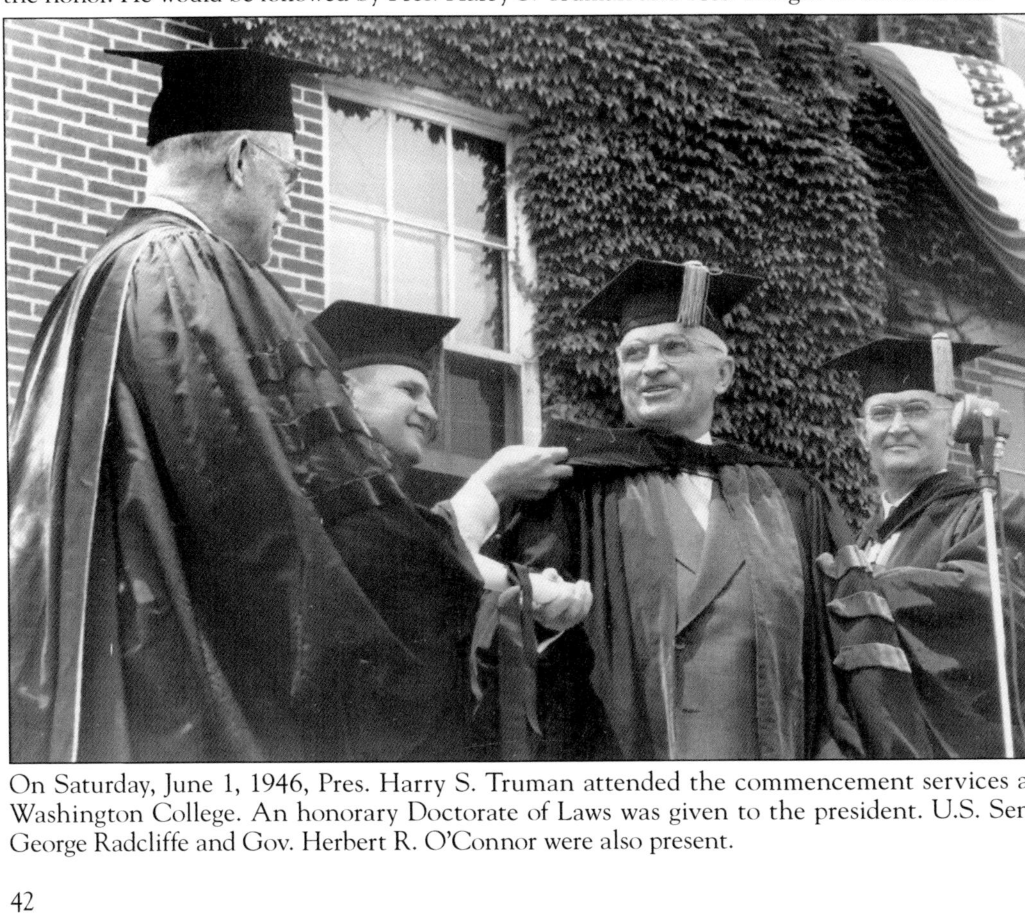

On Saturday, June 1, 1946, Pres. Harry S. Truman attended the commencement services at Washington College. An honorary Doctorate of Laws was given to the president. U.S. Sen. George Radcliffe and Gov. Herbert R. O'Connor were also present.

Four

Our Historic Buildings, Houses, Manors, and Farms

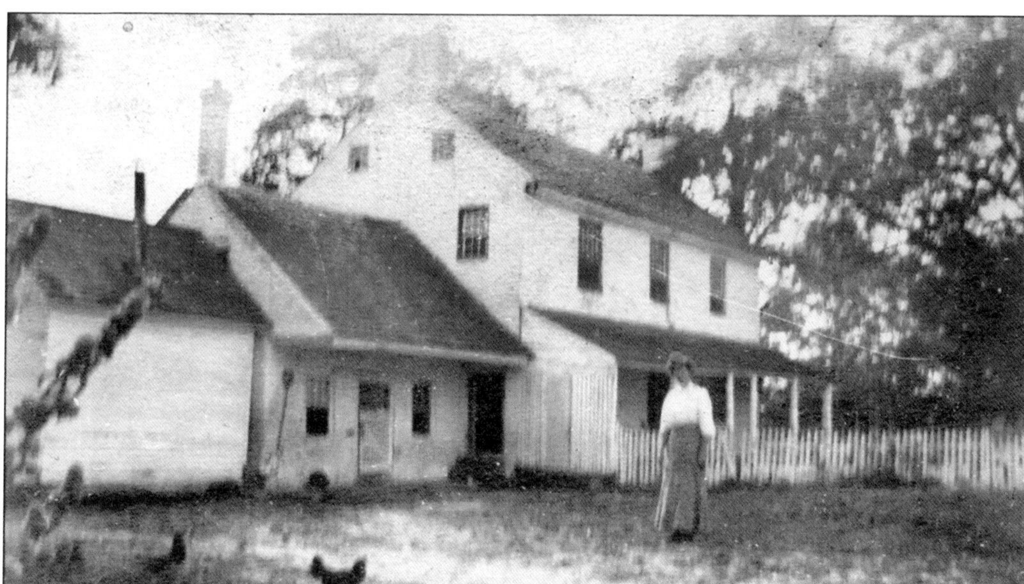

Buck Neck Farm was the home of James Henry and Elizabeth Lord Shuster from 1856 to 1888. On November 19, 1856, their granddaughter, Mary Shuster Groves, shown in front of the Shusters' home, was born here. She was the daughter of John Asbury and Sarah Sureten Shuster Groves.

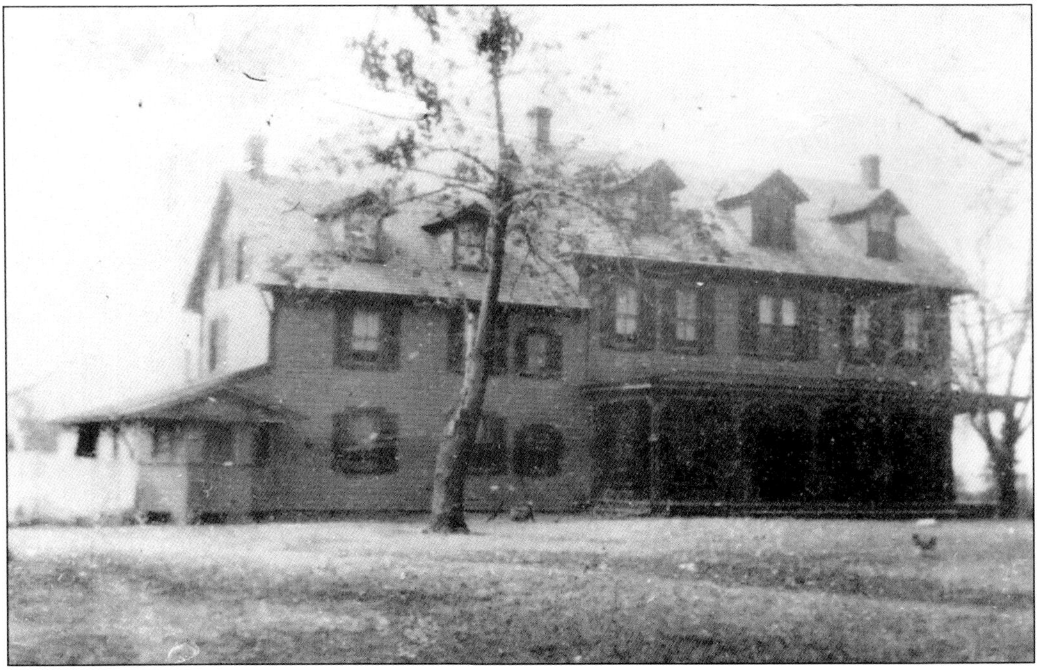

This picture was taken in front of Cedar Grove, home of Benjamin F. and Frances Ann Wickes Sappington, on East Neck Island, Rock Hall, Maryland, *c.* 1910.

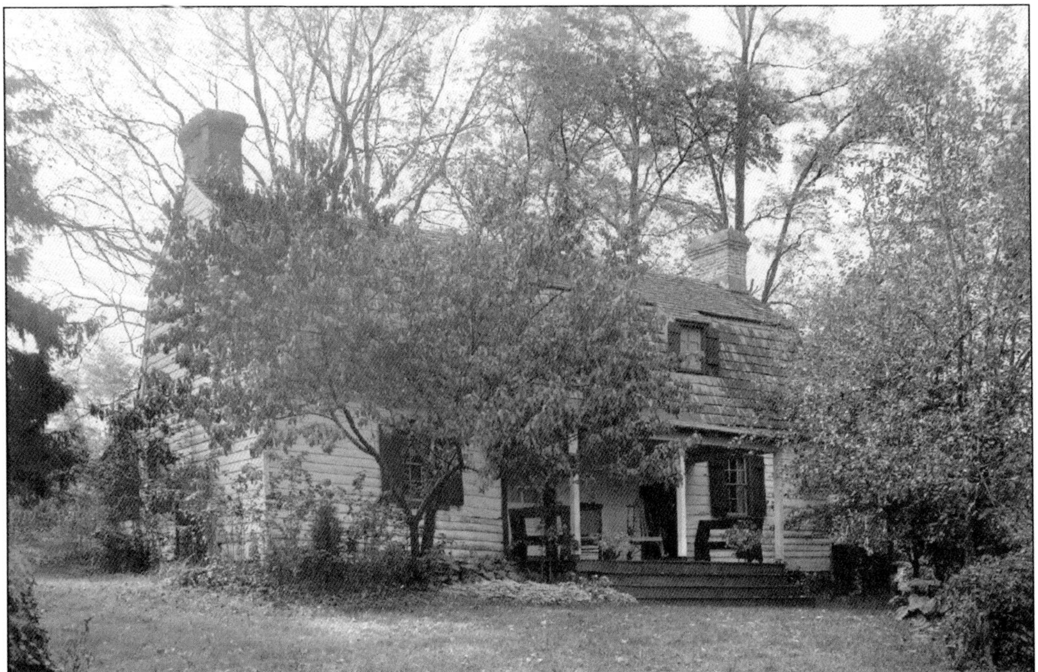

Valley Cottage was built in 1737 on lot number 51 in the village of Georgetown. It is one of the few houses in Kent County that has remained in the same family for eight generations.

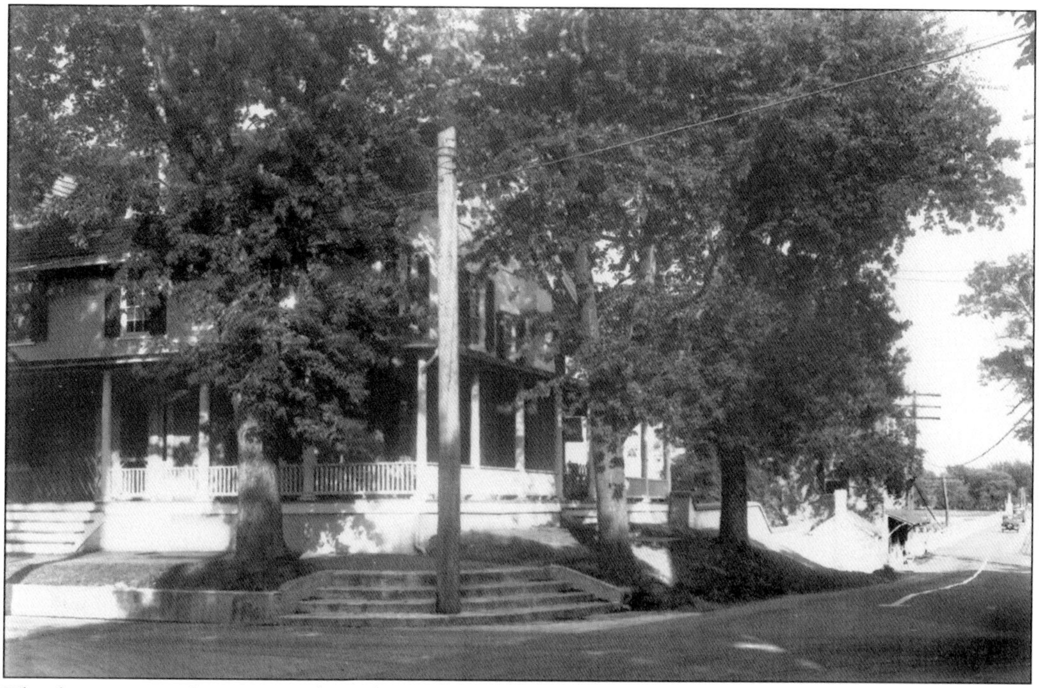

This house is on the corner of Maple Avenue and North Water Street in Chestertown, just before crossing the Chester River Bridge. It is known as the Perkins House and was built in the third quarter of the 18th century. A small toll house at the edge of this property was where bridge tolls were collected until tolls were lifted in 1890 by Kent and Queen Anne's Counties.

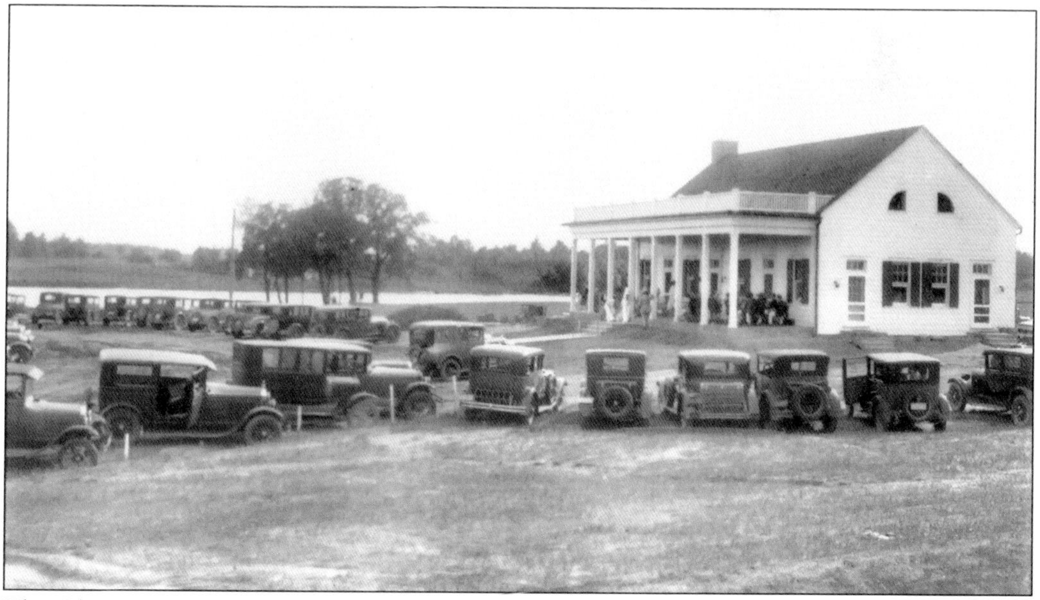

The Chester River Yacht and Country Club, located on Quaker Neck Road just a few miles from Chestertown, was conceived by a group of 27 men. The clubhouse was built in 1928 as an all-purpose family club offering swimming, boating, tennis, and nine holes of golf. The wooden Chester River Bridge reportedly had been recently dismantled around this time. Its wood apparently floated down the river and was used to create a 14-slip pier at the club.

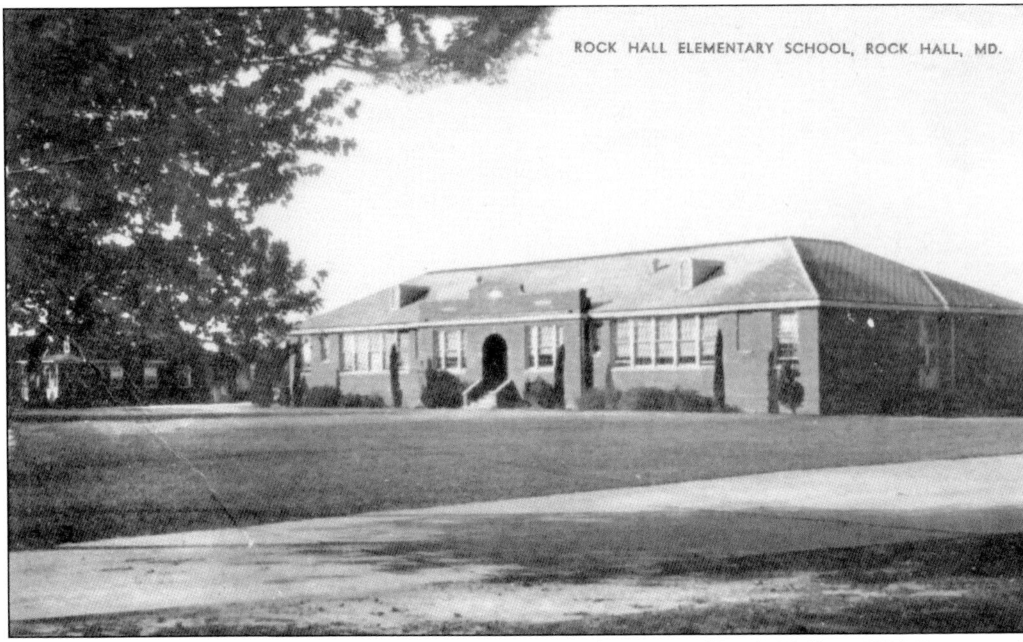

The former Rock Hall Elementary School was given to the town of Rock Hall in 1976. It presently houses all of Rock Hall's administrative offices along with meeting rooms, the Rock Hall Museum, a branch of the Kent County Public Library, and a Head Start program. It also serves as a senior center with cafeteria service, and a private insurance company rents space there as well.

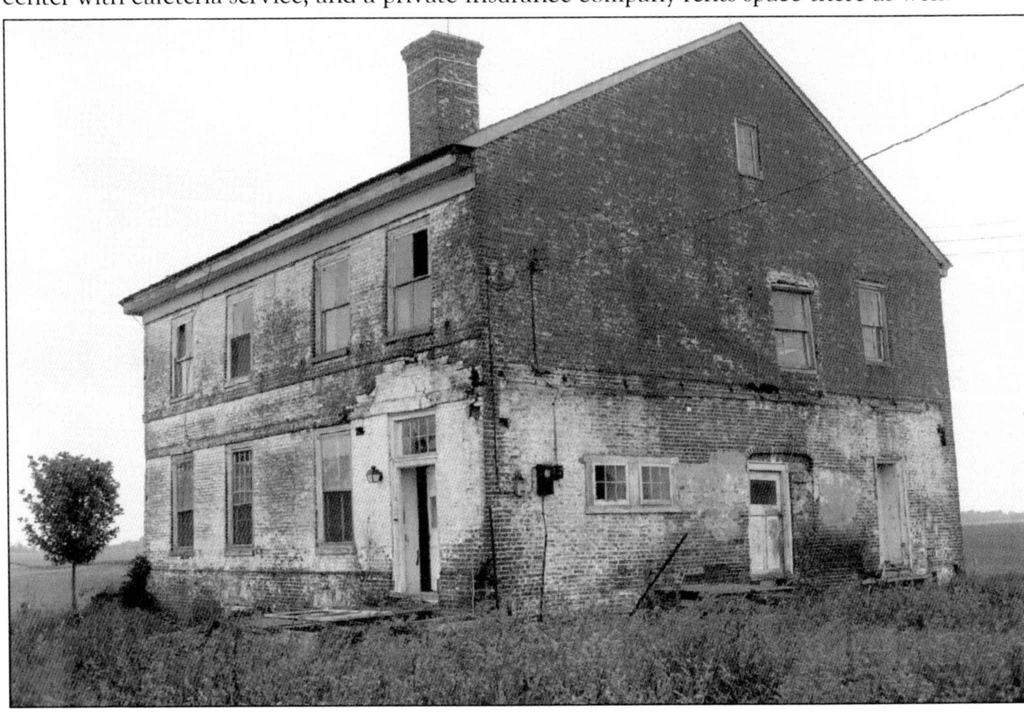

Rose Hill is located on the old road between Chestertown and Georgetown. This house was built in 1760 by Alexander Calder. The house is shown here in a 1936 photograph. It has been beautifully restored and is listed on the National Register of Historic Houses.

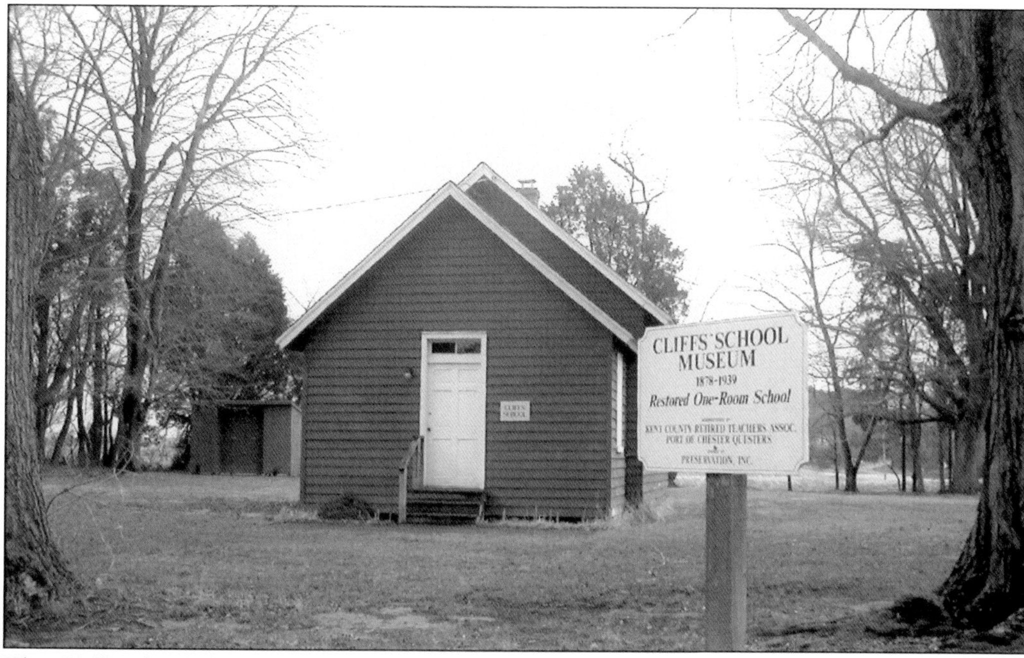

The Cliff School, located on Quaker Neck Road south of Chestertown, is the last one-room school in Kent County. The school property (one acre, more or less) was purchased in 1878 by the Kent County school commissioners for $50 to serve as a fishing and farming community. The schoolhouse was in use until 1939. One teacher taught seven grades. It is owned by Preservation, Inc. and administered by the Kent County Retired Teachers Association and the Port of Chester Questers, a local club.

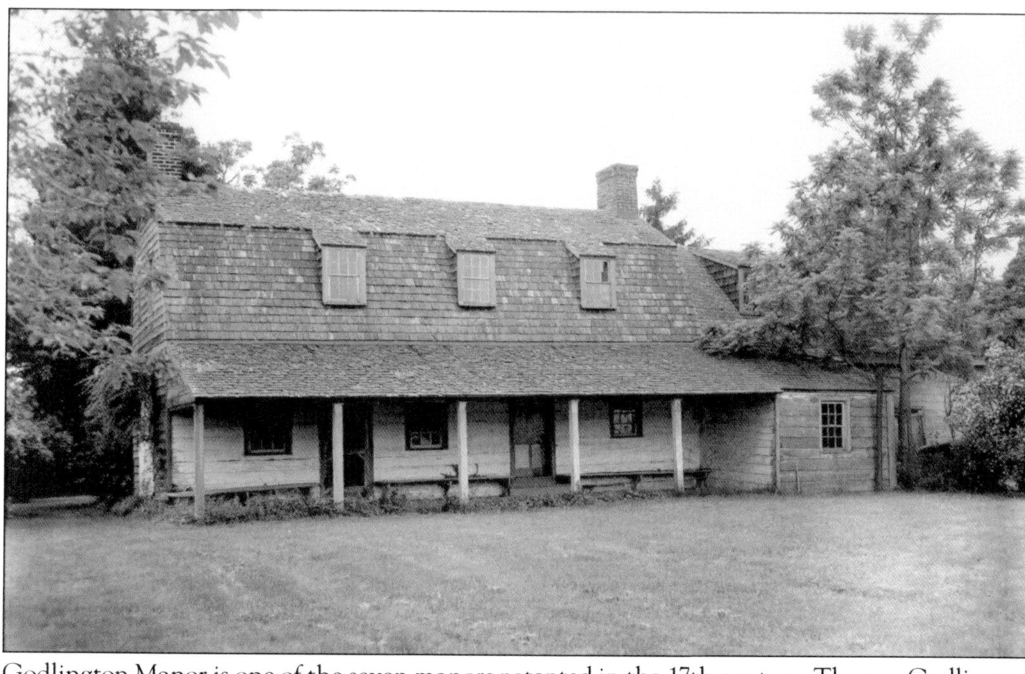

Godlington Manor is one of the seven manors patented in the 17th century. Thomas Godlington received a land grant of 1,000 acres for the manor in 1659.

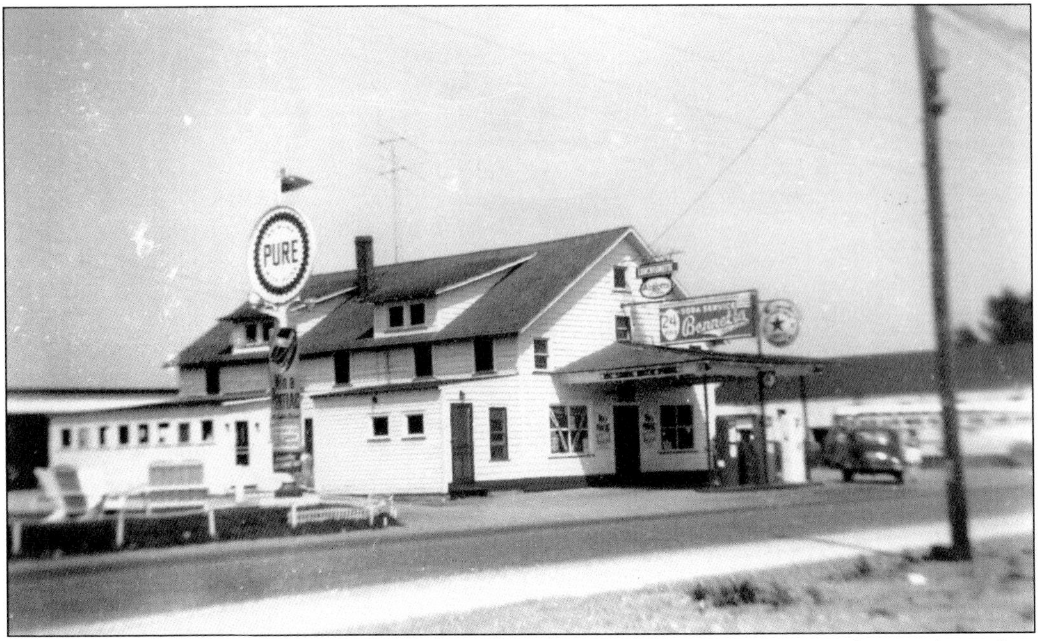

Bill Bennett's Service Station, on Washington Avenue in Chestertown, was the Trailways bus station in 1945. It was located to the left of the present-day Watkin's Auto Supply Company.

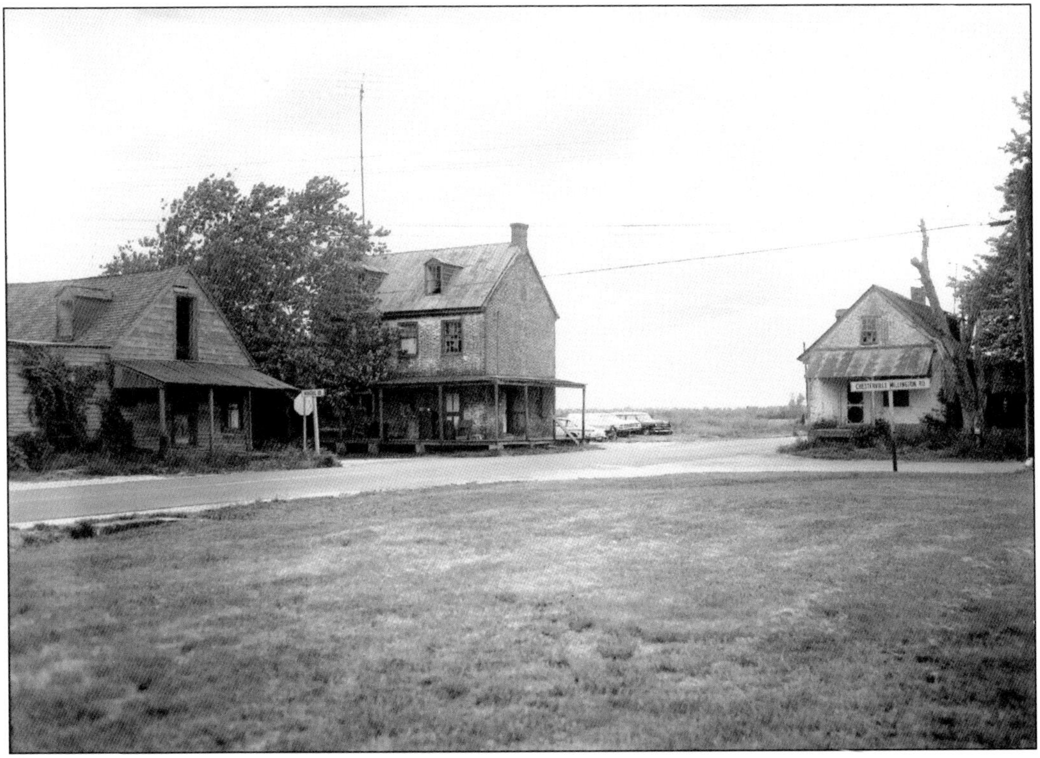

Shown here is Chesterville Crossroads with the Chesterville Hotel on the left, Spencer Store in the center, and Chesterville Store and the post office on the right. These buildings do not exist today. Chesterville, called New Market in the 1720s, was considered a small village.

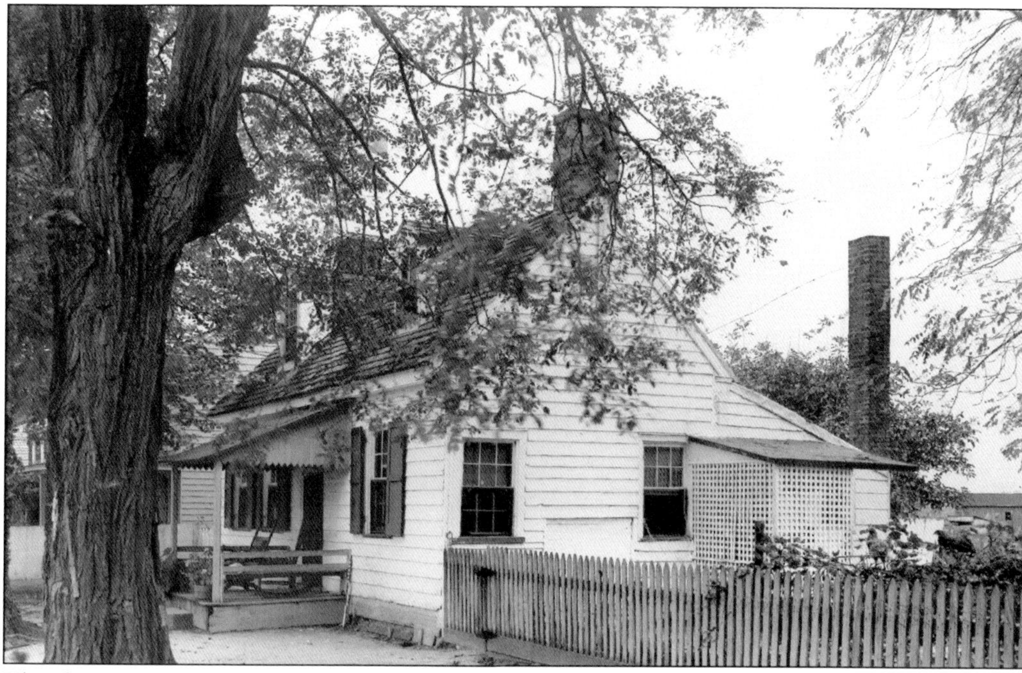

This frame cottage was located on Route 213 in Galena. It was built *c.* 1846 and was included in the photographic documentation of the Historic American Building Survey that was completed in the 1930s. It is now referred to as the Cochran House.

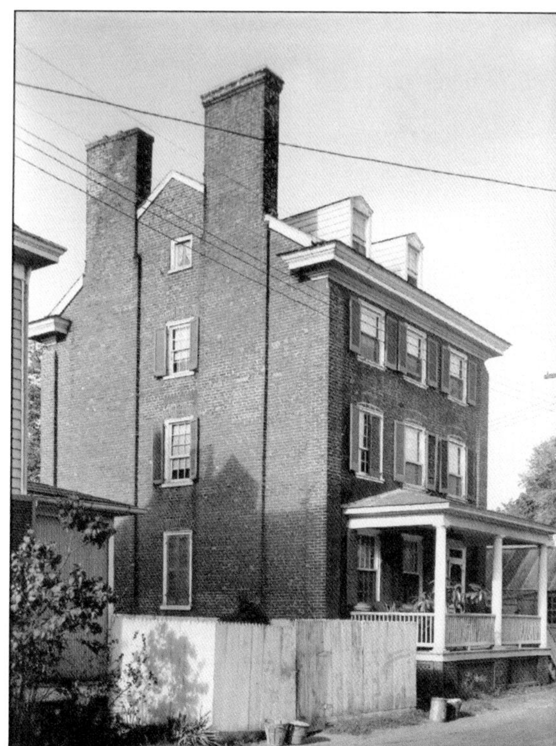

The Geddes-Piper House is the headquarters of the Historical Society of Kent County. It represents the first use of a townhouse plan in Chestertown. Willaim Geddes, customs collector of the Port of Chestertown, completed the house in the early 1700s and sold it soon after completion to James Piper, a Chestertown merchant. The brigantine *Geddes*, presumably owned by William Geddes, was the scene of Chestertown's Tea Party on May 23, 1774.

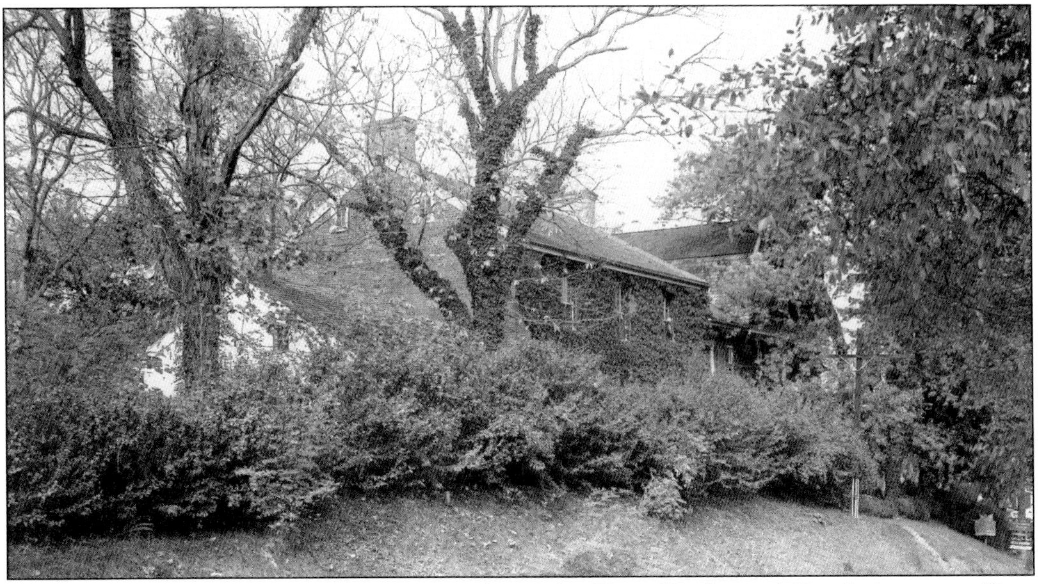

The Kitty Knight House in Georgetown is where Miss Kitty (Catherine) Knight became a Kent County and American heroine. The British troops advanced up the Sassafras River in May 1813, burning, looting, and causing many Georgetown residents to flee. The legend states that Miss Kitty stood her ground to protect an invalid neighbor's and her own house. She was 38 when she confronted Rear Admiral Cockburn at the two adjacent houses on the Georgetown hill and convinced him not to burn them, and she was also able to save a church and several other houses. Today the two adjoining brick residences she saved (with the front entrance facing the Sassafras River) is the Kitty Knight Restaurant and 11-room inn. The restaurant is often referred to as "Miss Kitty," where one can dine overlooking the Georgetown Yacht Basin and the Sassafras River. There is also a tavern named Cockburn's Tavern, named after the British admiral.

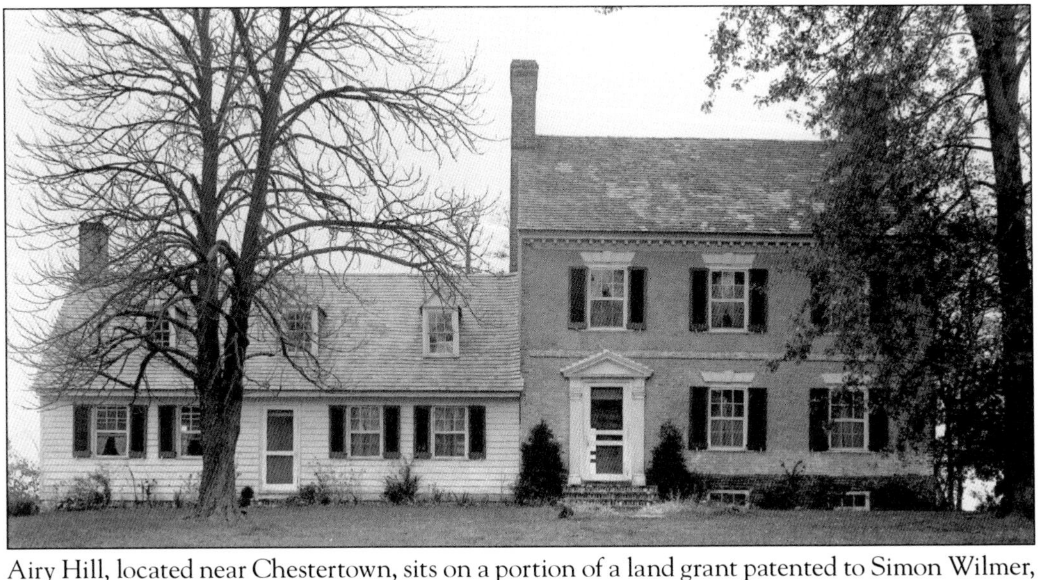

Airy Hill, located near Chestertown, sits on a portion of a land grant patented to Simon Wilmer, one of Kent's early pioneers. It was built by John and Anna Maria Rowles *c.* 1790. There is a small family graveyard on the property that contains the graves of Mary Thomas (1781–1850) and her husband, George Thomas (1781–1842).

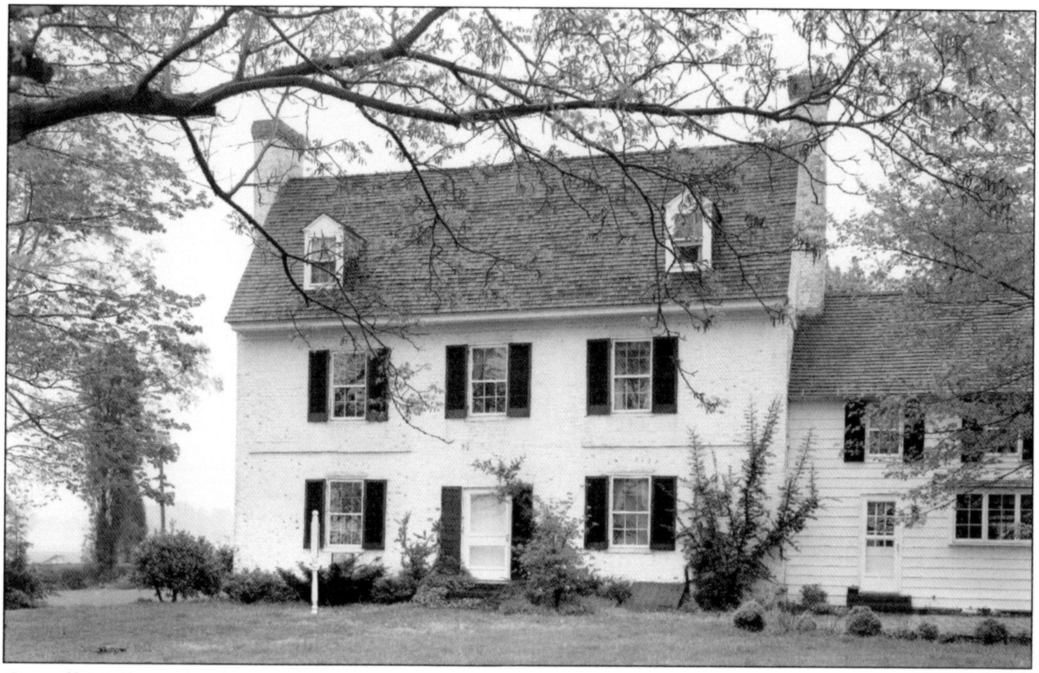

Carvill Hall was built in 1695 on a 26-acre tract of land called Carvill's Prevention. Carvill Hall stands as the oldest residence in Kent County. It was built by John Carvill, who served as high sheriff of Cecil County and as a delegate of the Maryland General Assembly. Carvill Hall is still used as a residence and is now part of the Great Oak Club. Carvill Hall is on the National Historic Register of Historic Places.

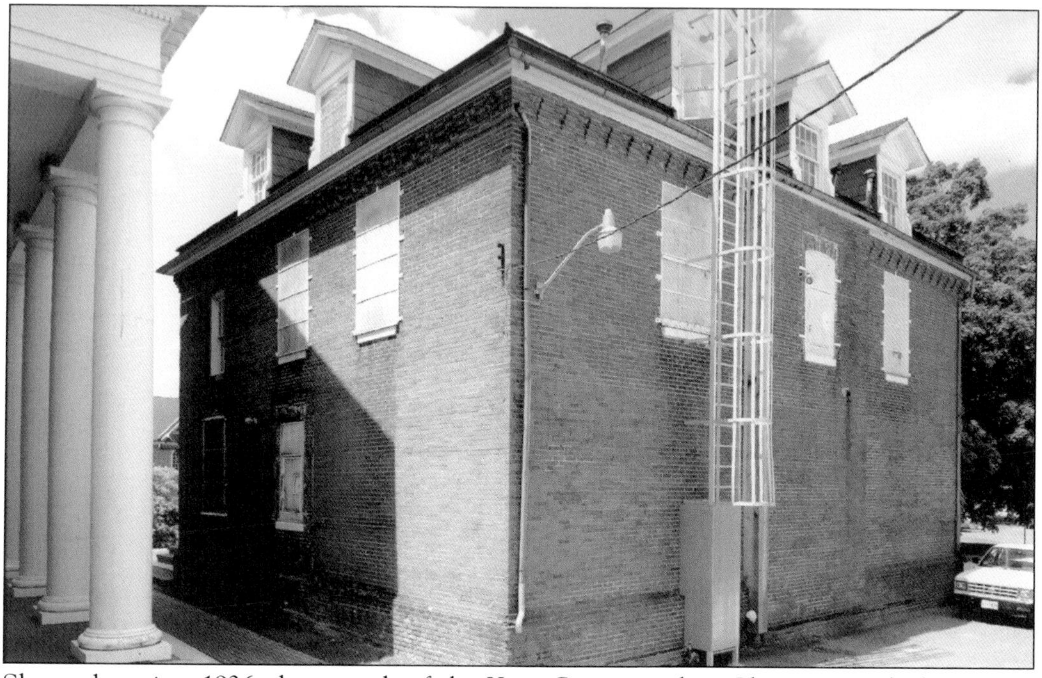

Shown here is a 1936 photograph of the Kent County jail in Chestertown before it was torn down.

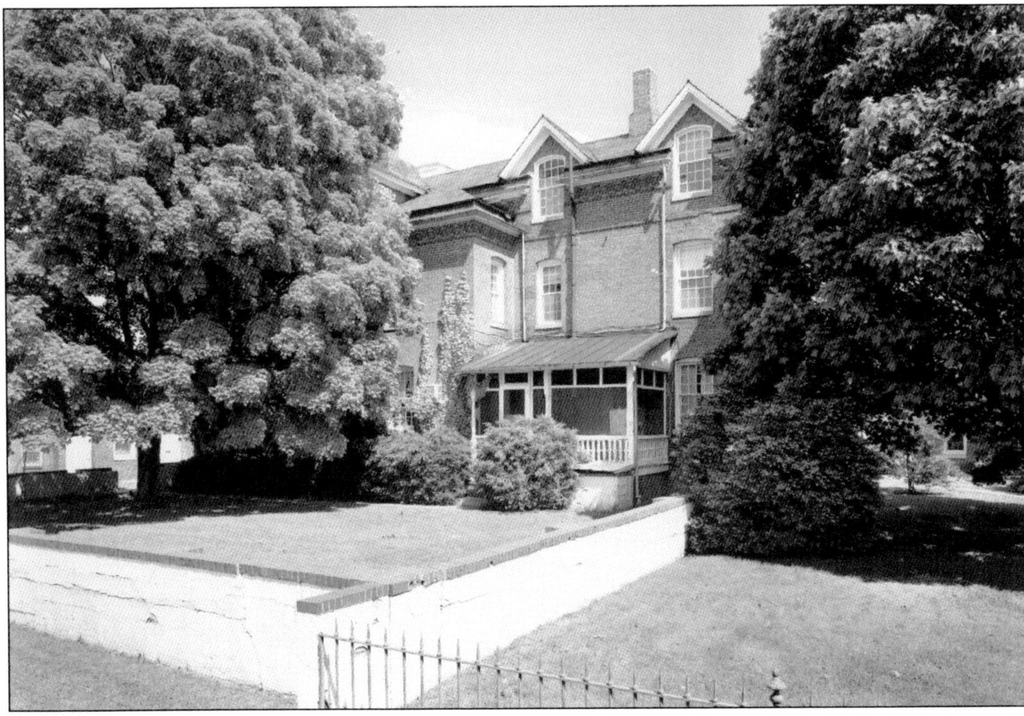

In this photograph, the Kent County Jail, now demolished, faces Cross Street in Chestertown. It was erected in 1884. H. M. Stuart was the builder.

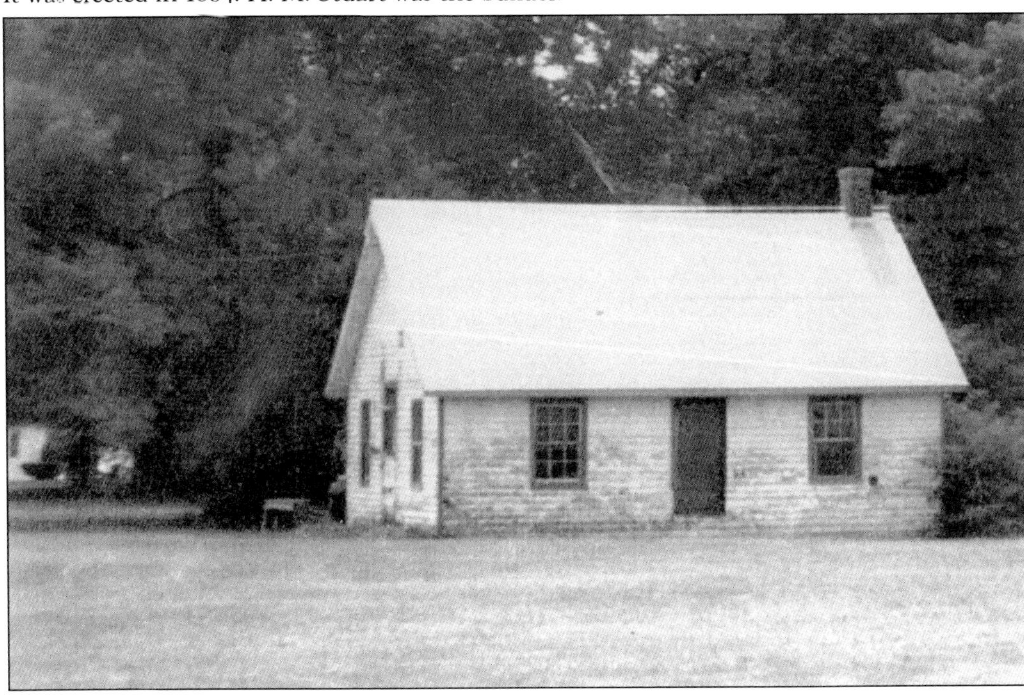

Worton Point Colored School No. 2 is now the African American Schoolhouse Museum, housing a collection of photographs, artifacts, and memorabilia. The community was settled in the 1700s, and many Worton Point residents can trace their ancestry to slave days.

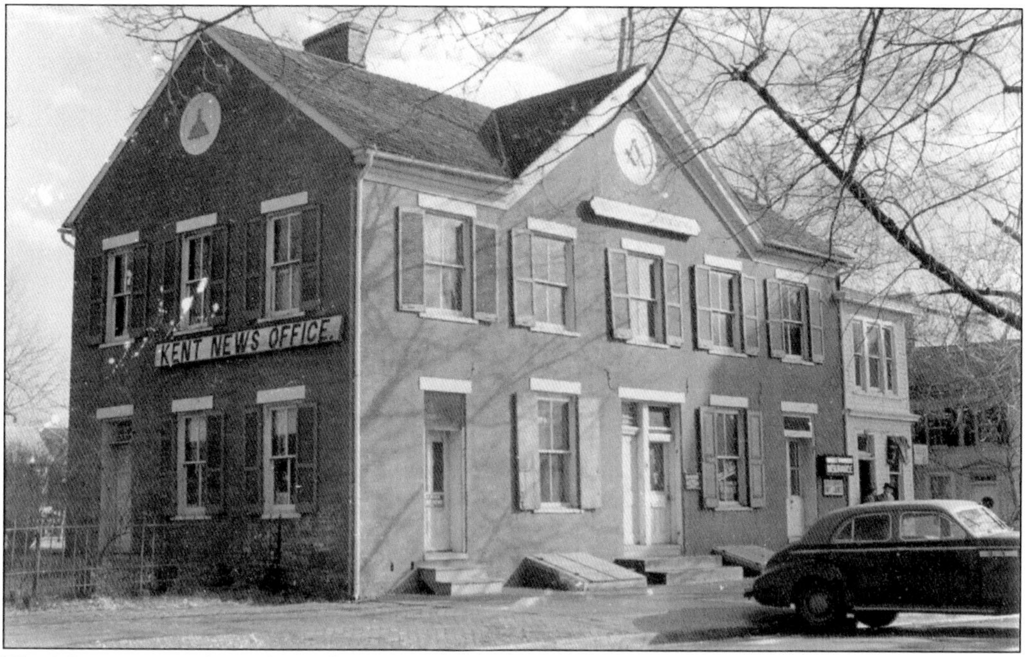

The Masonic Temple Building faces High Street in Chestertown. It was built between 1826, when the Maryland General Assembly granted the lot to the Masons, and 1835, when a deed from the Clinton Lodge to the president and directors of Masonic Hall Company referred to a building on the property. As early as 1849, the building was being used as a newspaper establishment when it became known as the Kent News Building. Masonic emblems appear in both gable ends and in the central pediment.

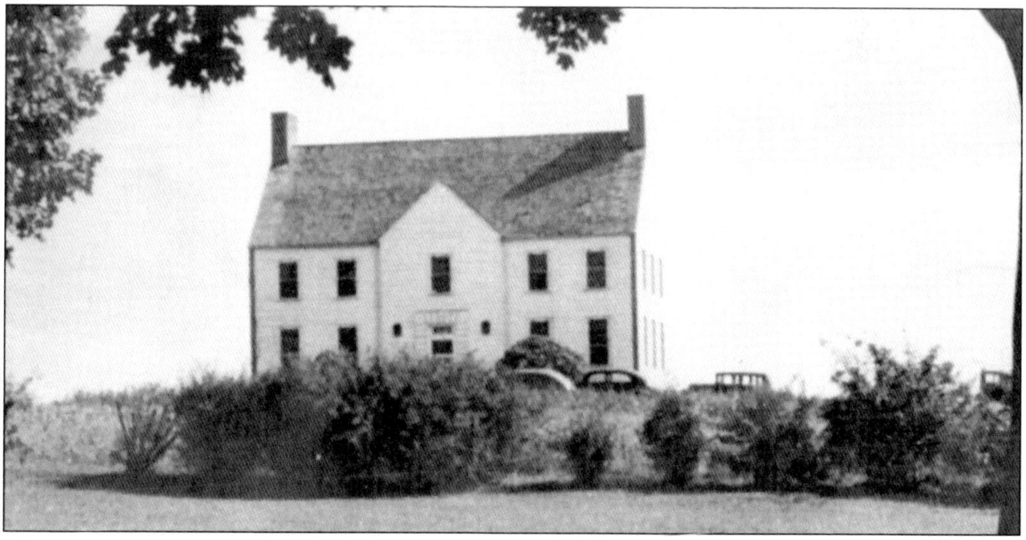

This is the original building of the Kent and Queen Anne's Hospital located in Chestertown, Maryland. It had its beginnings is 1928 in four rented rooms on the second floor of William Rodney's home on High Street. In March of 1930, the hospital was a two-story building behind Washington College's Reid Hall. From humble beginnings, the hospital has grown to a 56-bed facility. The hospital is now called Chester River Hospital Center and is part of the Chester River Health System.

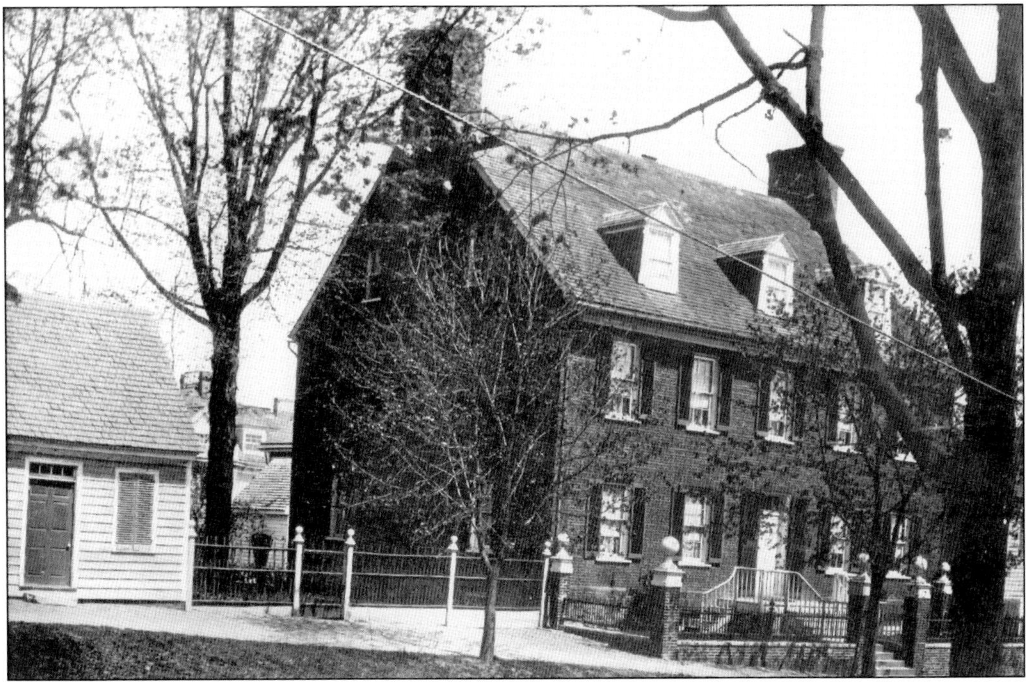

The Wickes House was home to one of Chestertown's most prominent families. It also was a tavern and a hotel. A large garden, which is a Chestertown landmark, adjoins the northwest corner of the house and is surrounded by a brick wall.

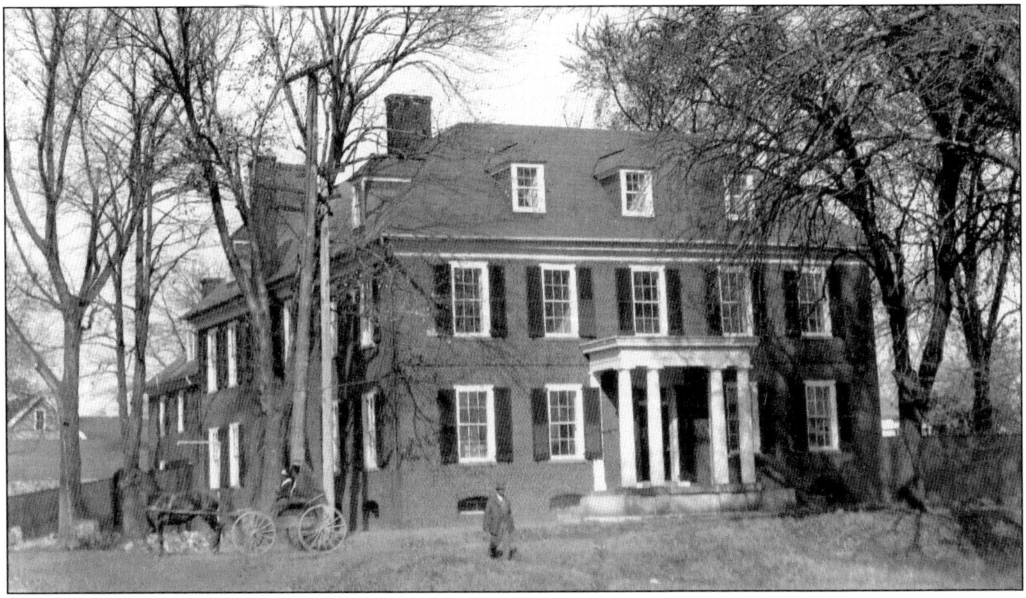

The Hynson Ringgold House, sometimes called "The Abbey," is home to the president of Washington College. A mid-section houses one of Chestertown's most beautiful staircases. The interior once boasted a room by William Buckland that was removed to the Baltimore Museum of Art in 1932. The house was built in two stages on land that had been owned by Nathaniel Hynson in 1735. Dr. William Murray purchased the lot in 1743, built the front section, and sold it to Thomas Ringgold, a wealthy Chestertown merchant.

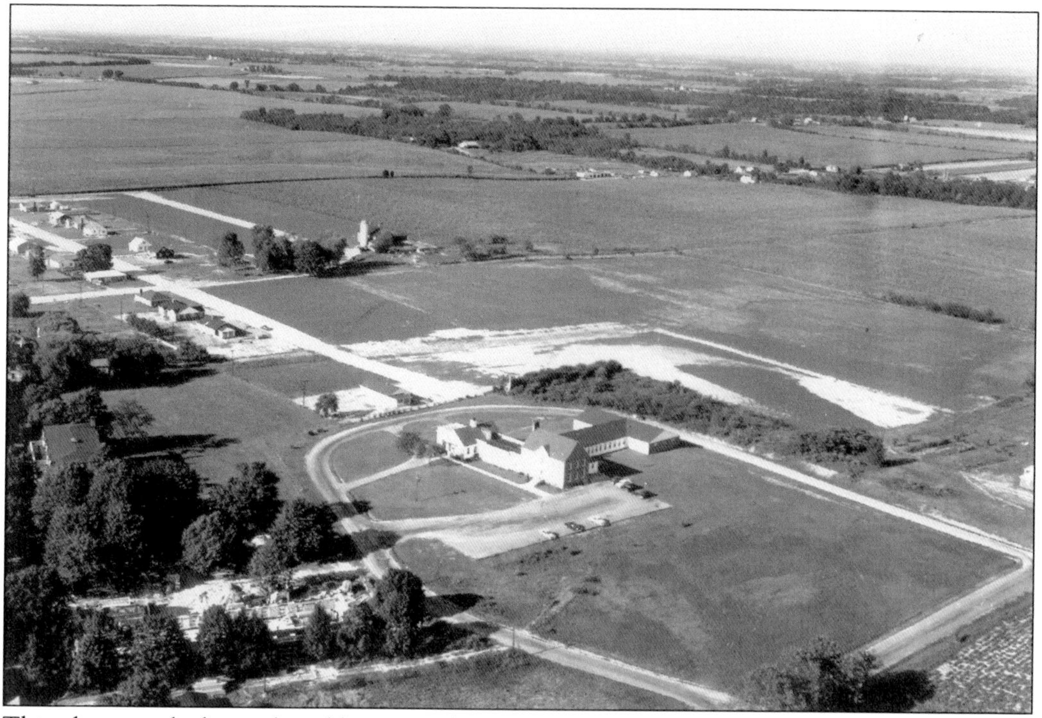

This photograph shows the additions to the Kent and Queen Anne's Hospital in Chestertown. Pine Street in the College Heights subdivision is shown to the left.

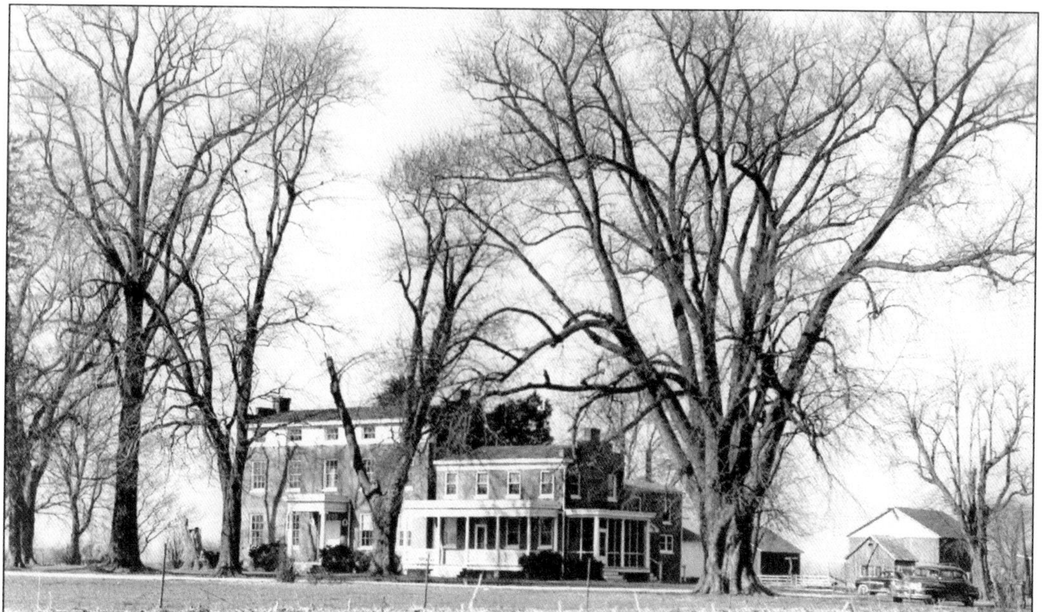

The Stephney farmhouse was built in Broad Neck by Benjamin Beck in 1850. The name Stephney Farm is derived from the name "Stephenheath Manor," which was a 1,000-acre tract that was patented in 1659 to Samuel Pensax, a London mariner. The National Society of Descendants of Lords of the Maryland Manors erected a plaque in 2005 marking the manor of Stephenheath.

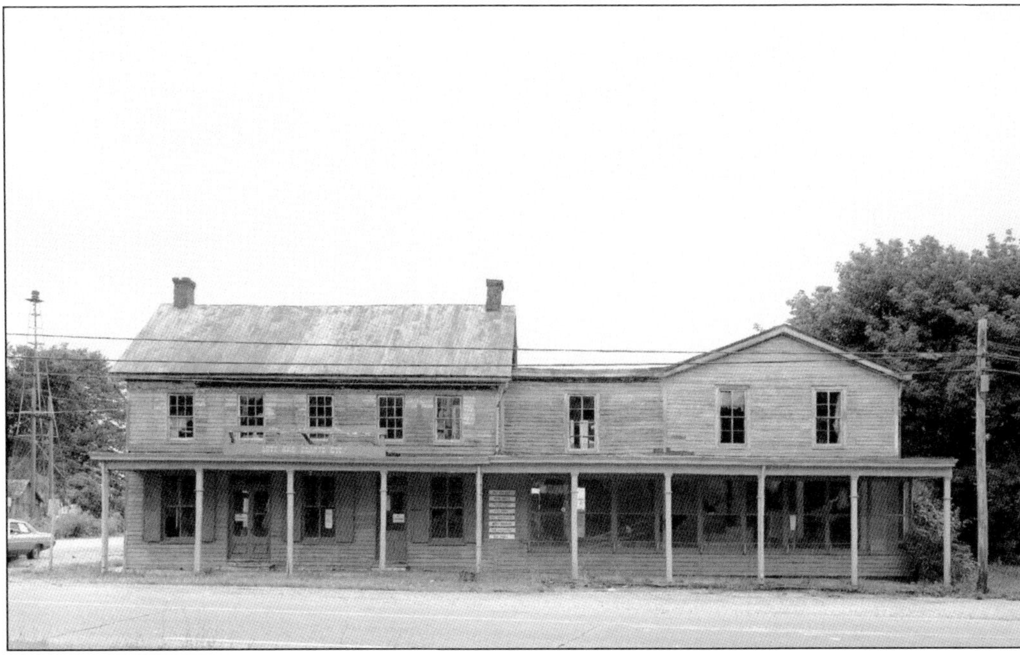

George Harper's store is a mainstay in the small crossroad village of Still Pond. Still Pond, which derives its name from Steelpond Creek, was the first place south of the Mason-Dixon Line where women could vote. Three women voted in local elections in 1908, 12 years before women would win that right in 1920 with the ratification of the 19th Amendment.

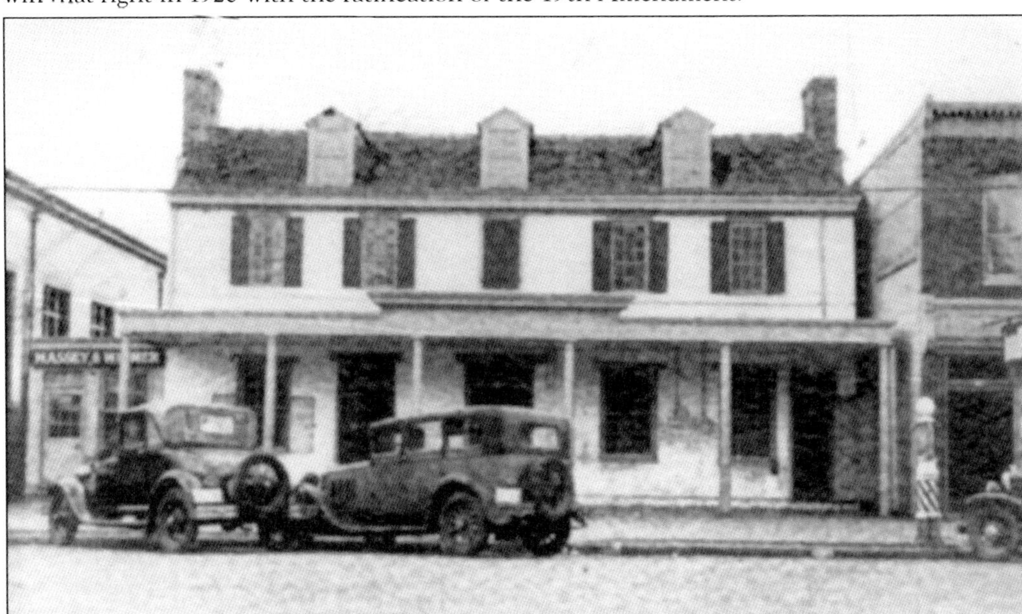

In 1932, this High Street building in Chestertown was the office of Mr. Thomas W. Eliason. Constructed as a residence by Joseph Nicholson in 1733, it was enlarged into a tavern in the 1790s and operated as such until the 1850s, when it became a general store. The tavern was eventually restored to its 1795 appearance in the late 1970s and re-opened in 1981 as a bed and breakfast named the White Swan Tavern.

Five

Sundays in Kent

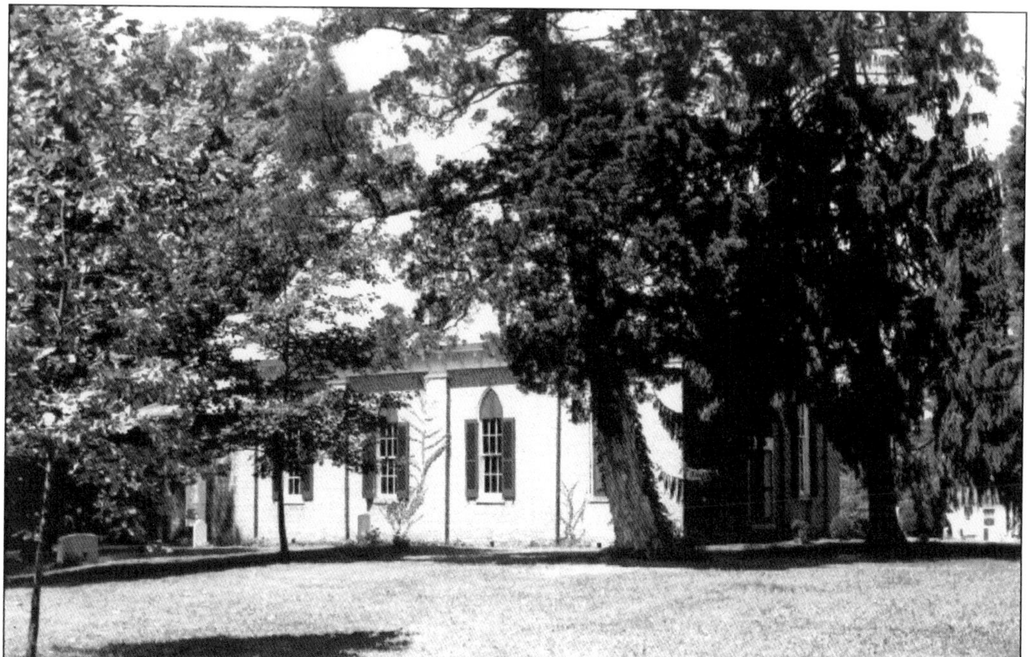

I. U. Christ Church is located just outside the village of Worton. Katherine Hepburn, the famed actress, left the tiny parish $10,000 when she died on June 29, 2003. Her grandfather, Sewell Hepburn, was the parish minister from 1913 until 1925. Hepburn still has relatives in Kent County.

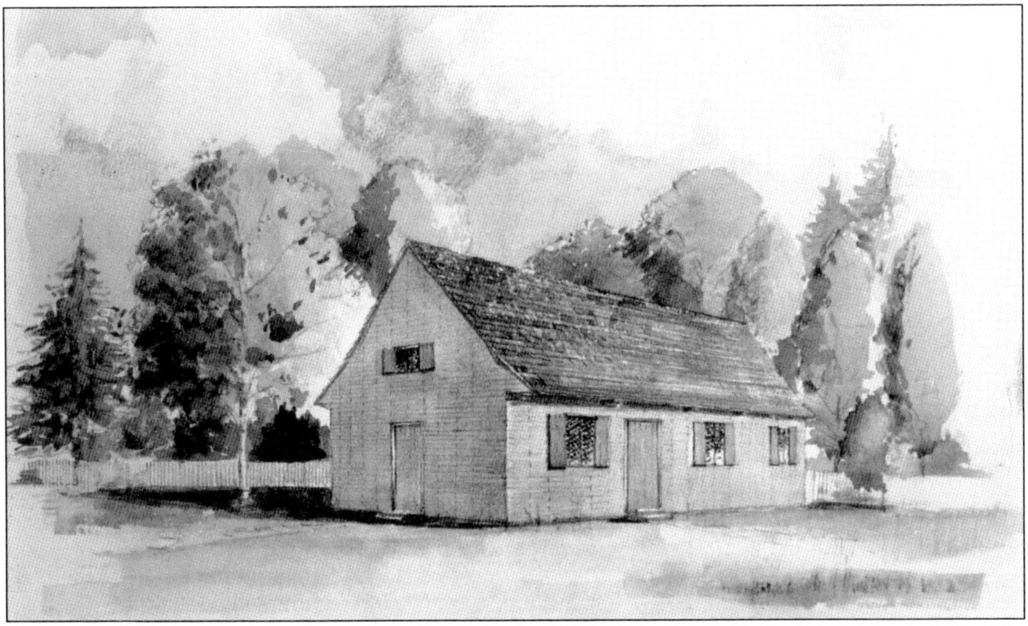

Shrewsbury Parish was one of the first Anglican parishes in Maryland. Similar to St. Paul's Parish, Shrewsbury was officially established in 1692. Originally named South Sassafras Parish because of its location on the southern banks of the Sassafras River, Shrewsbury has been part of Kent County's religious landscape since before 1680. It moved to its new location near Kennedyville shortly after 1692 as a more centralized location for its parishioners. It continues as an active parish today.

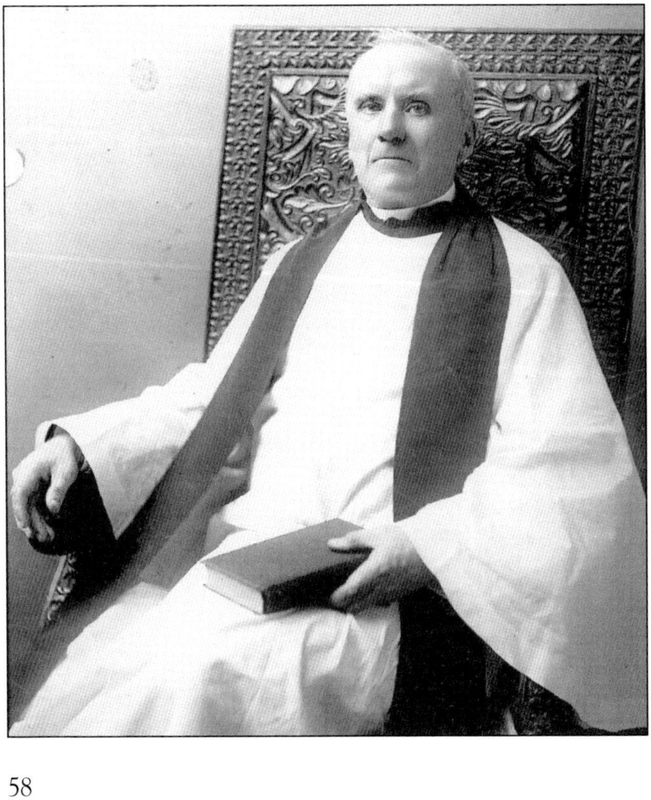

Rev. Stephen C. Roberts, D.Min., was the rector of the Emmanuel Episcopal Church of Chestertown in 1871. He served for 28 years until his death in November 1899. A memorial plaque to Dr. Roberts was placed in the church on the south wall of the chancel.

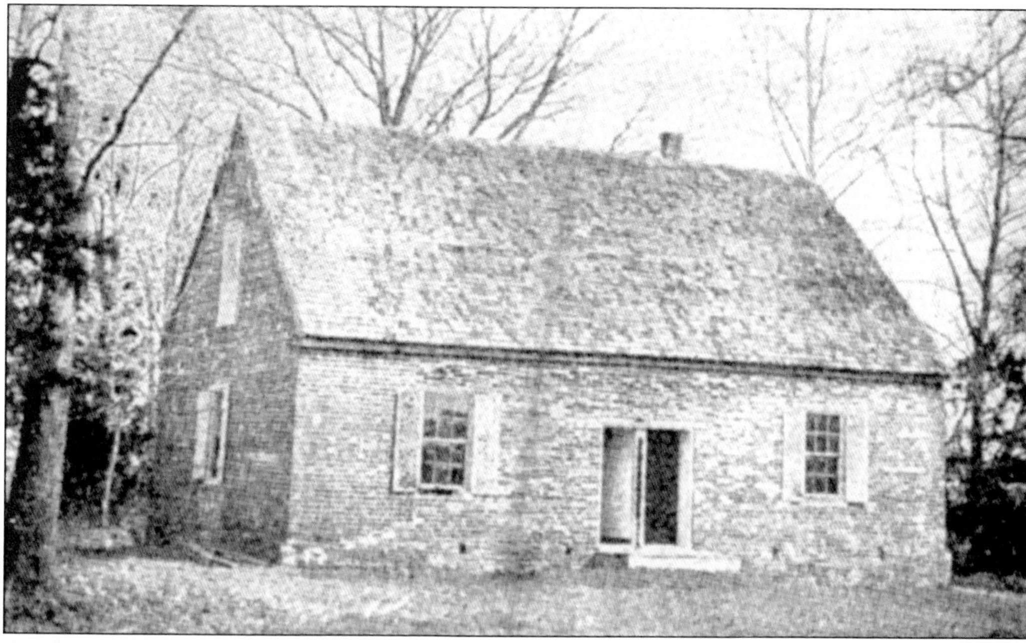

Cecil Meeting House near Lynch, Maryland, is no longer standing. John Lynch, after whom the town is named, was a Quaker, and the meeting house stood on land once owned by him. The Cecil Burial Ground is located just outside of Lynch. It was called Cecil Meeting House because in 1698 Kent County was part of Cecil County.

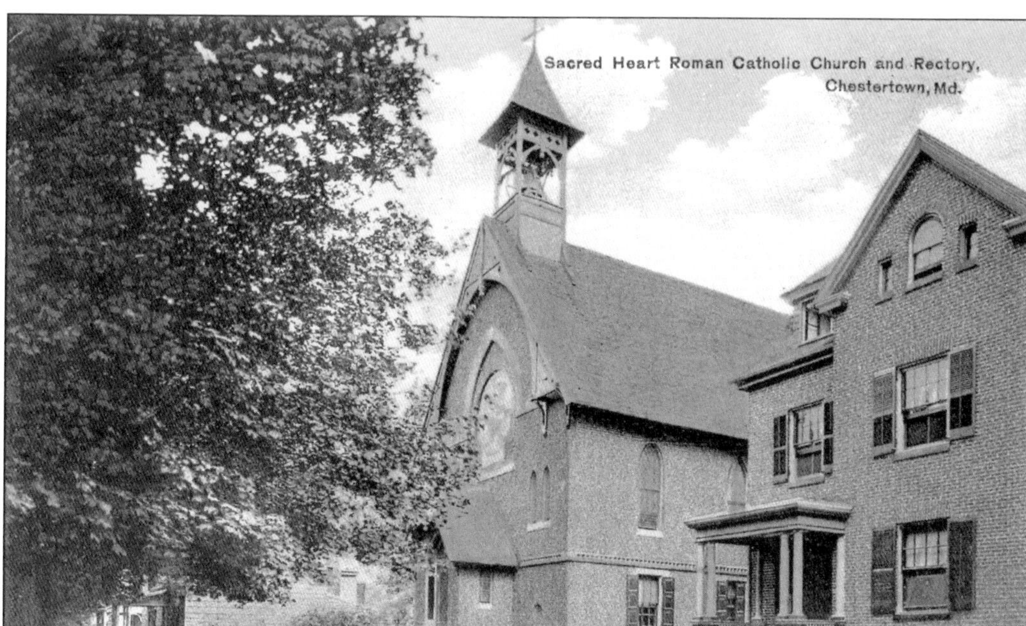

This postcard photograph of Sacred Heart Roman Catholic Church and Rectory was taken shortly after the parish was founded in Chestertown in 1947.

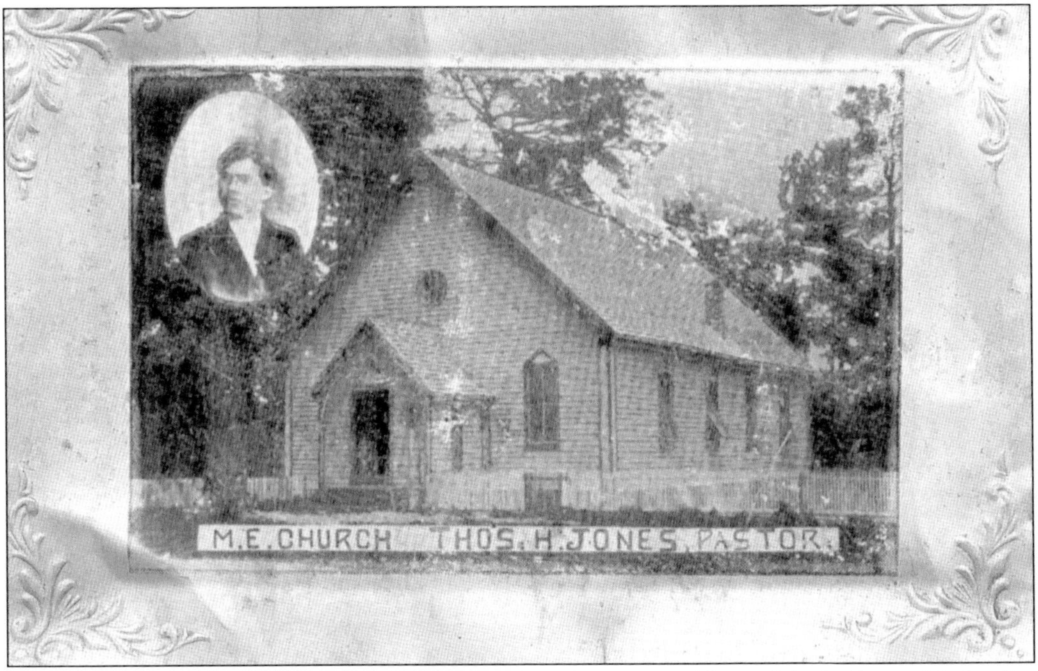

Constructed in 1850, this small white frame church is named Piney Neck Grace Methodist Episcopal Church. It was located at the intersection of Edesville and Crosby Roads in Piney Neck, near the village of Rock Hall.

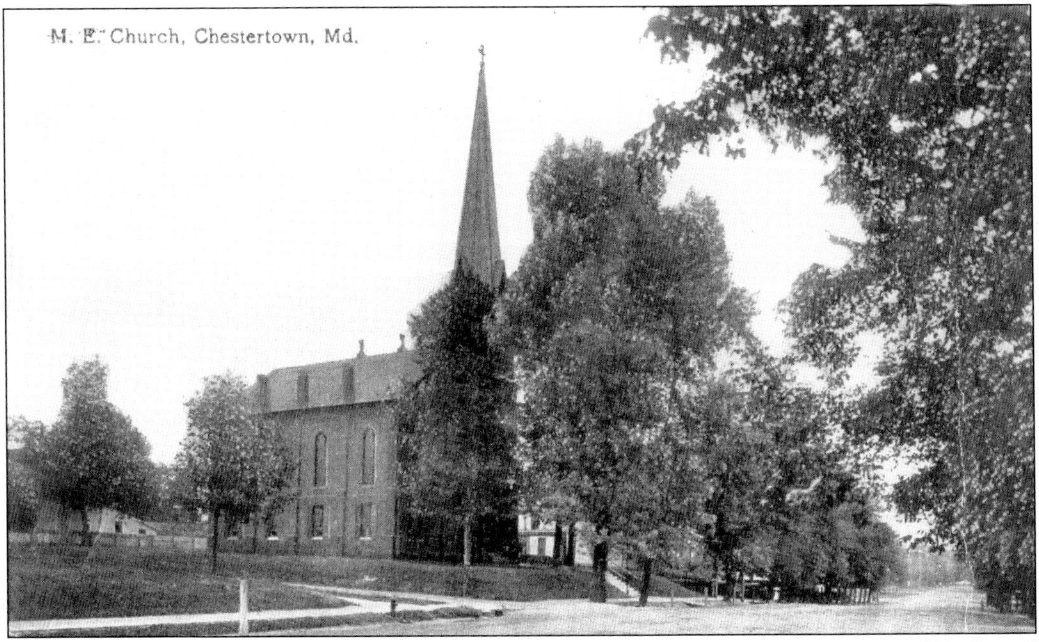

The Methodist Episcopal church was founded in 1780. It is located on the corner of High and Mill Streets in Chestertown. This picture postcard was taken in the 1920s. In 1939, the building became First Methodist Church.

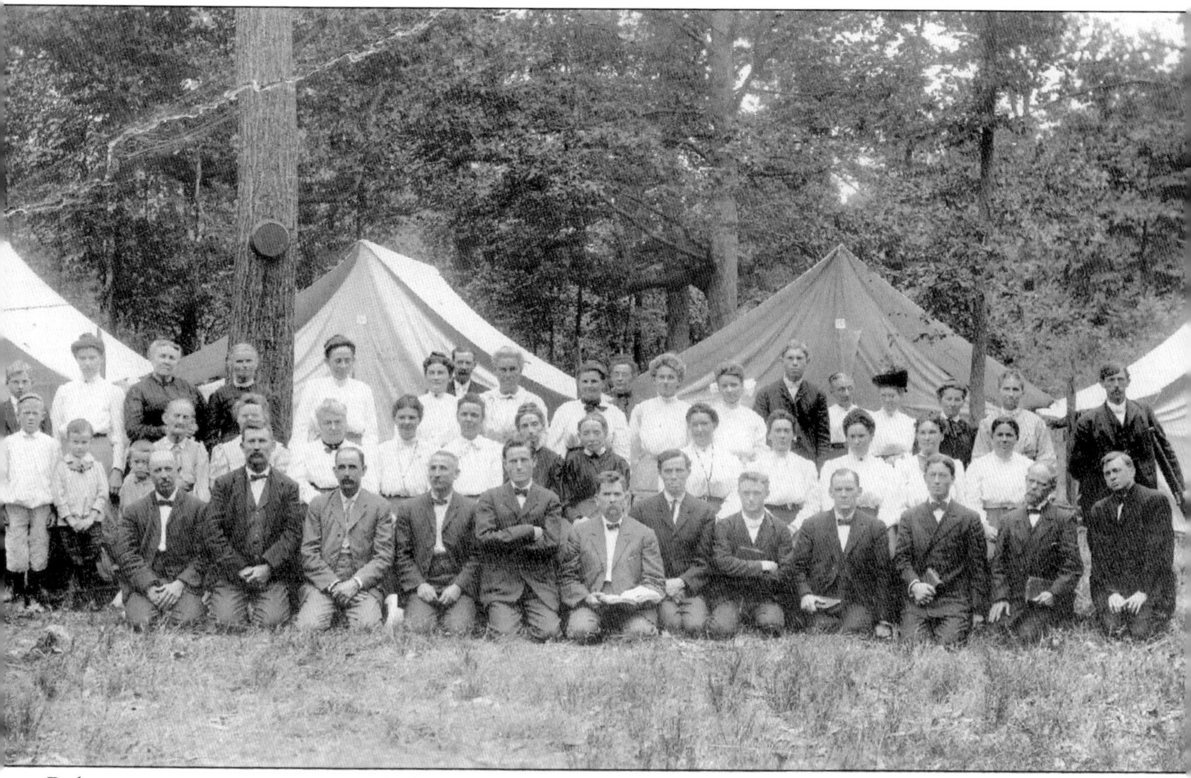

Religious camp meetings were held in various parts of Kent County in the late 19th and early 20th centuries. This is a photograph of the William Wiggins Holiness camp meeting.

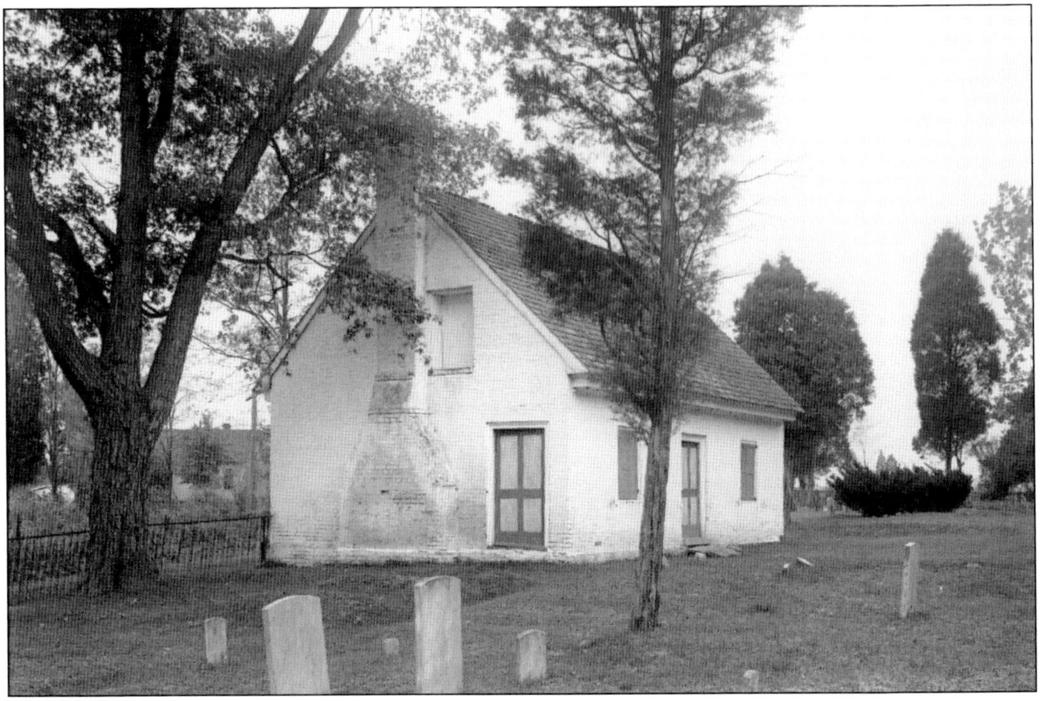

The bricks have been white-washed in this 1930s photograph of St. Paul's Vestry House near Chestertown. It was built in 1766.

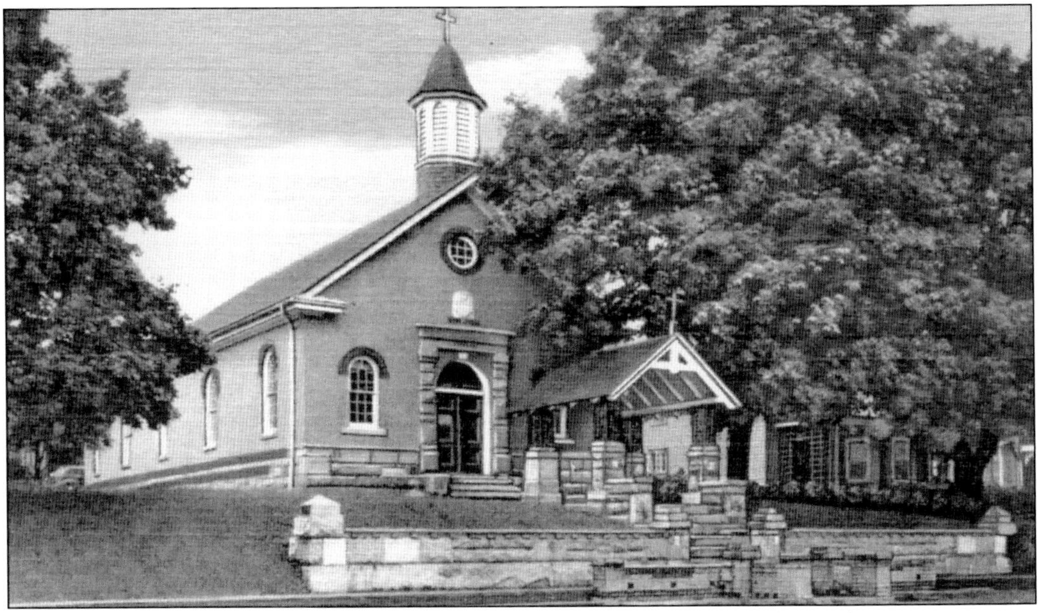

Betterton's Most Precious Blood Catholic Church, built in 1910, is shown here in a picture postcard. It is now closed. The community is considering turning the building into the Betterton Town Community Center.

The Methodist Protestant Church, or Christ Methodist Church, is located on High Street in Chestertown. The church is shown on this 1912 picture postcard, which was published by G. C. Rote of Chestertown.

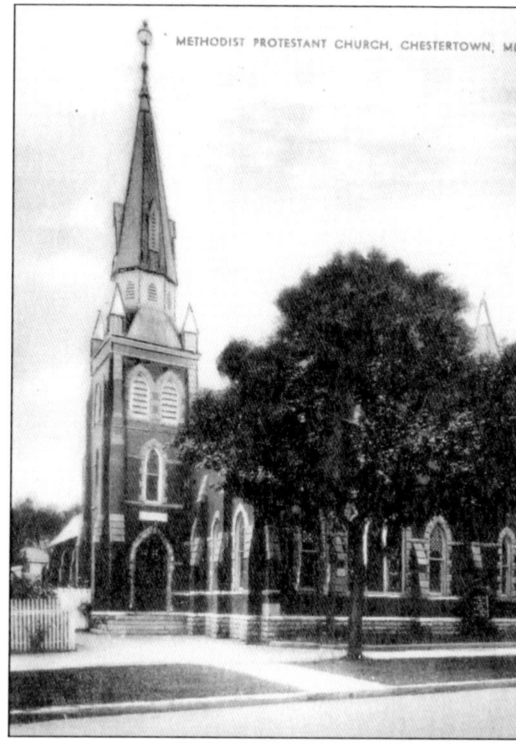

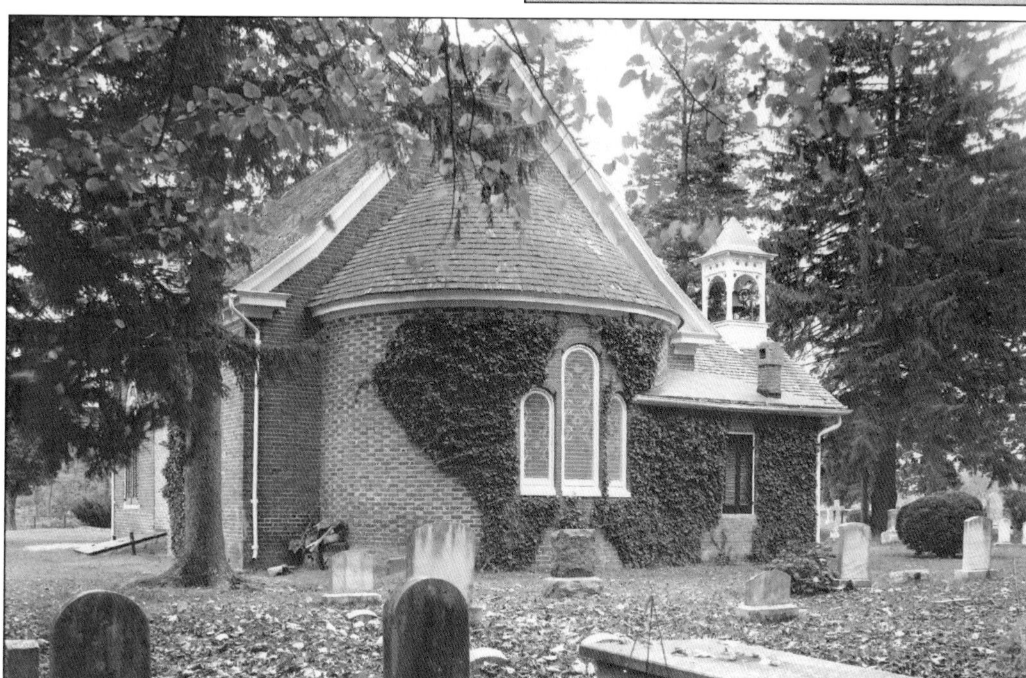

Old St. Paul's Church is the oldest church in continuous service in Maryland. It was built near the village of Fairlee in 1711. The parish was one of the original 30 parishes laid out in Maryland by the "Act for the Service of Almighty God, and the Establishment of the Protestant Religion in the Province."

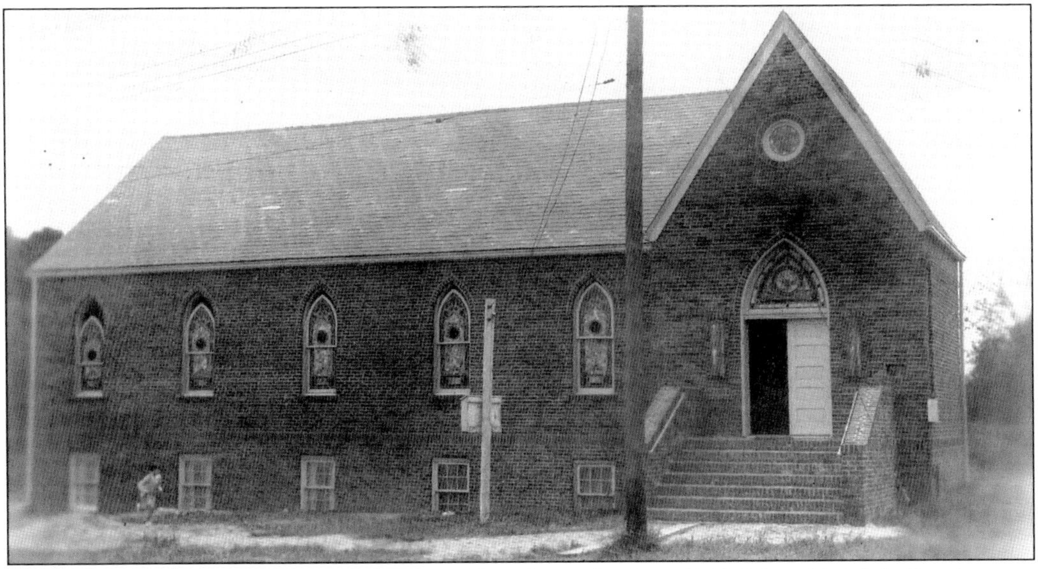

The Chestertown Seventh Day Adventist Church was built in 1945. The official dedication was held in September of that year.

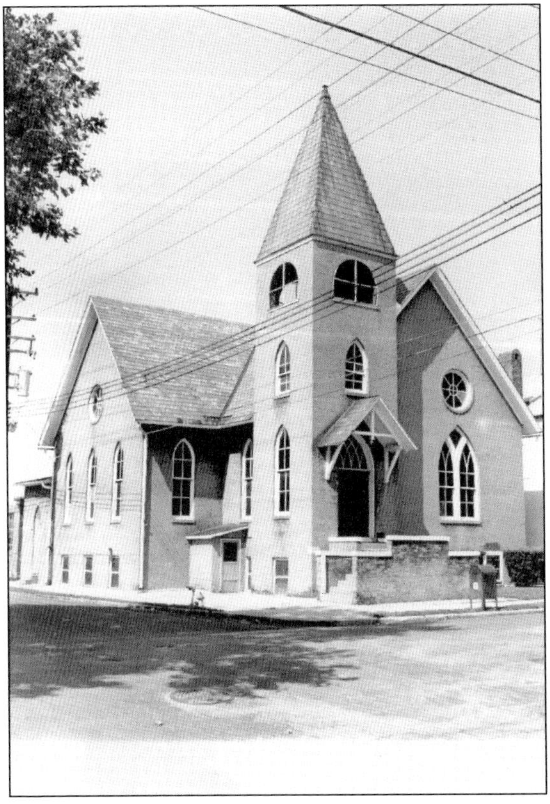

An achievement for Eastern Shore African American Methodism, the Janes United Methodist Church was built in 1914 for $15,000.

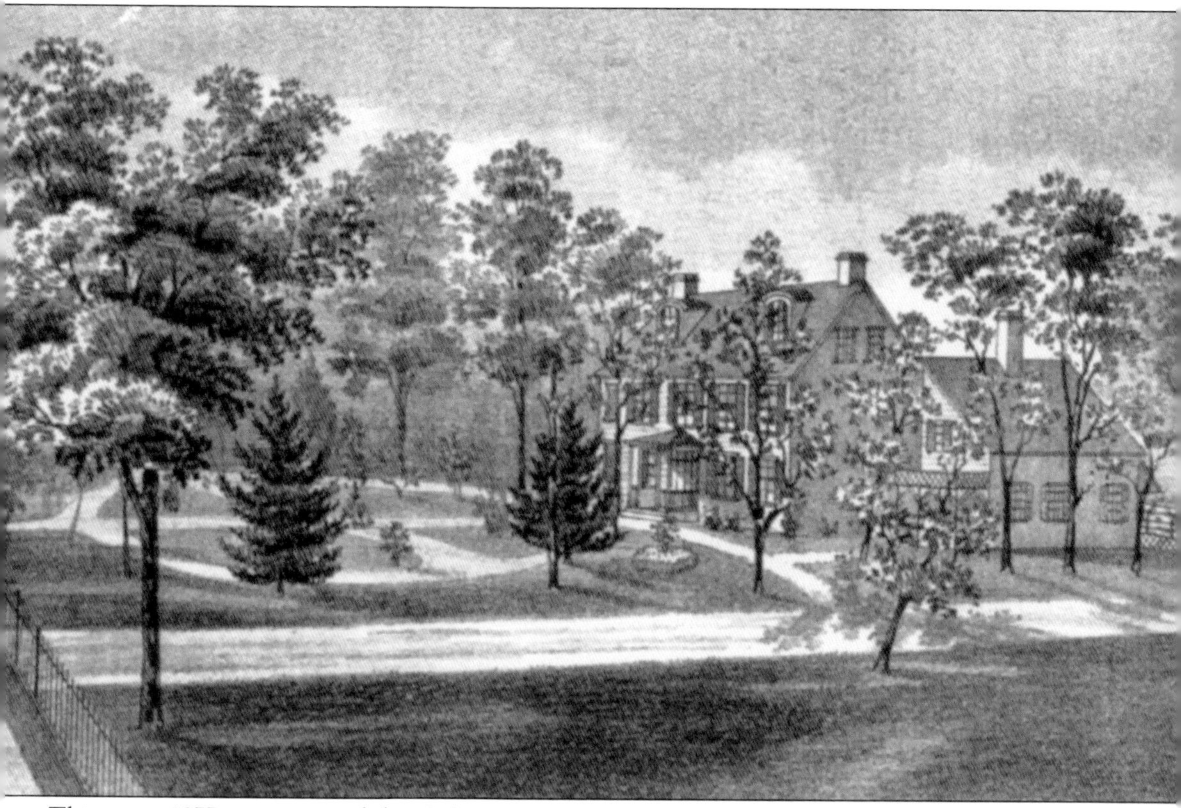

This is an 1877 engraving of the Galena Seminary Home for Young Ladies. Miss E. Lavinia Benny was the principal.

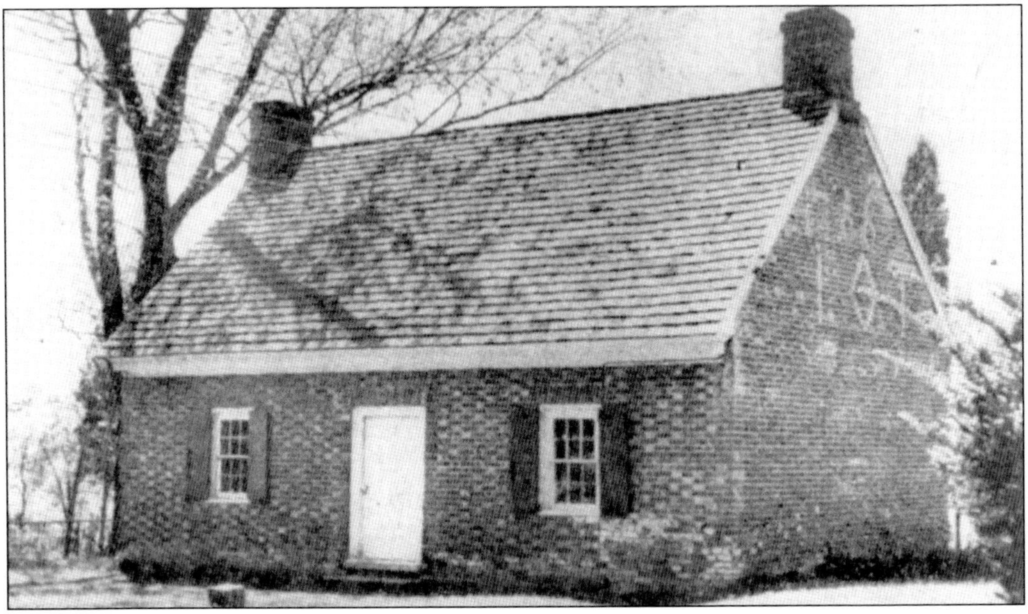

St. Paul's Vestry House near Fairlee was constructed in 1766. Thomas Slipper was the pastor during the construction. Slipper's salary was 2,500 pounds of tobacco per year. It was contracted by Charles Tilden, grandson of one of the original vestrymen of St. Paul's Parish. The year 1766 can be seen in the brick work.

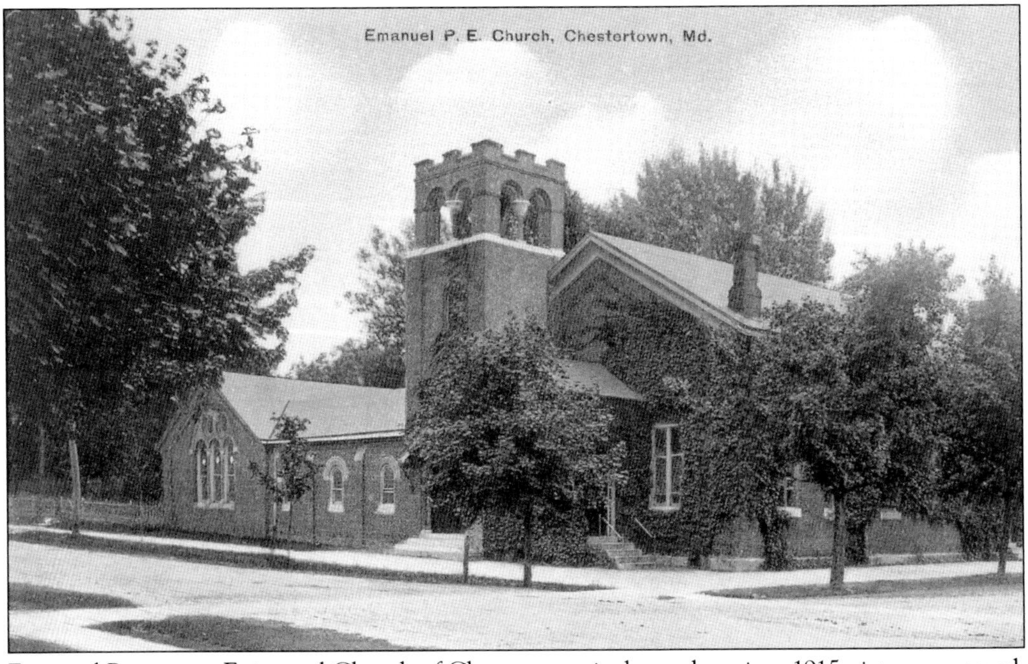

Emanuel Protestant Episcopal Church of Chestertown is shown here in a 1915 picture postcard. On November 9, 1780, a convention of clergy and laymen met here at the call of the incumbent rector (and future founder of Washington College) William Smith, D.D. They proclaimed the former Church of England with American Colonies independent of the British crown and adopted the name Protestant Episcopal Church of America.

Six

FACES OF KENT COUNTY

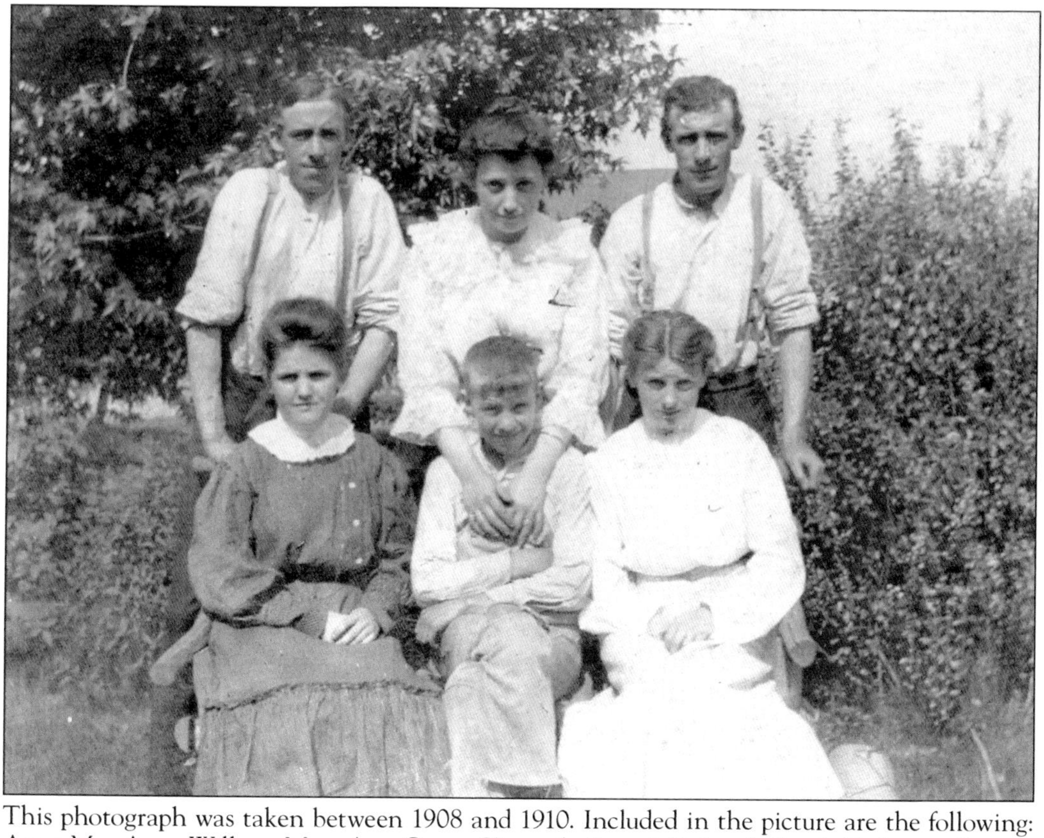

This photograph was taken between 1908 and 1910. Included in the picture are the following: Anna May Ayres Willson, Mary Ann Groves Kennedy, Francis D. Lamb, Sarah Catherine Groves, Walker Ball Lamb Sr., and an unidentified person.

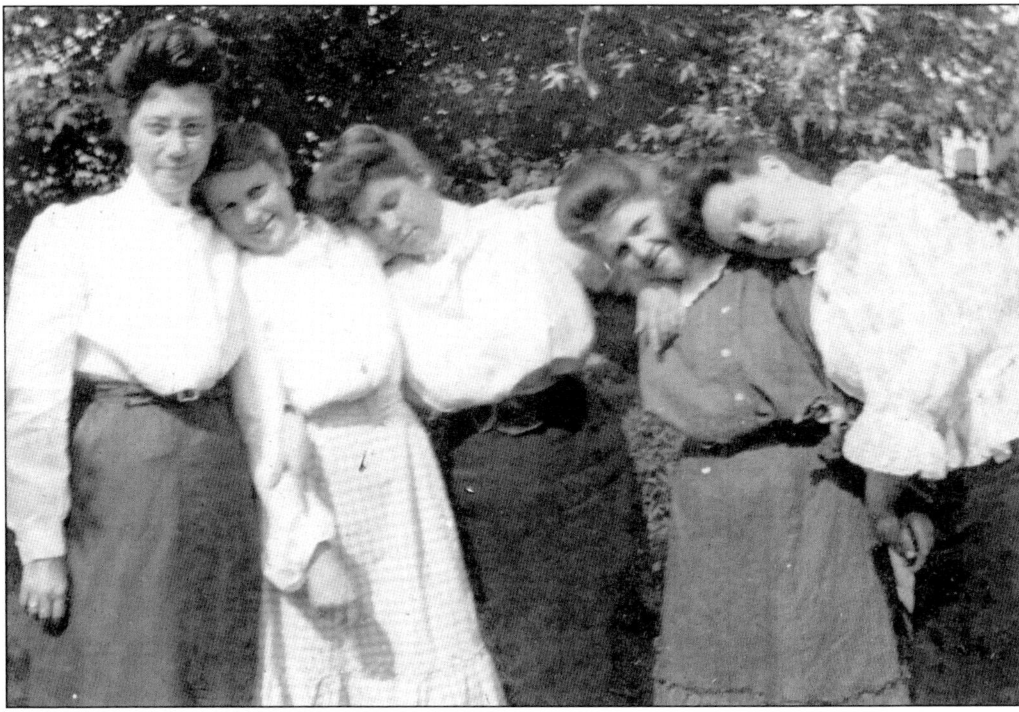

This photograph was taken in Kent County in the early 1900s and shows Bella Groves Kramer, Mary Ann Groves Kennedy, Mary Alberta Lamb, Anna Mae Ayres Willson, and Sarah C. Groves.

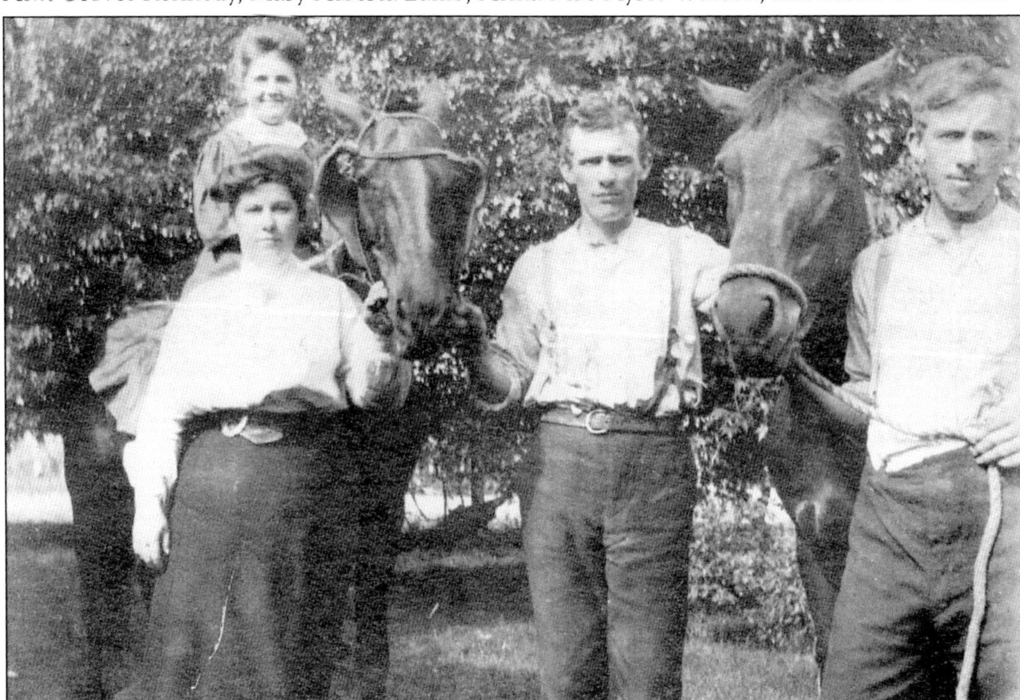

Standing from left to right are Mary Alberta Lamb, William Groves Lamb, and Francis David Lamb. Anna Mae Ayres Wilson is pictured on the horse.

Sparkes VanZant, son of James and Elleanora Boots VanZant of Kent County, is pictured here on his bicycle.

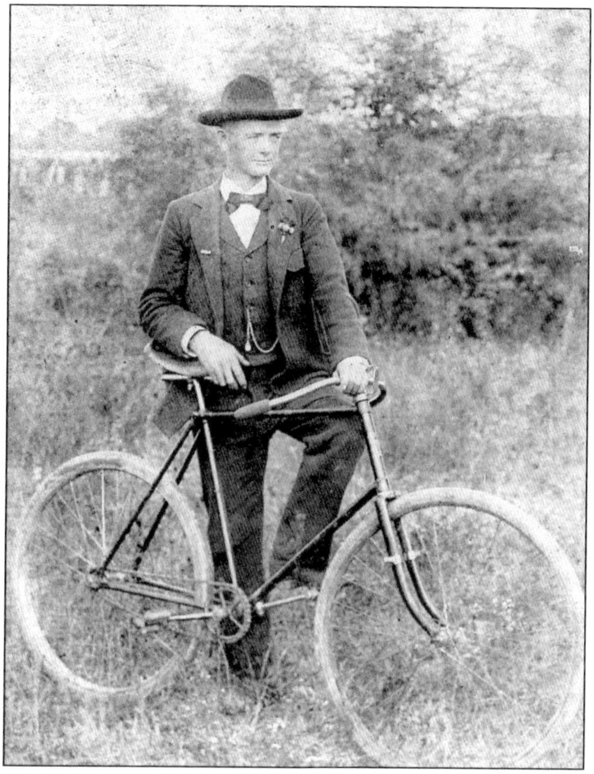

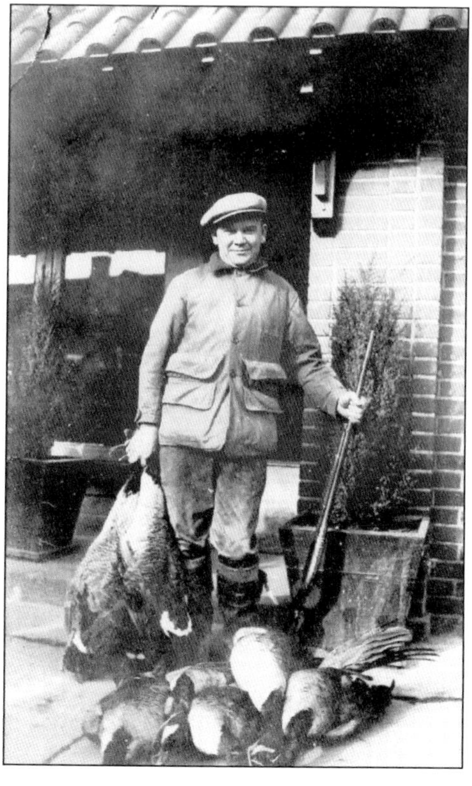

Henry C. Gill of Chestertown returns from hunting geese in Kent County.

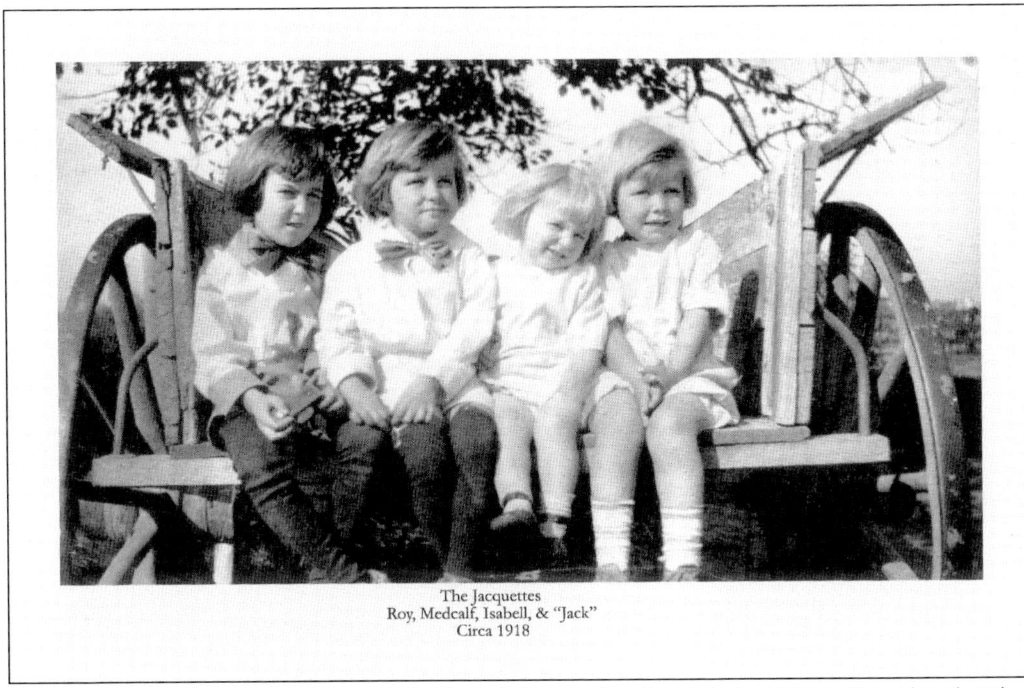

The Jacquettes of Kent County include, from left to right, Roy, Medcalf, Isabell, and Jack. They were photographed *c.* 1918.

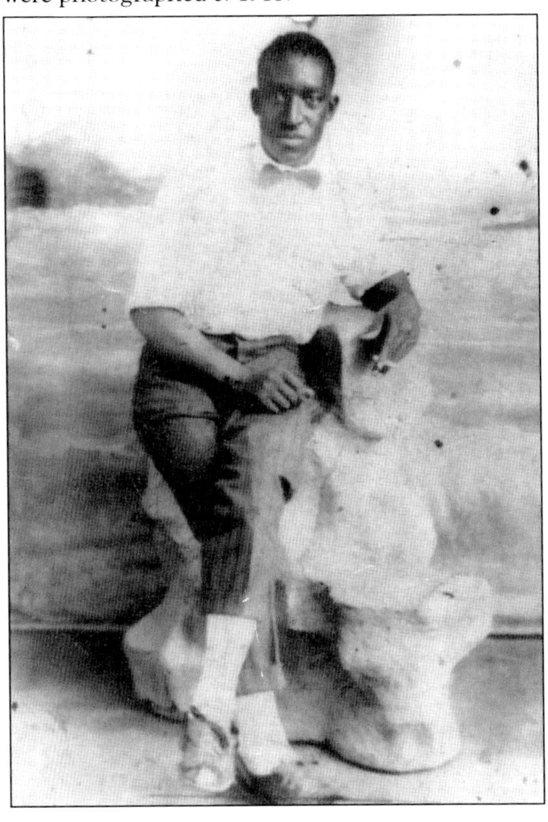

Melvin Cole of Still Pond, Maryland, is pictured here in the 1920s. He was an African American born and raised in the Coleman's Corner area of Kent County. His grandfather was Henry Brown, a Native American.

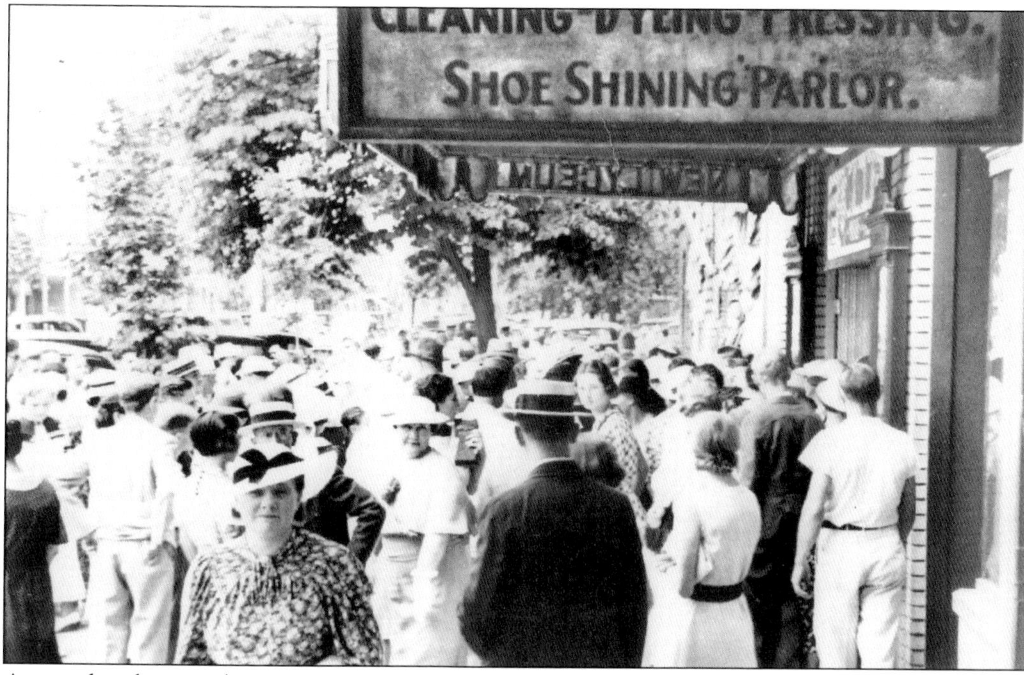

A crowd gathers at the New Lyceum Theater in downtown Chestertown.

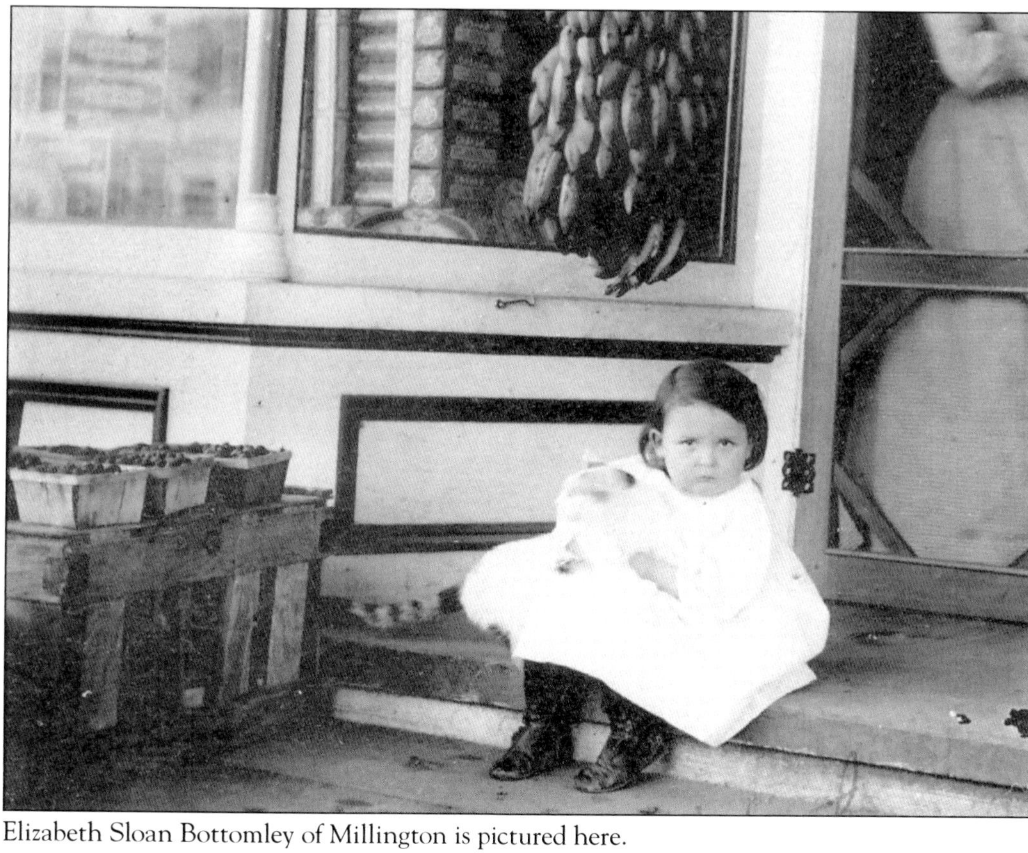

Elizabeth Sloan Bottomley of Millington is pictured here.

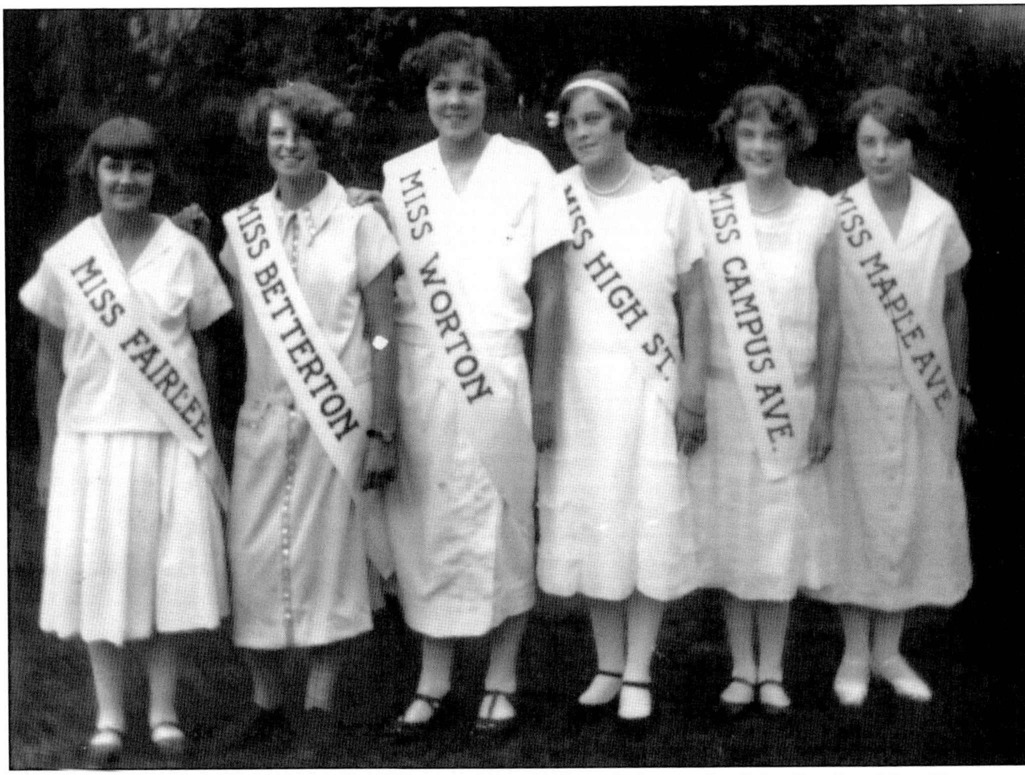

Photographed together here are the following women from left to right: Miss Fairlee, Miss Betterton, Miss Worton, Miss High Street, Miss Campus Avenue, and Miss Maple Avenue.

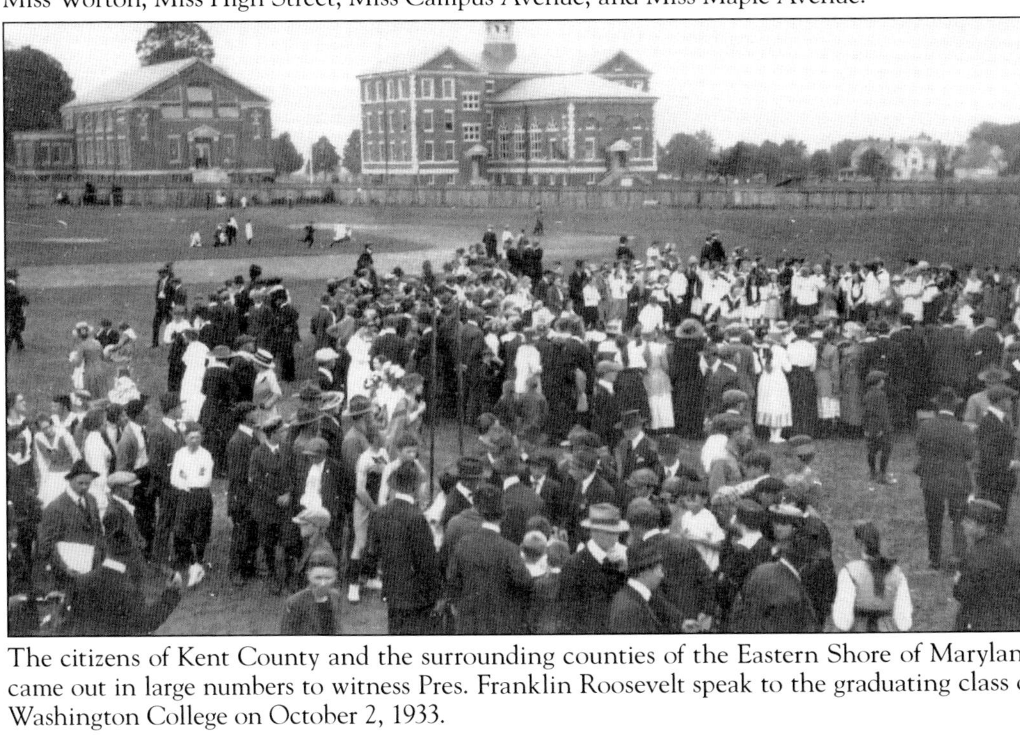

The citizens of Kent County and the surrounding counties of the Eastern Shore of Maryland came out in large numbers to witness Pres. Franklin Roosevelt speak to the graduating class of Washington College on October 2, 1933.

Alexander Murray was born on July 12, 1755, in the Hynson-Ringgold House in Chestertown, Maryland. He was the highest ranking naval officer from 1811 until his death on October 6, 1821. He commanded several ships during the American Revolution and thereafter. The *Constellation* was one of the ships he commanded.

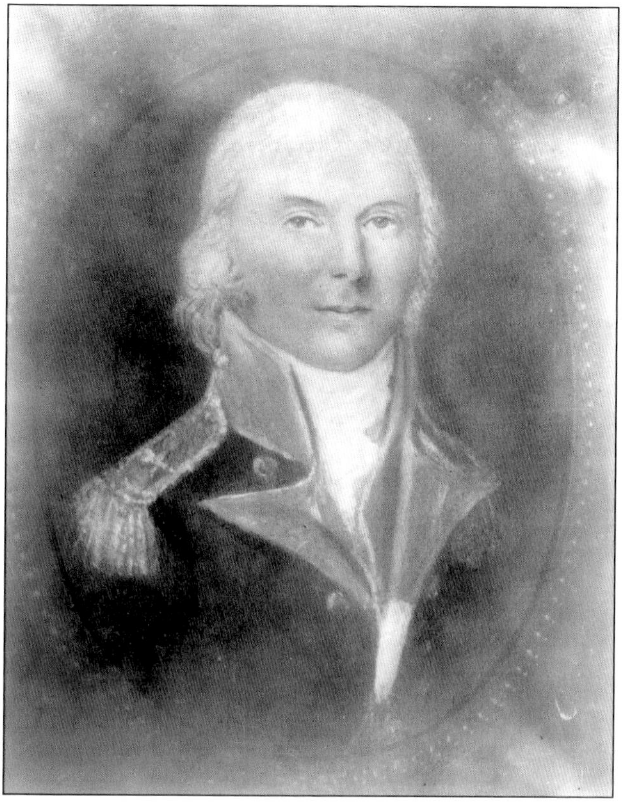

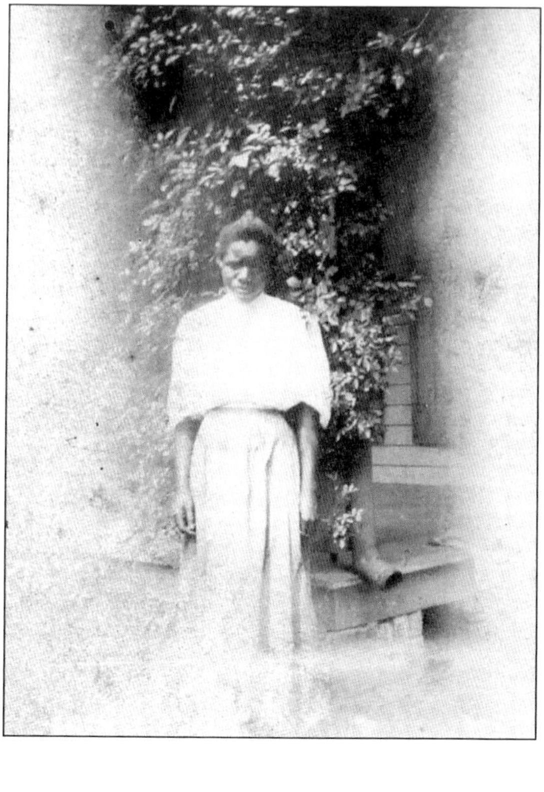

Pictured is Sarah (Sadie) Houston, who was born in Kent County in 1885.

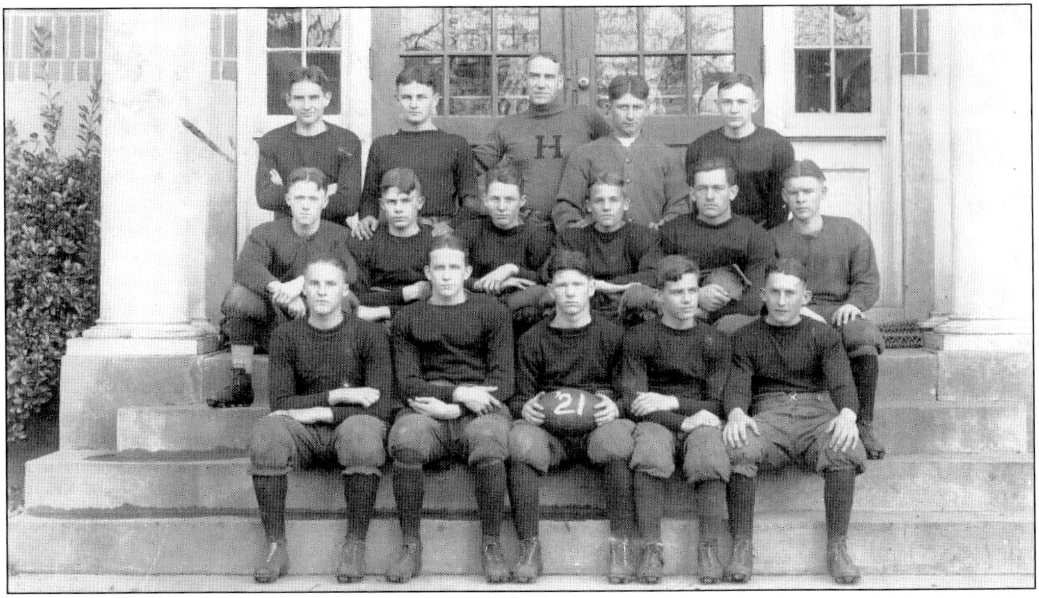

Among those on the 1921 football team at Chestertown High School were M. Estes, Gilpin Brown, Reds Armstrong, Dr. Charles Atwater, and Vernon Kirby.

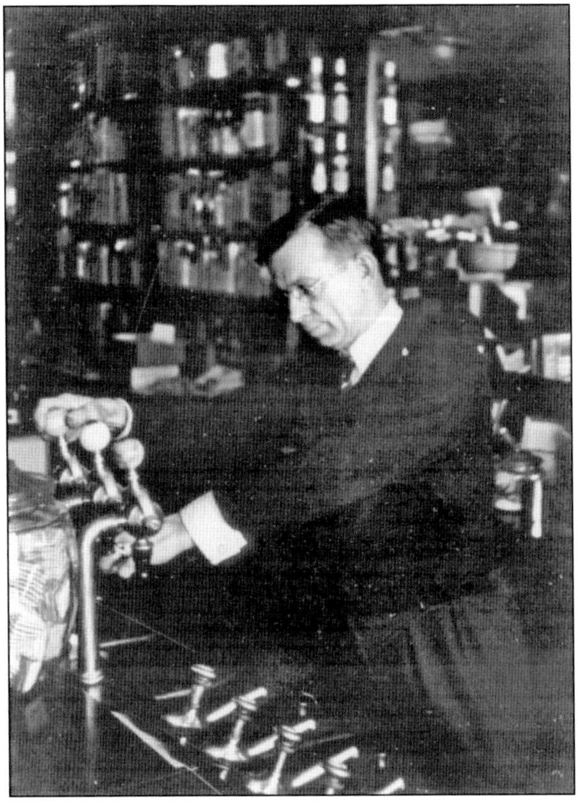

Pharmacist Dr. A. L. Sterling is pictured behind the soda fountain at his drug store on High Street (now part of the Sterling Suite at the White Swan Tavern) in downtown Chestertown. He opened his drug store in 1917 and remained in business at this location for 47 years. He would give away shamrocks and serve chocolate cake to his customers once a year on the anniversary of his store's opening. A relative recalled he could place an order for his store in the morning and it would arrive at the foot of High Street by boat late the same afternoon. Dr. Sterling died in 1964.

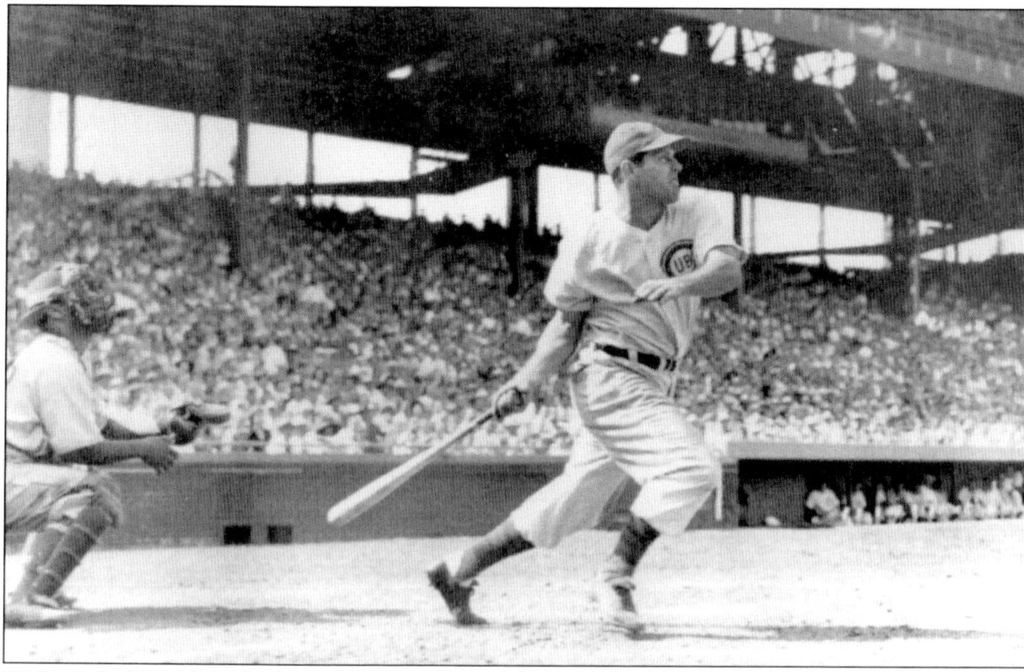

William B. (Swish) Nicholson played professional baseball from 1936 to 1953. He signed a contract with the Philadelphia Athletics in 1935. The Chicago Cubs bought his contract in 1939, and he was traded to the Philadelphia Phillies in 1948. He tied the record for most runs batted in during one series (seven games out of eight) in 1945; it was an outstanding World Series performance. He was named as outfielder for *The Sporting News* All-Star Major League Team in 1945 by the Baseball Writers Association of America.

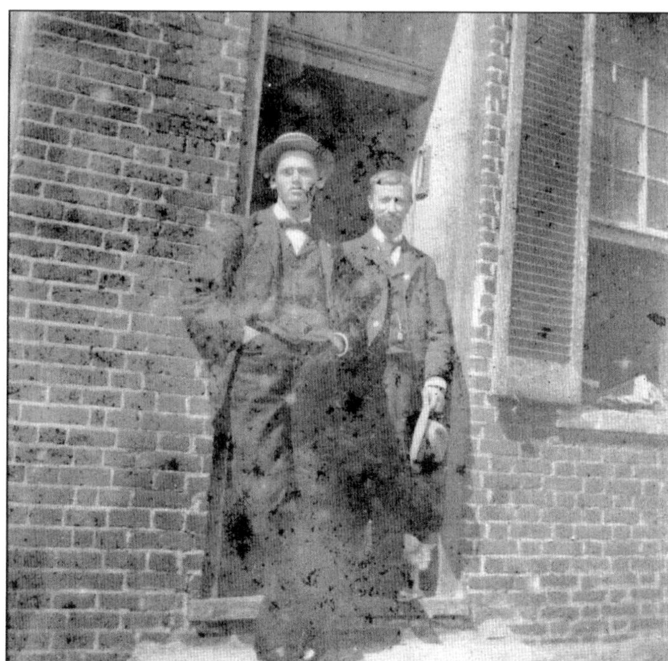

C. C. Hoppin and Clarence W. Perkins are pictured in the door of the old Chestertown Transcript Building. *The Chestertown Transcript* was known as a pro-Southern paper. It was a weekly and established on May 20, 1862, reportedly by Eben F. Perkins. It merged with *Kent News* on February 1, 1946, to form the *Kent County News*.

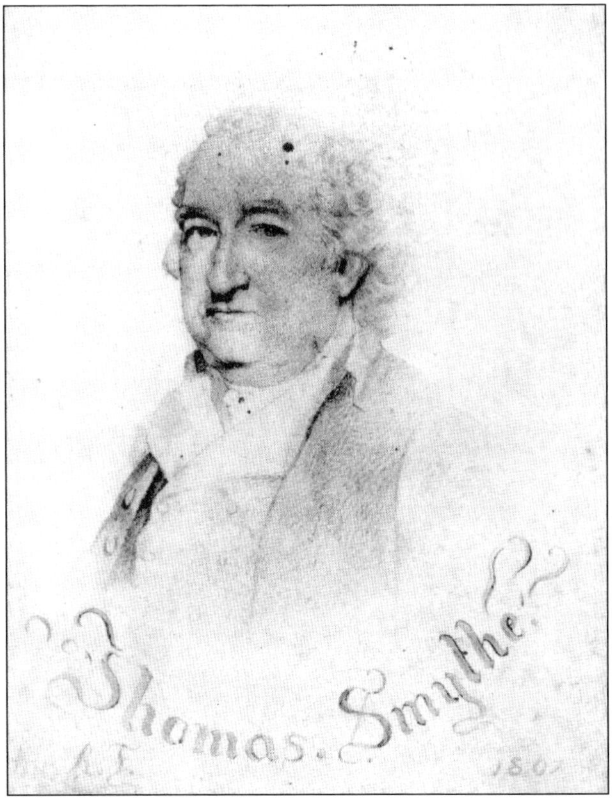

This is an image of Thomas Smythe in 1802. Smythe was the wealthiest merchant in Kent County in his time. His house, Widehall, was Chestertown's most ornate residence. Smythe was head of Maryland's revolutionary provisional government as well as Washington College's first treasurer.

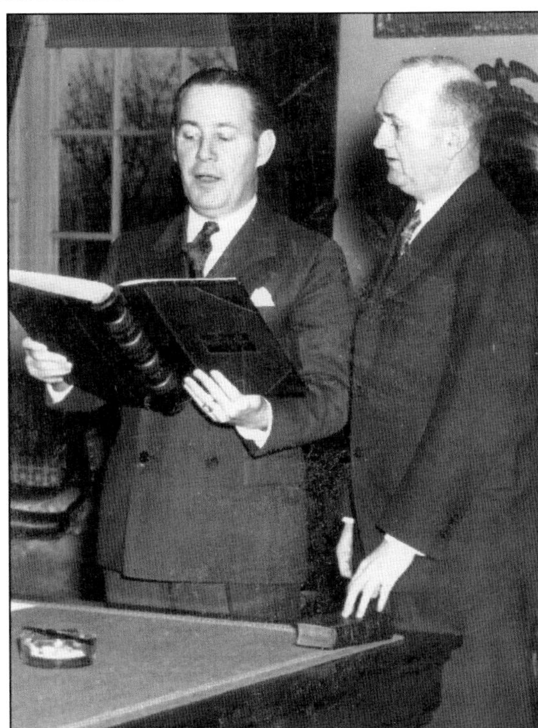

Judge Stephen R. Collins, situated at the right in this photograph, and Democratic governor Herbert R. O'Conner are pictured here in the early 1940s.

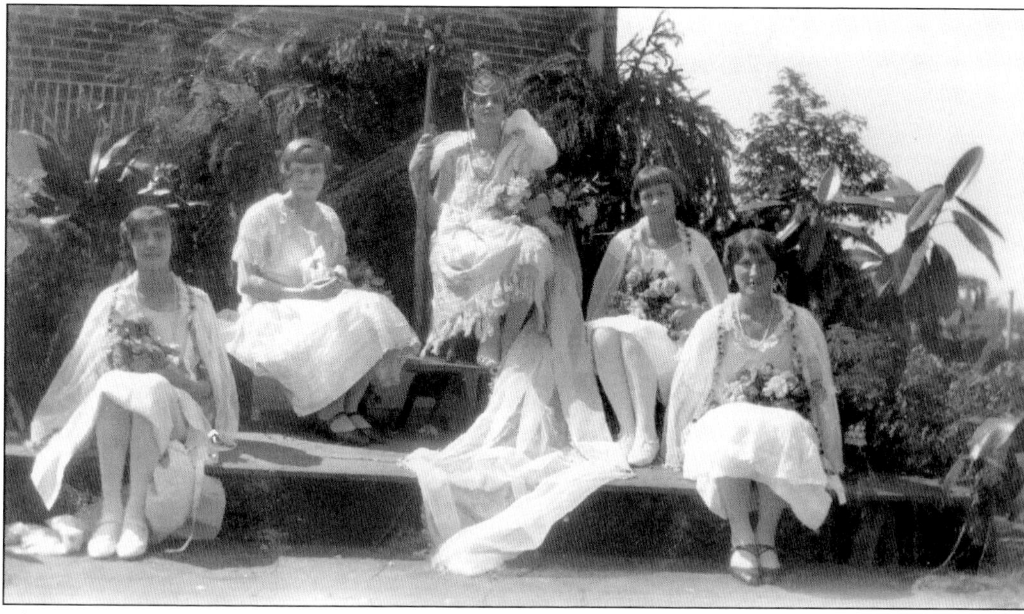

These ladies were in the Rock Hall High School May court in the mid-1920s. Sitting on the far left is Thelma Moffett Vansant of Chestertown.

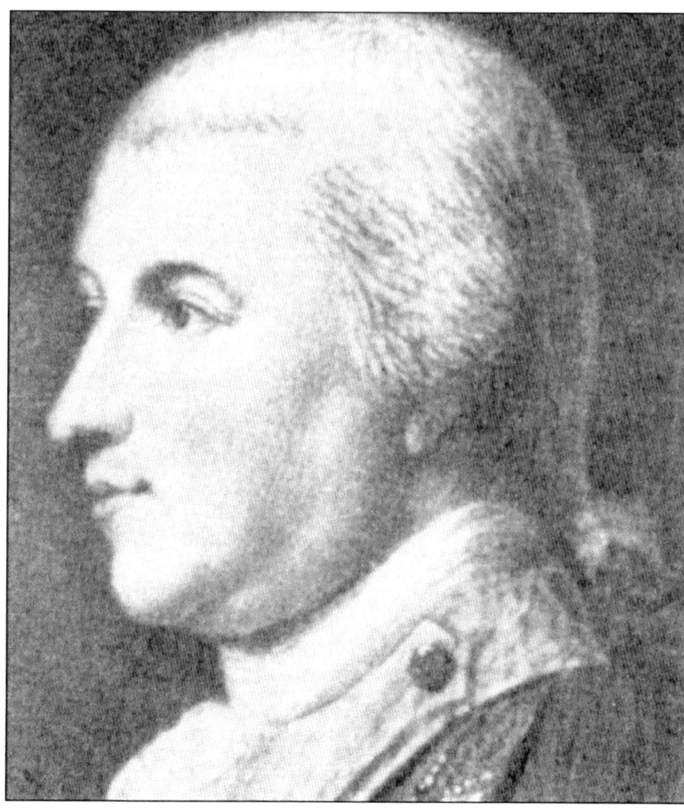

Col. Tench Tilghman was Gen. George Washington's aide-de-camp during the Revolutionary War. It was Tilghman who rode on horseback through Kent to carry the news of Great Britain's surrender at Yorktown. Tilghman's ride through Kent County has been immortalized in a poem by Confederate general Bradley T. Johnson entitled "Tench Tilghman's Ride Through Kent."

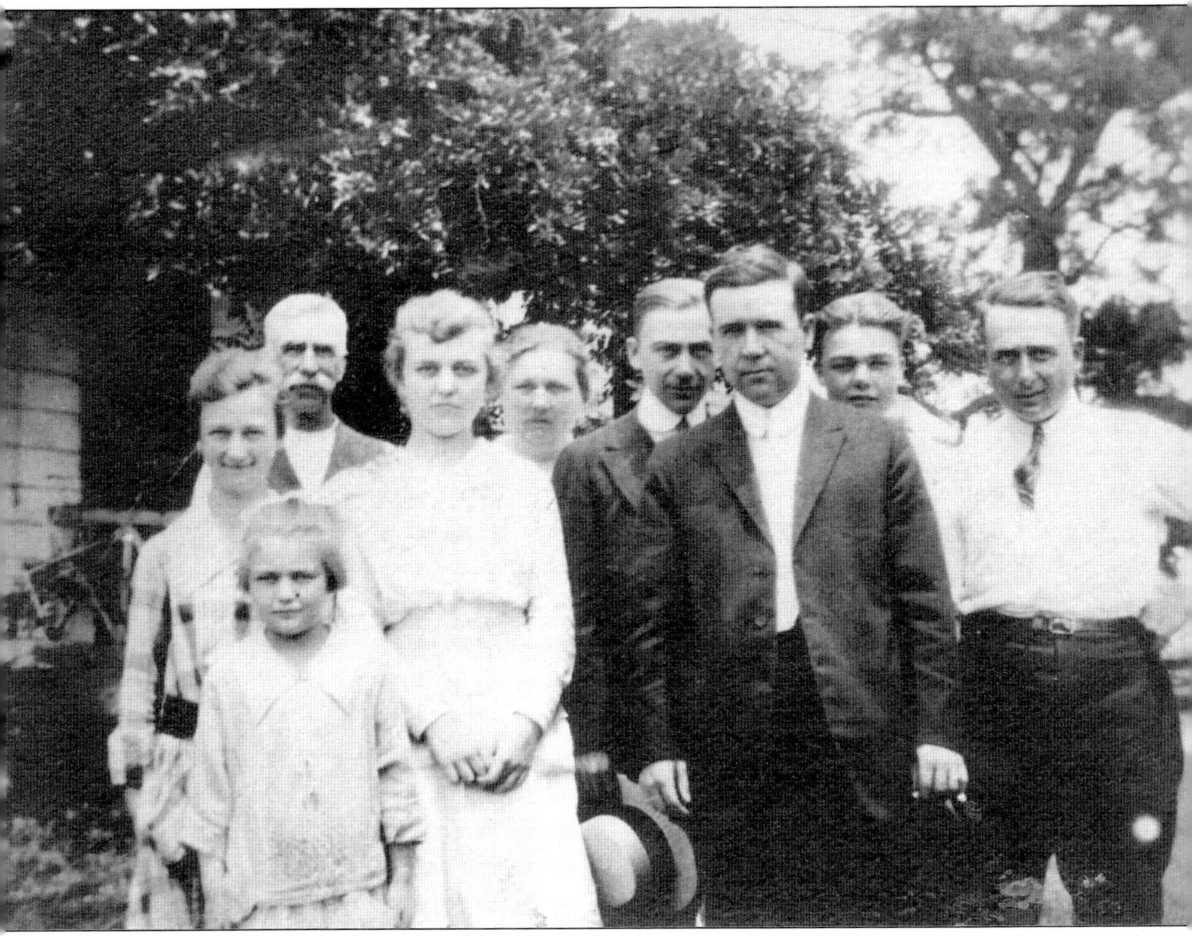

The Willson family of Trumpington near Rock Hall includes the following, shown here: Isabel Tilden Willson, Julia Madeline and Alan Willson, Alexander Carroll Willson, Gertrude Hadaway Willson, Carroll Elmer Willson, Daniel Carroll Willson, and James Ernest Willson.

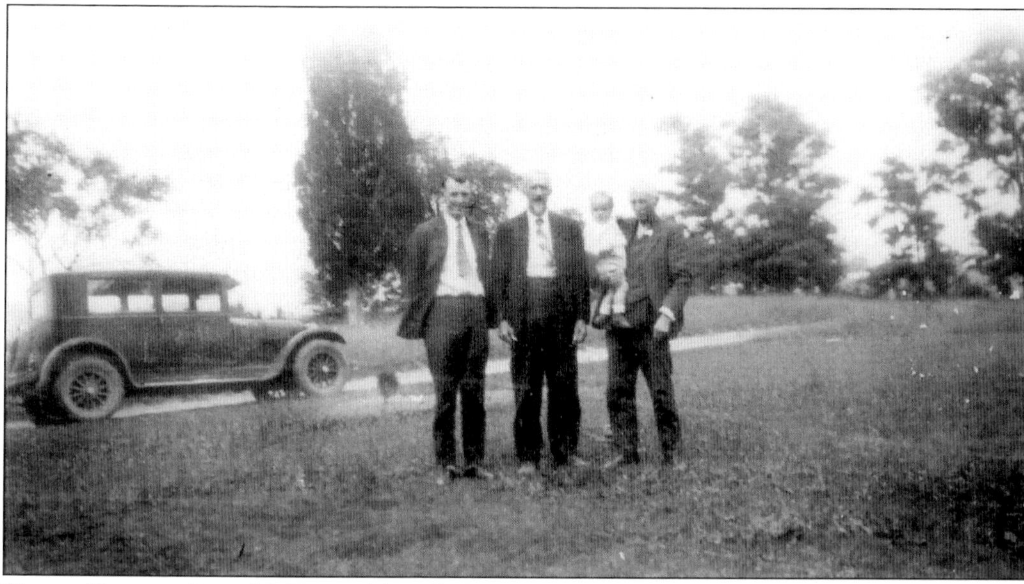

Pictured here are Lionel J. Keyser (sheriff of Kent County from 1903 to 1905), Lionel J. Keyser Jr. (his son), and Anna Kendall Usilton (baby).

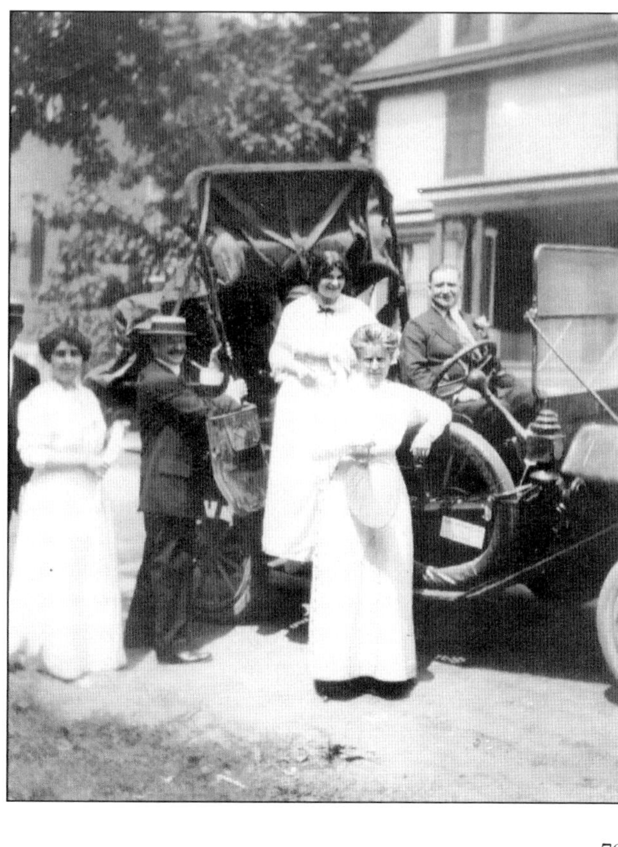

Standing in the front, center, is Mrs. W. W. Hubbard, founder of the Women's Improvement Society. Her leadership helped create Chestertown's beautiful town park. Also pictured are Mr. Hubbard, Wilbur Hubbard, and Miriam Hubbard Morris. They lived at Widehall on Water Street in Chestertown.

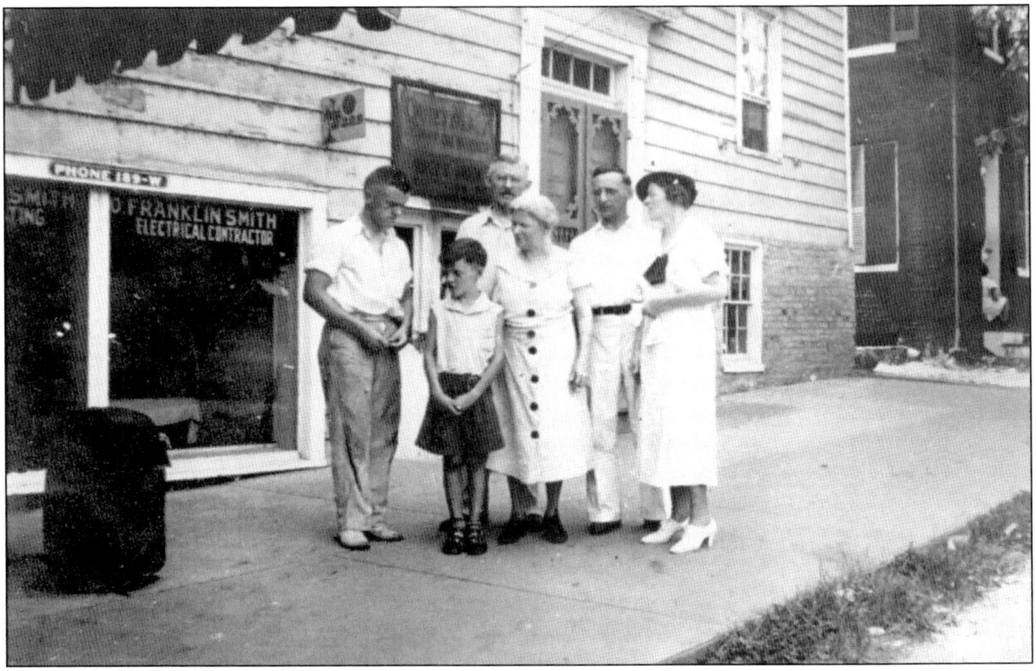

This photograph was taken on High Street in Chestertown in front of the business of Mr. Owen Smith and his son, Franklin, who were electrical contractors. The building is now occupied by Andy's, a local drinking establishment.

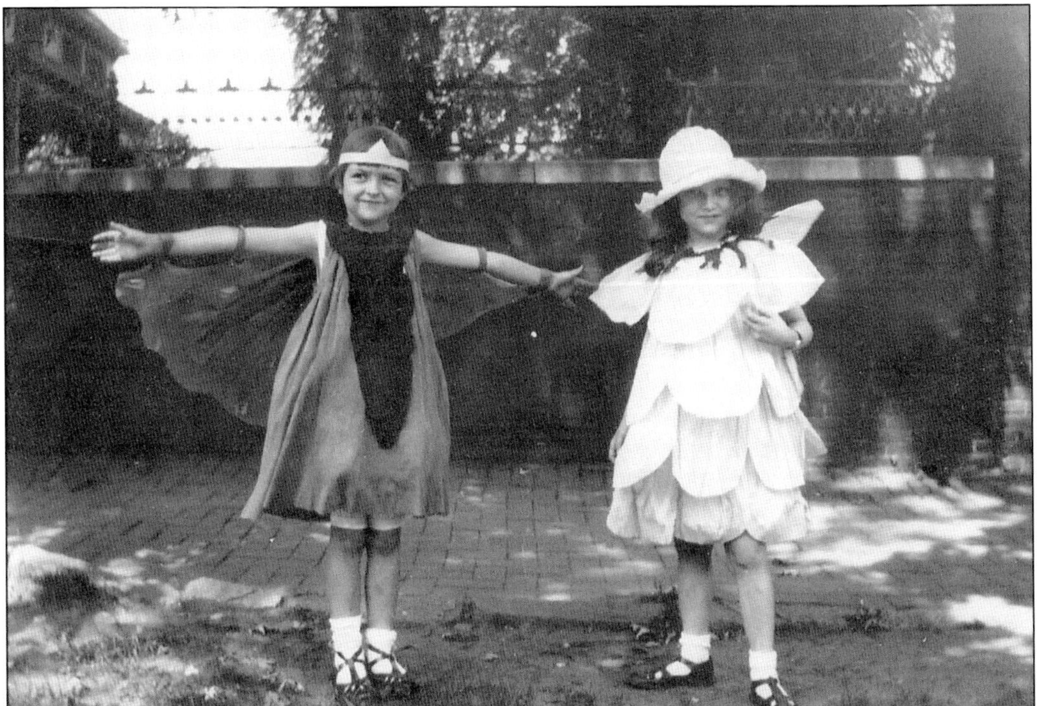

In this image, Carrie Schreiber, on the left, and Betty Thibodeau dress up in costumes for a play in Chestertown.

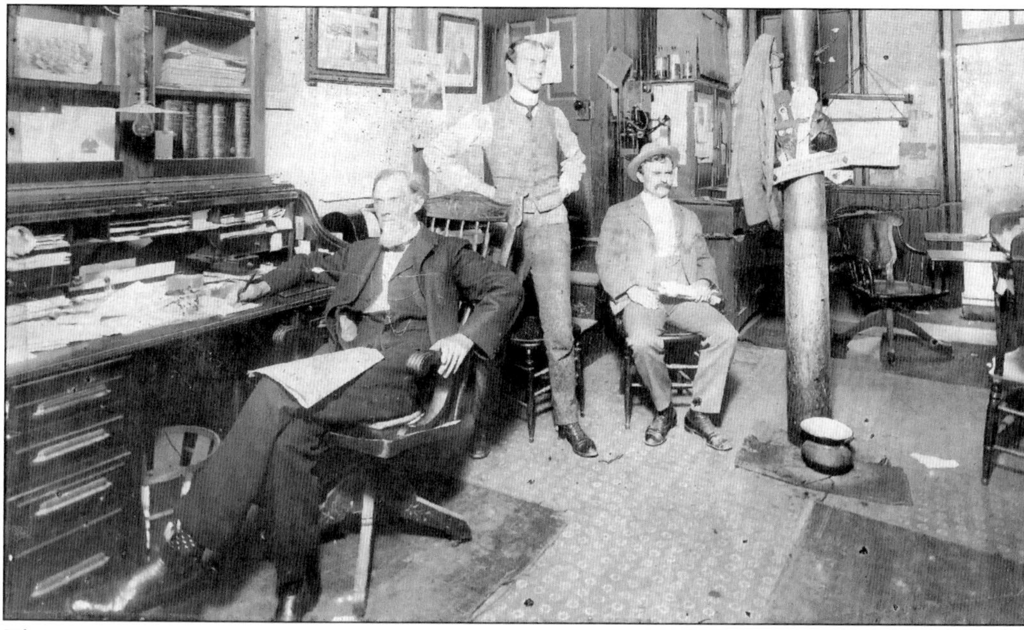

This is an 1890 photograph of the *Kent News* office, which was located in the former Pinder Building in Chestertown. Included in the picture are William B. Usilton Sr. and Jr.

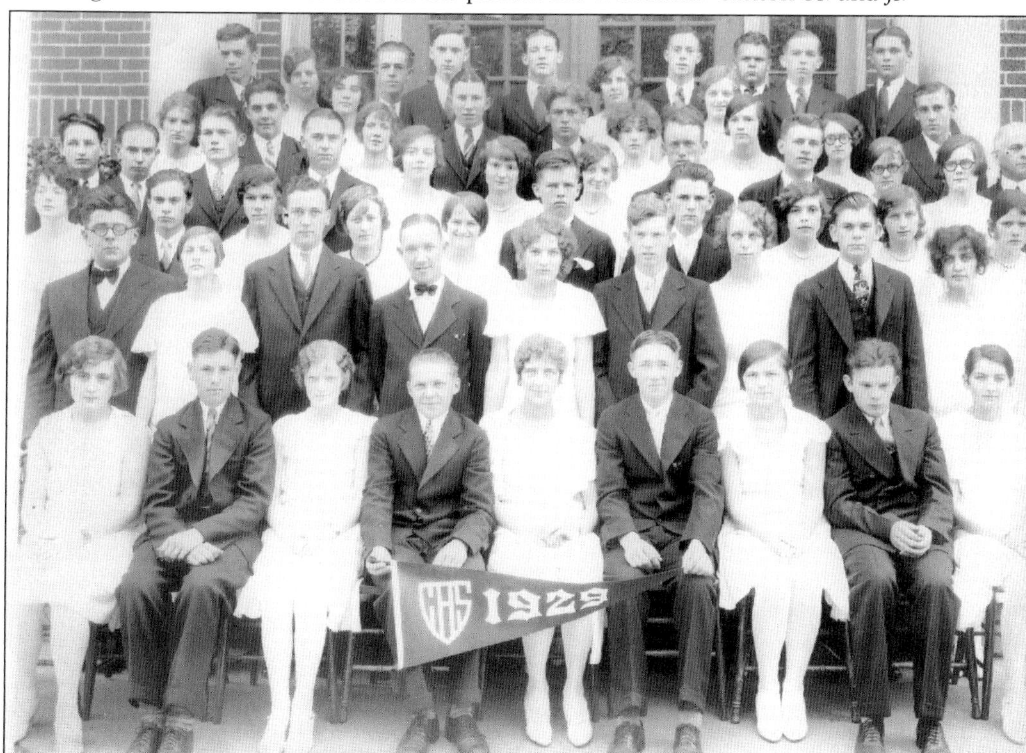

Among these Chestertown school class members are Miriam Ford Hoffecker, Anna Harris Briggs, Catharine Hepbron Harris, Margaret Ann Brown, Barbee Humphries Roe, Nancy Jean Usilton Ellis, and Lucille Rasin.

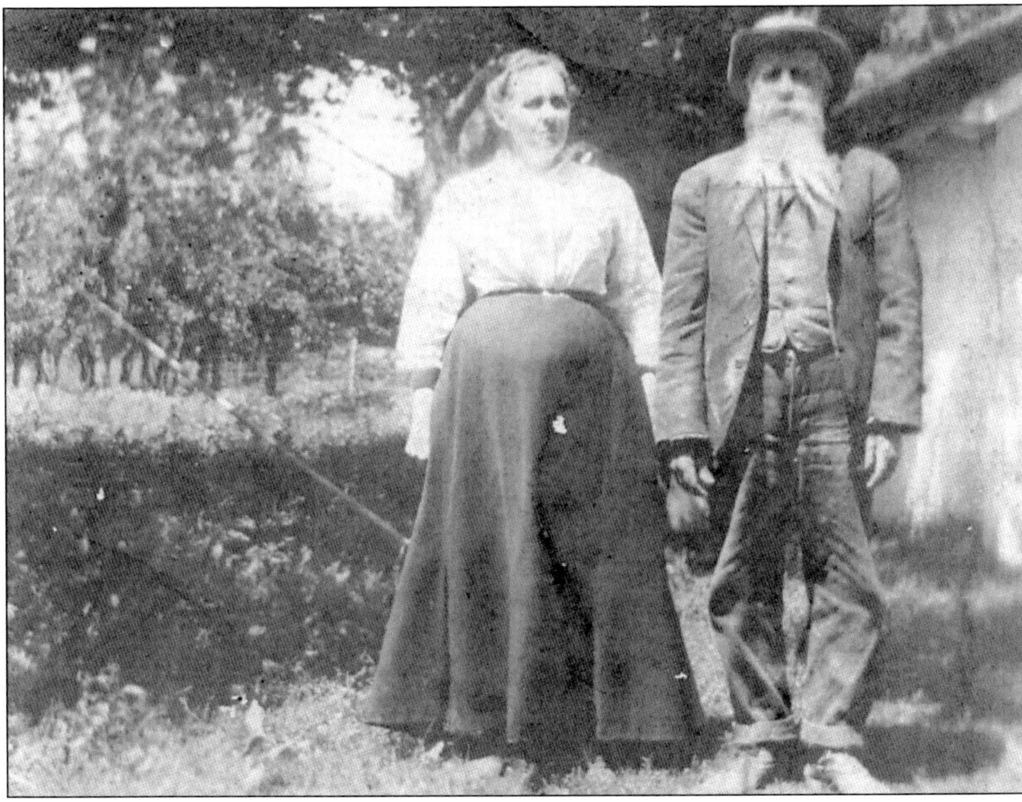

Mary Shuster Groves Lamb and Francis David Lamb are pictured here in Fairlee.

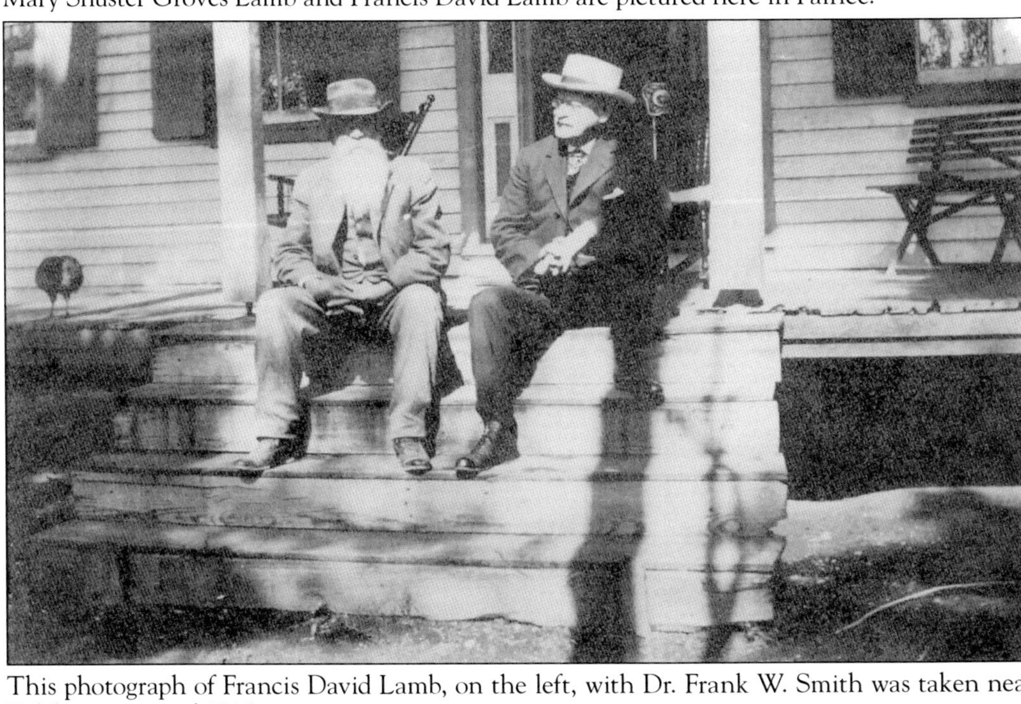

This photograph of Francis David Lamb, on the left, with Dr. Frank W. Smith was taken near Tolchester around 1916.

Seven

JUST FOR THE FUN OF IT

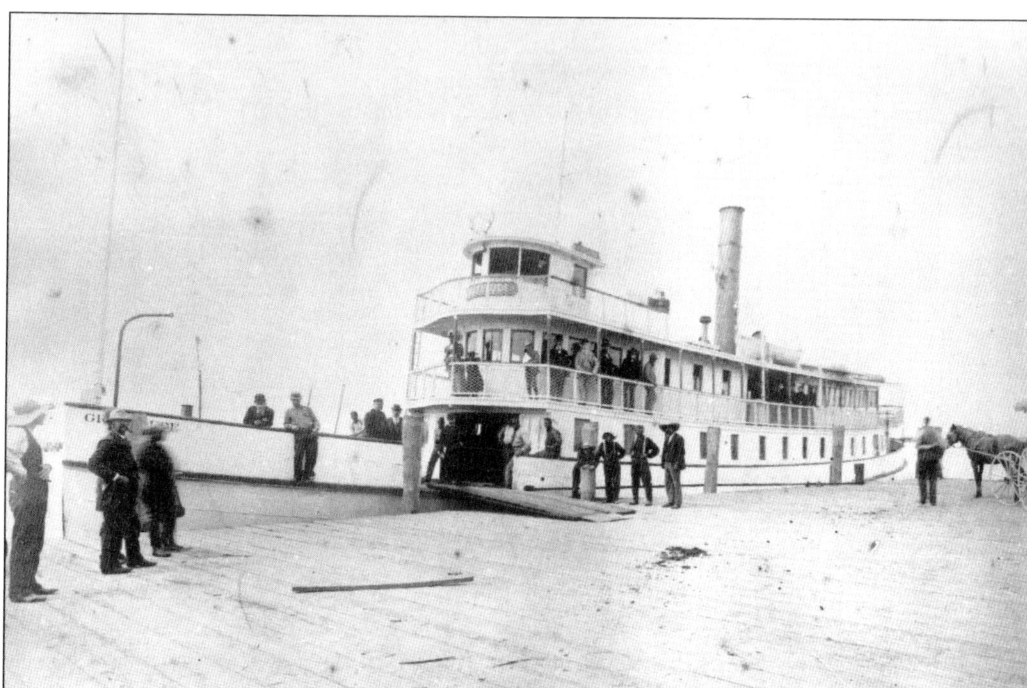

A steamboat is pictured here docked at Gratitude Harbor in Rock Hall, Maryland.

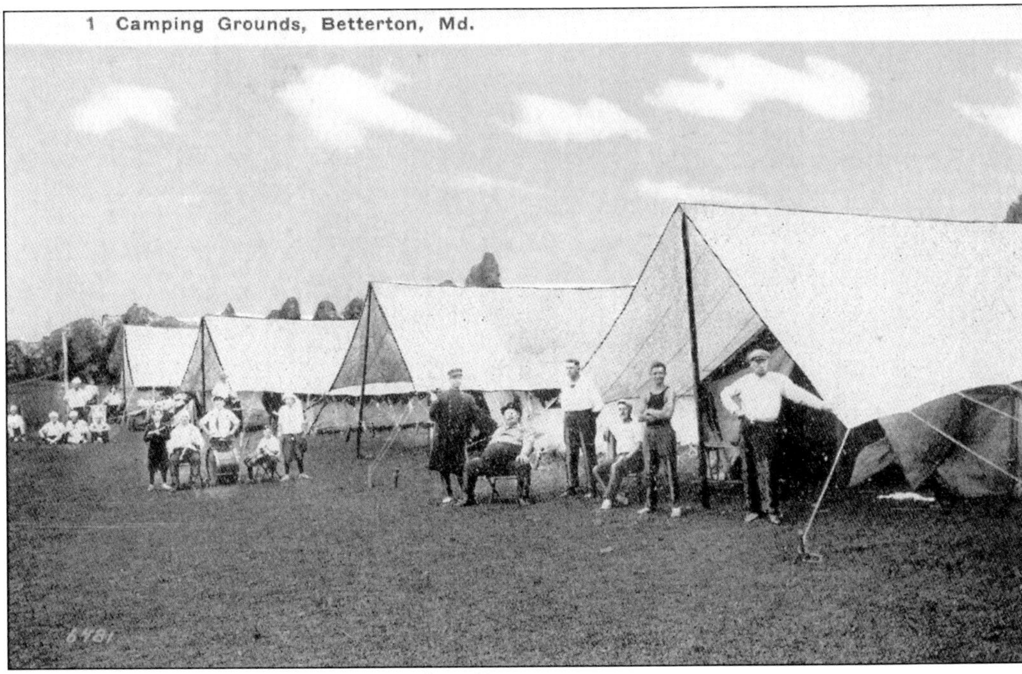

This is the Maryland Camping Grounds in Betterton.

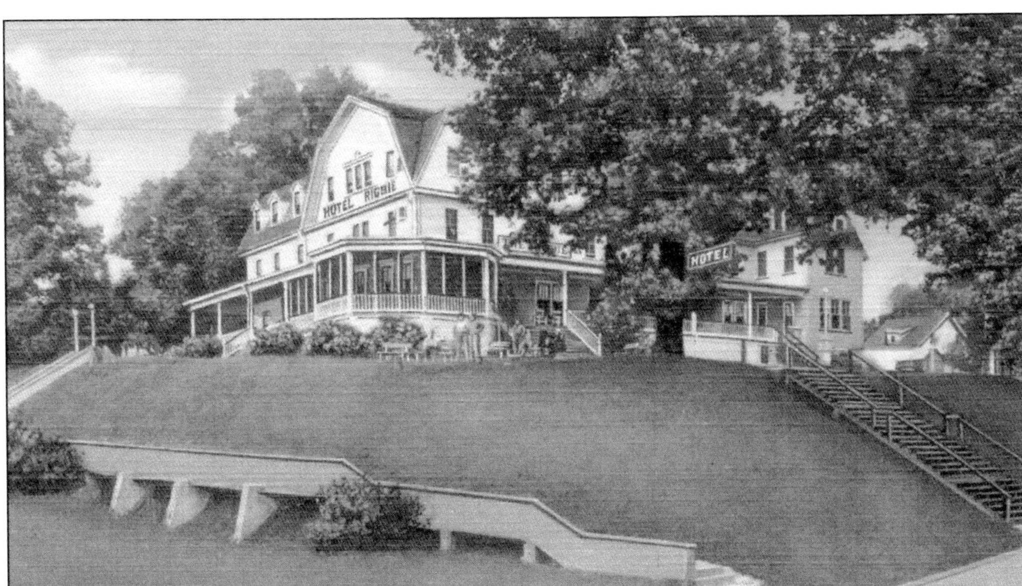

These stone stairways along the front of the bluff are all that remain of the Hotel Rigbie. Once the grandest of all the hotels overlooking the Chesapeake Bay in Betterton, it was demolished to make way for the Rigbie Bluff Condominiums.

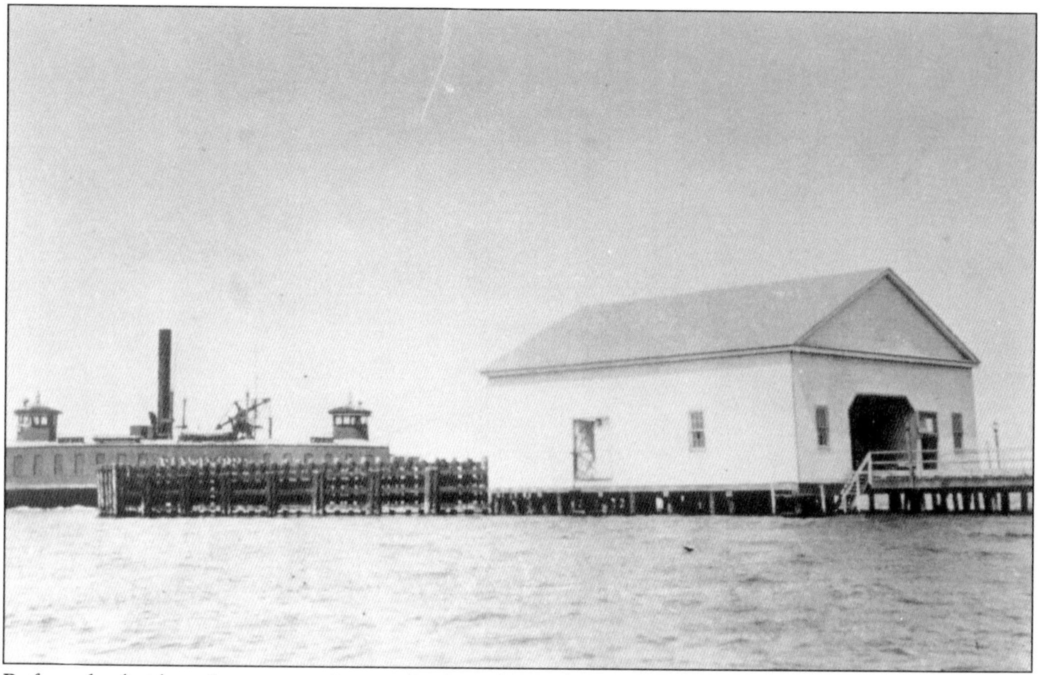

Before the bridge, there was a ferry, which is shown here either docking or leaving Rock Hall.

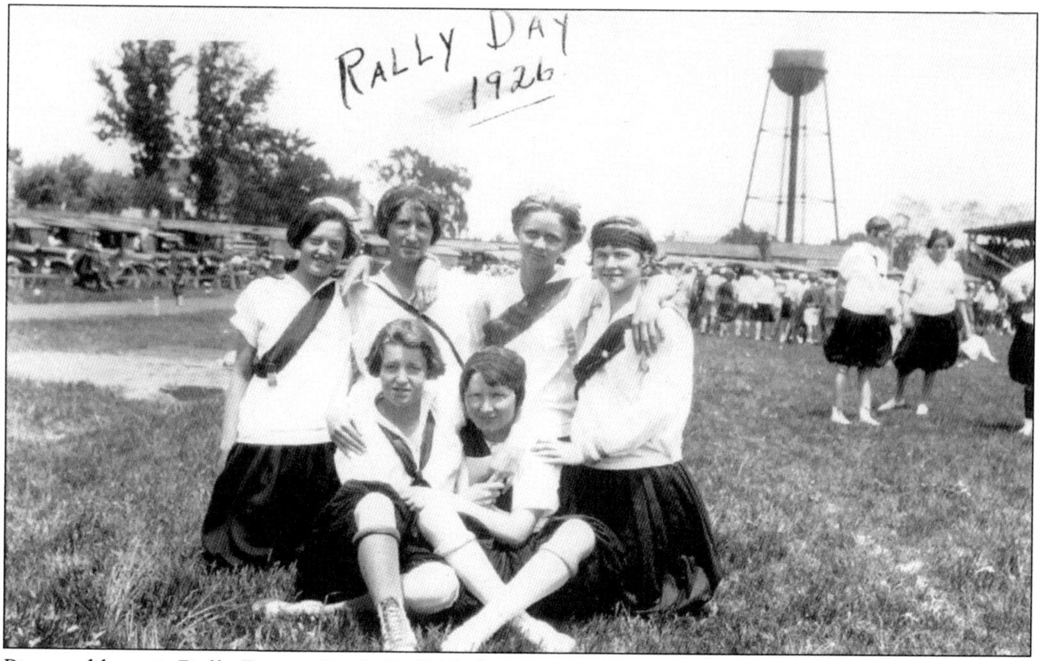

Pictured here is Rally Day at Rock Hall High School in 1926.

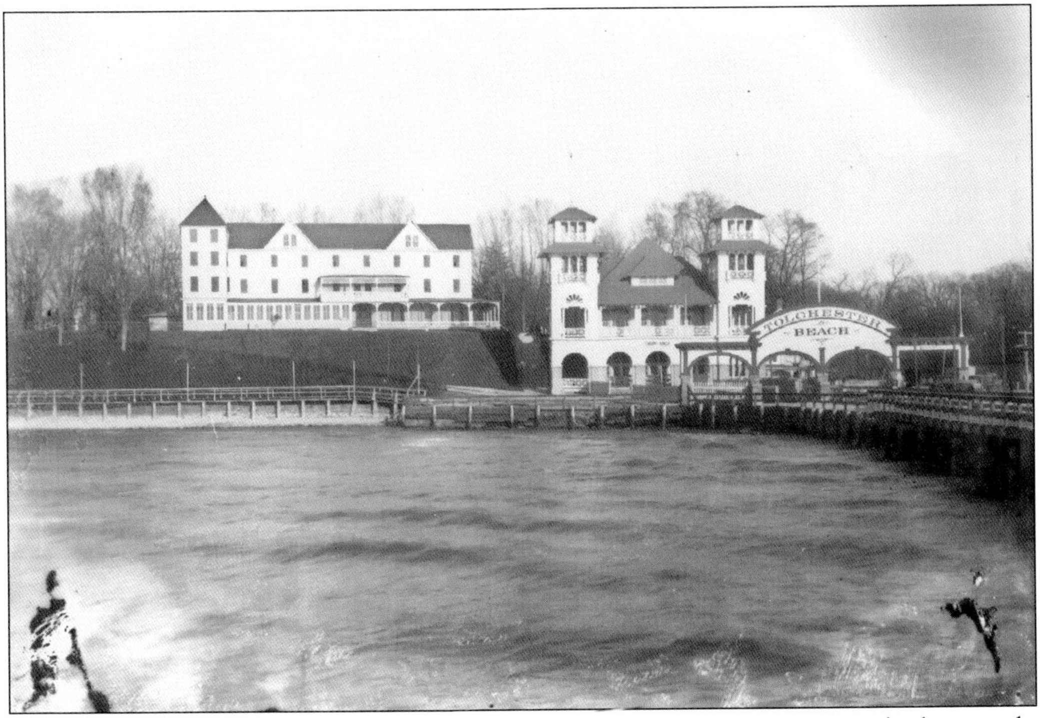

This is the Pavilion and Hotel at Tolchester Beach on the Chesapeake Bay in an early photograph. Shown here in its prime, Tolchester Beach consisted of 150 acres served by 6 steamers and a ferry. Visitors stayed at the great summer hotel pictured here at the top of the bluff. Tolchester attracted as many as 20,000 visitors a day from across the bay. It flourished for over 100 years until it closed in 1962.

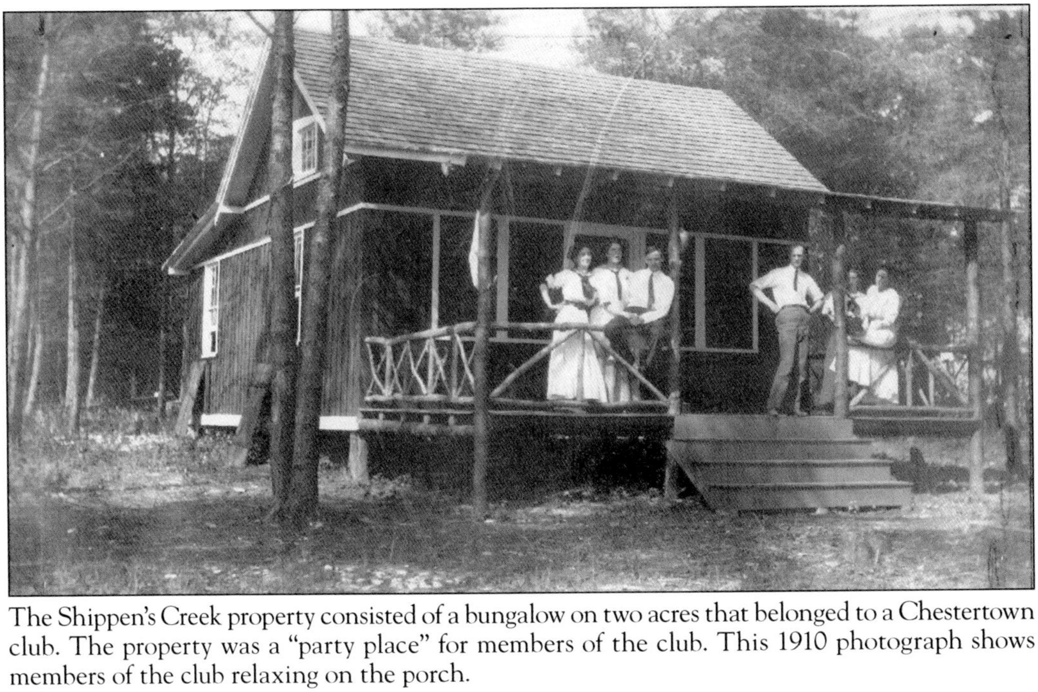

The Shippen's Creek property consisted of a bungalow on two acres that belonged to a Chestertown club. The property was a "party place" for members of the club. This 1910 photograph shows members of the club relaxing on the porch.

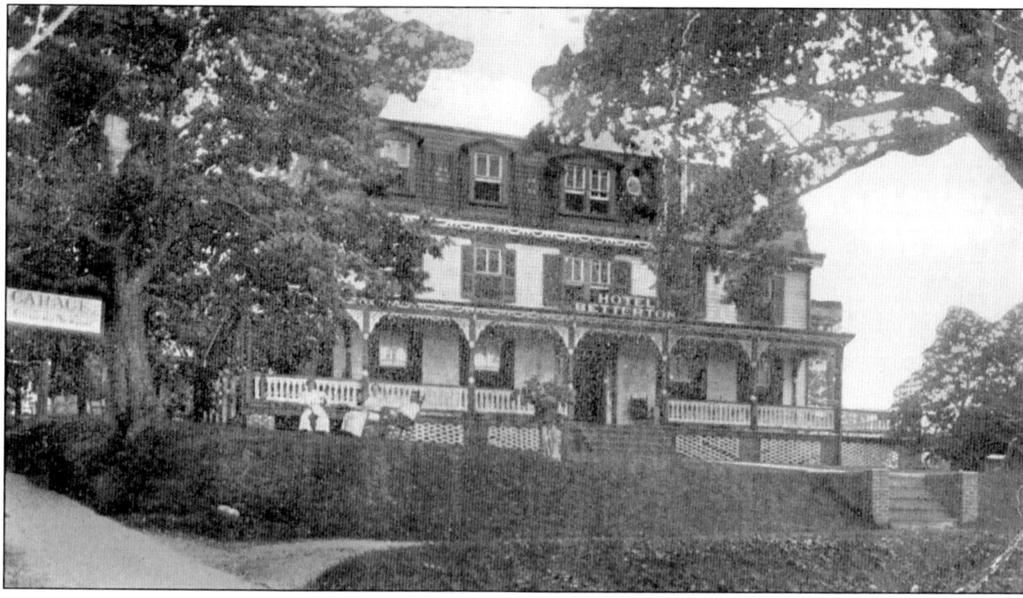

The Hotel Betterton is pictured here.

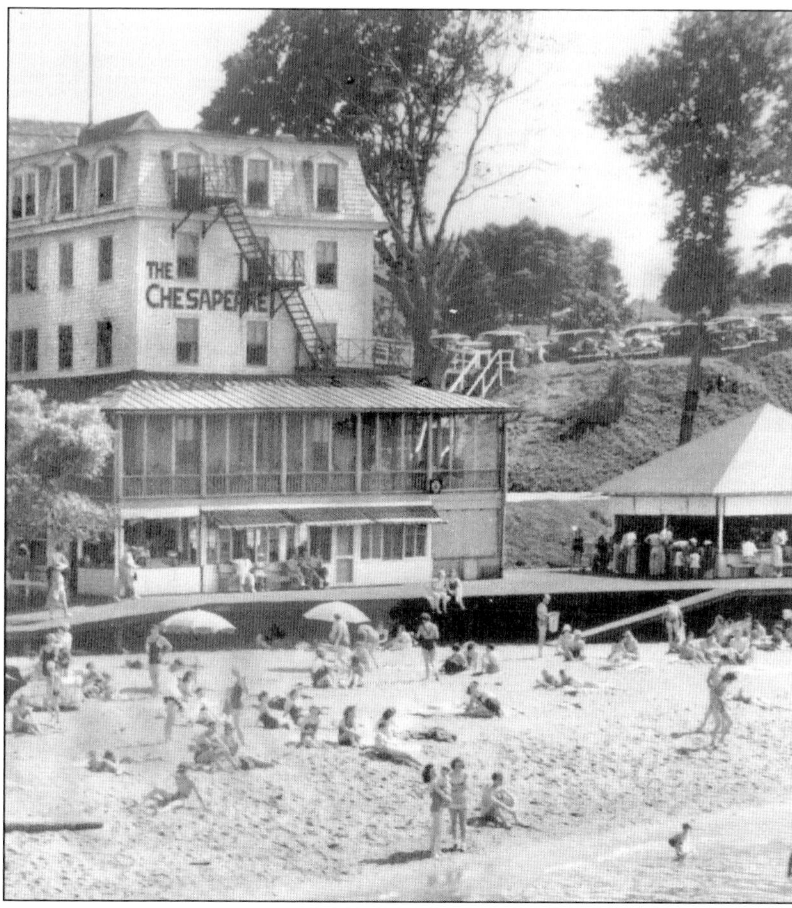

On Tuesday night, June 29, 1937, the Hotel Chesapeake in Betterton was partially destroyed by fire. This photograph was taken in the early 1920s before the fire.

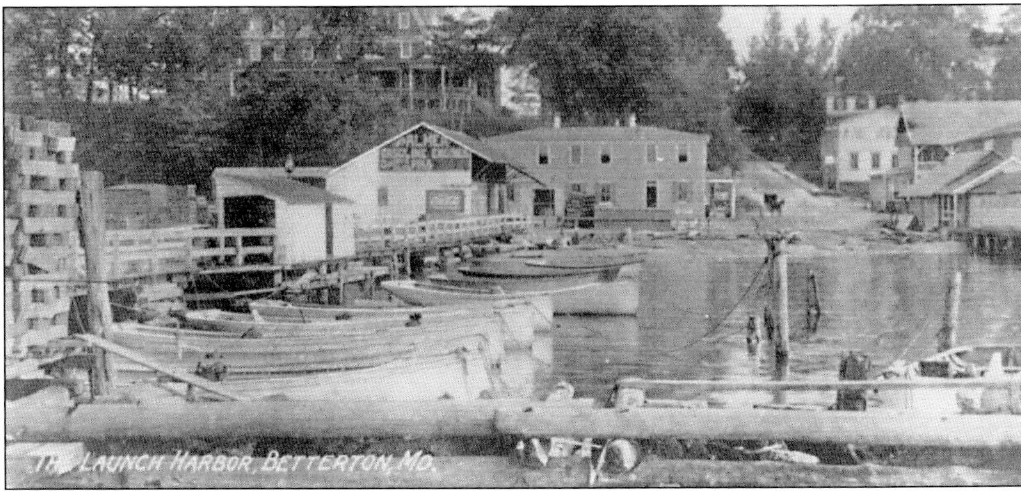

This early photograph is of the launch at Betterton. The Hotel Betterton is seen high on the bluff overlooking the Chesapeake Bay.

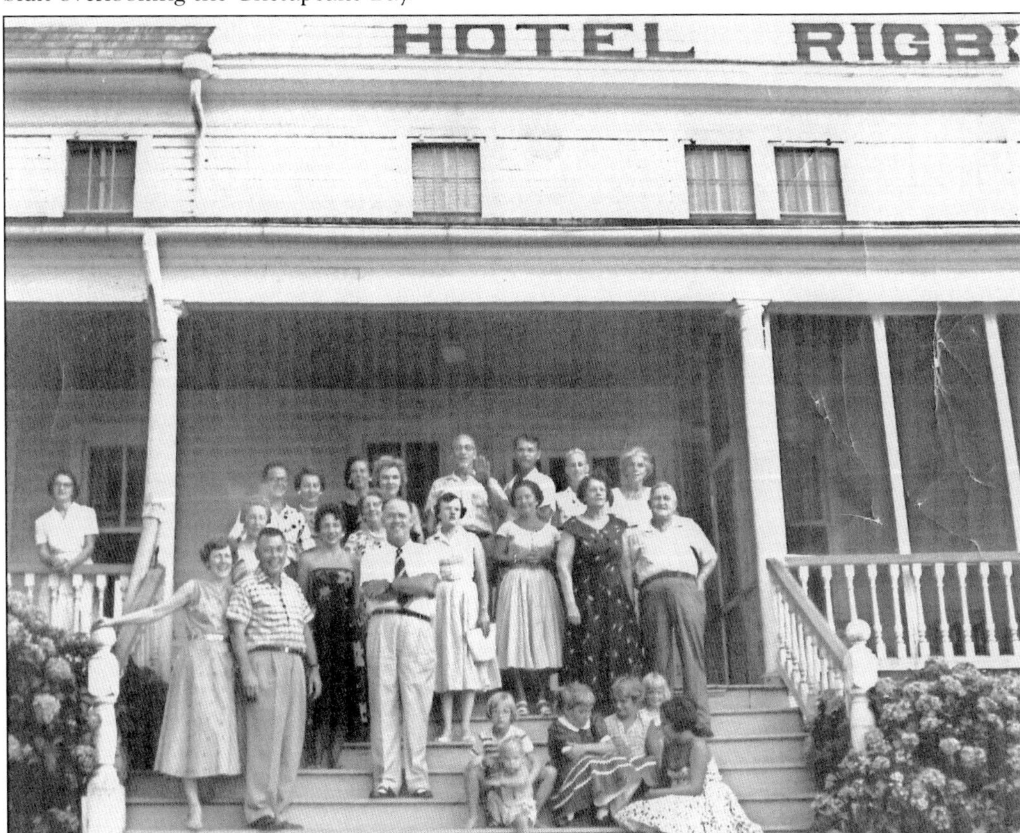

This group standing on the steps of the Hotel Rigbie in Betterton includes the following: Ruth Soltys, Mrs. Thompson, Dick Fellows, John Motter, Imogene Faulkner, Barbara Thompson, Vivian Motter, Nellie Greenwood, Buck Thompson, Scotty Fellows, Richard Soltys, Emily Bonwill, Helen Brice, and George Brice. Sitting on the steps, from left to right, are Libby Bonwill with Brice Bonwill, Linda Fellows, Louise Bonwill, Jackie Bonwill, and Peggy Motter.

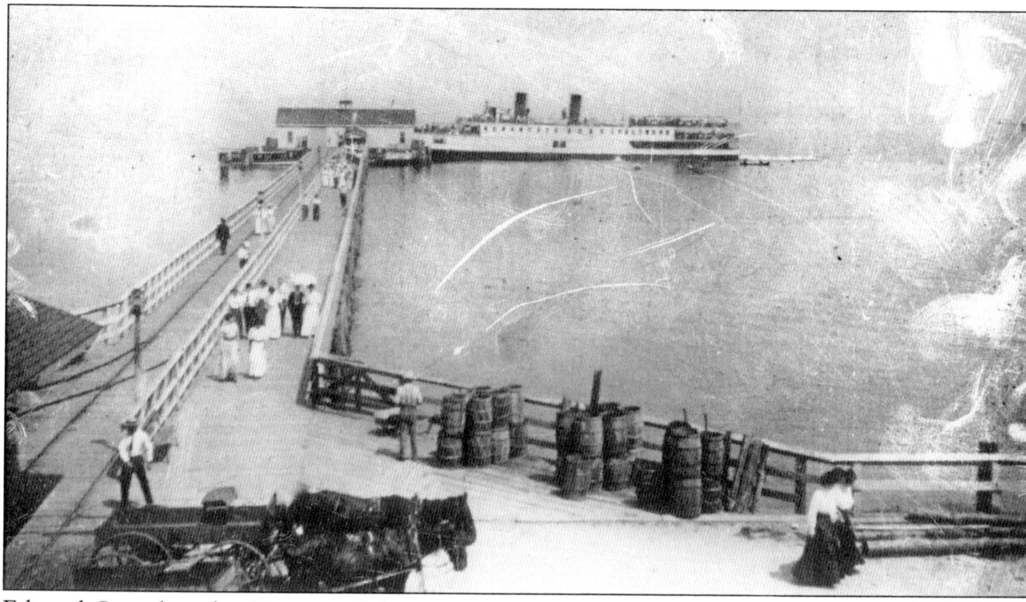

Edward Crew bought 60 acres of the original 225 acres of a land grant known as Fish Hall in 1726. He bought the remaining 165 acres of Fish Hall in 1728, and the property became known as Crew's Landing. In the 1850s, Richard Turner changed the name from Crew's Landing to Betterton in honor of his wife, Elizabeth Betterton. By 1900, this gracious town had become a popular vacation spot for summer visitors as well as locals. There were many boarding houses and hotels. As many as seven passenger boats arrived at the pier each summer day from Baltimore and Philadelphia.

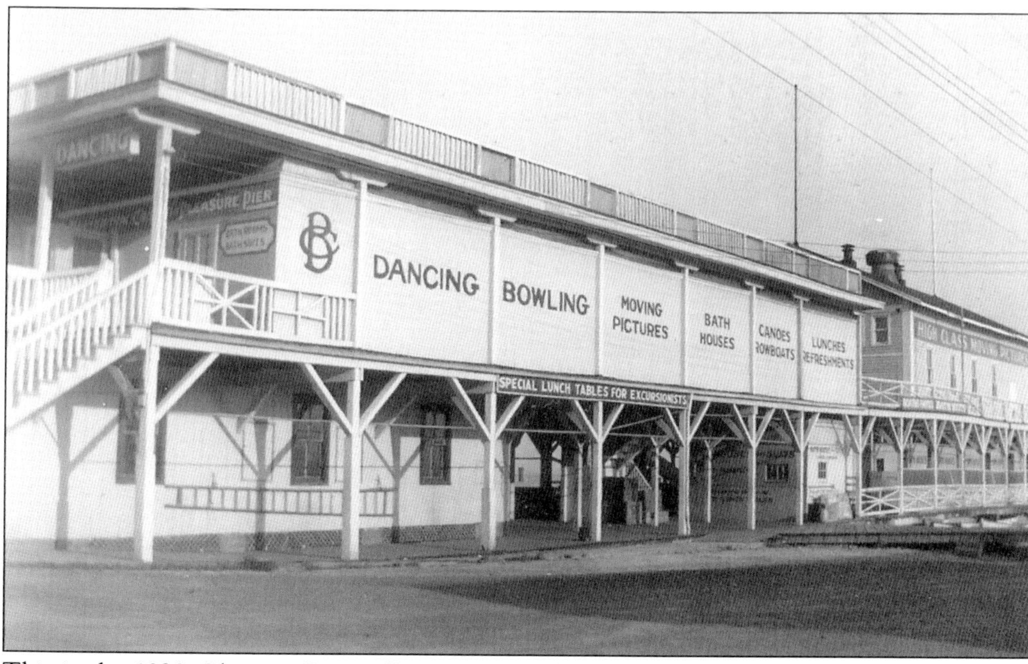

This is the 1930s Pleasure Pier at Betterton Beach on the Chesapeake Bay. The pier offered dancing, bowling, "high class" moving pictures, bathhouses, canoes, rowboats, and refreshments as well as special lunch tables for excursionists.

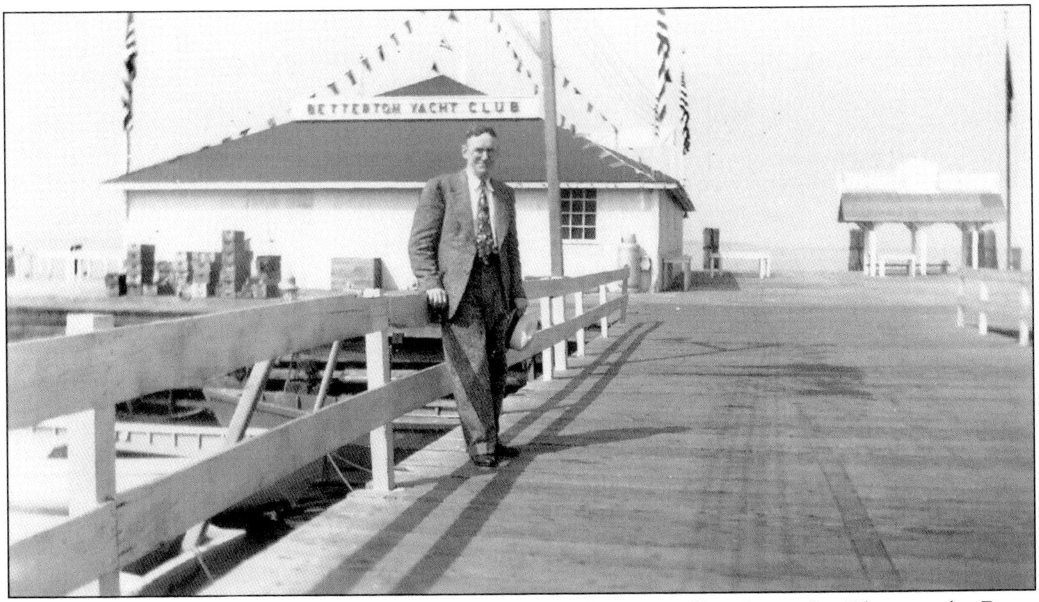

The Betterton Yacht Club was located on the pier at Betterton Beach on the Chesapeake Bay.

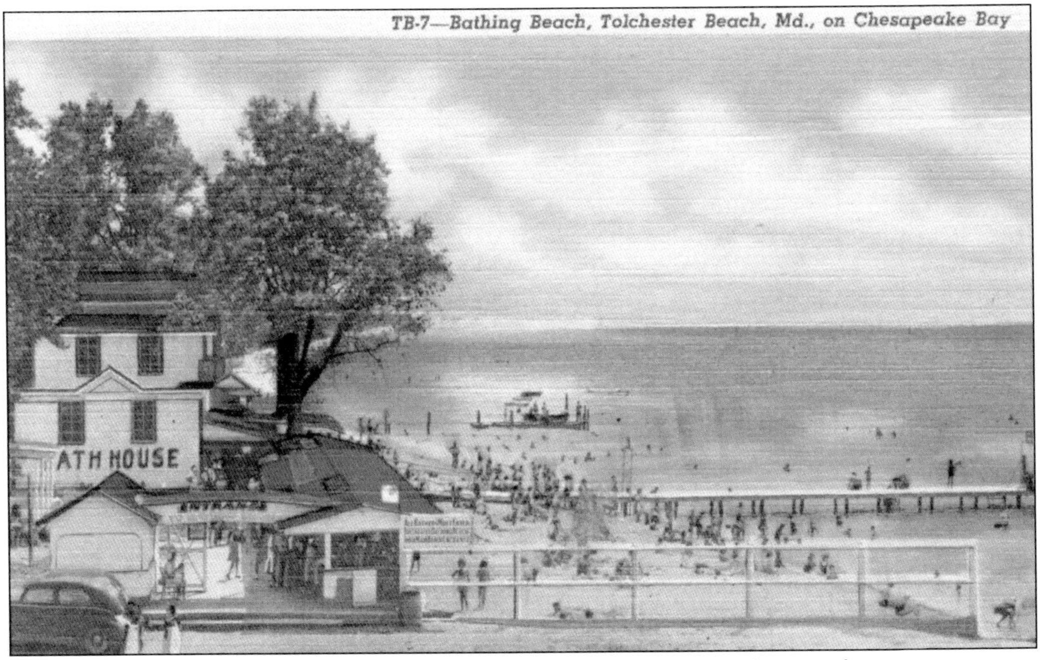

This bathing beach at Tolchester on the Chesapeake Bay was a popular spot for vacationers.

This menu was from the meeting of the Automobile Club at the Hotel Rigbie in Betteron on June 16, 1927.

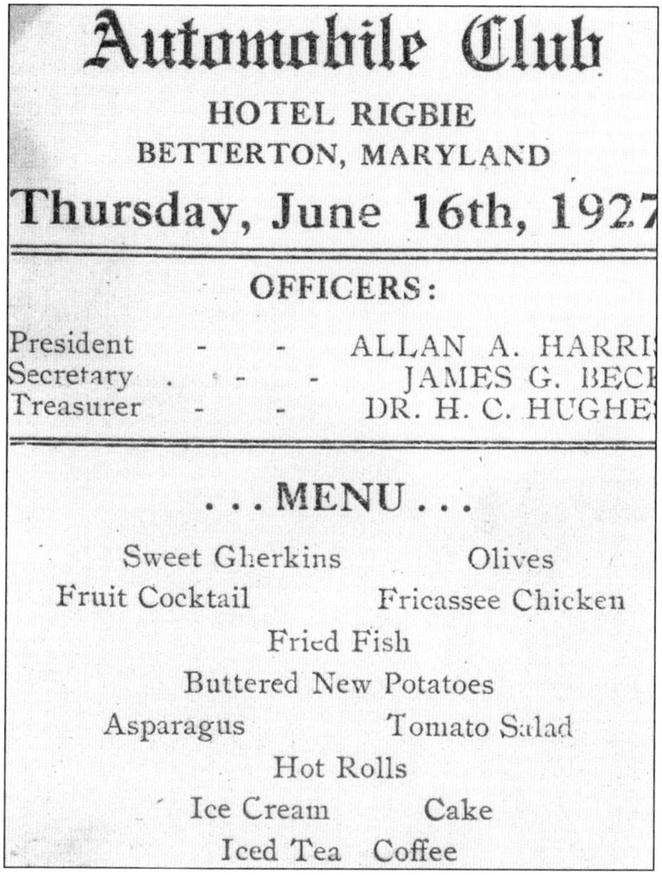
Automobile Club

HOTEL RIGBIE
BETTERTON, MARYLAND

Thursday, June 16th, 1927

OFFICERS:

President - - ALLAN A. HARRI
Secretary . - - JAMES G. BECI
Treasurer - - DR. H. C. HUGHE

. . . MENU . . .

Sweet Gherkins Olives
Fruit Cocktail Fricassee Chicken
Fried Fish
Buttered New Potatoes
Asparagus Tomato Salad
Hot Rolls
Ice Cream Cake
Iced Tea Coffee

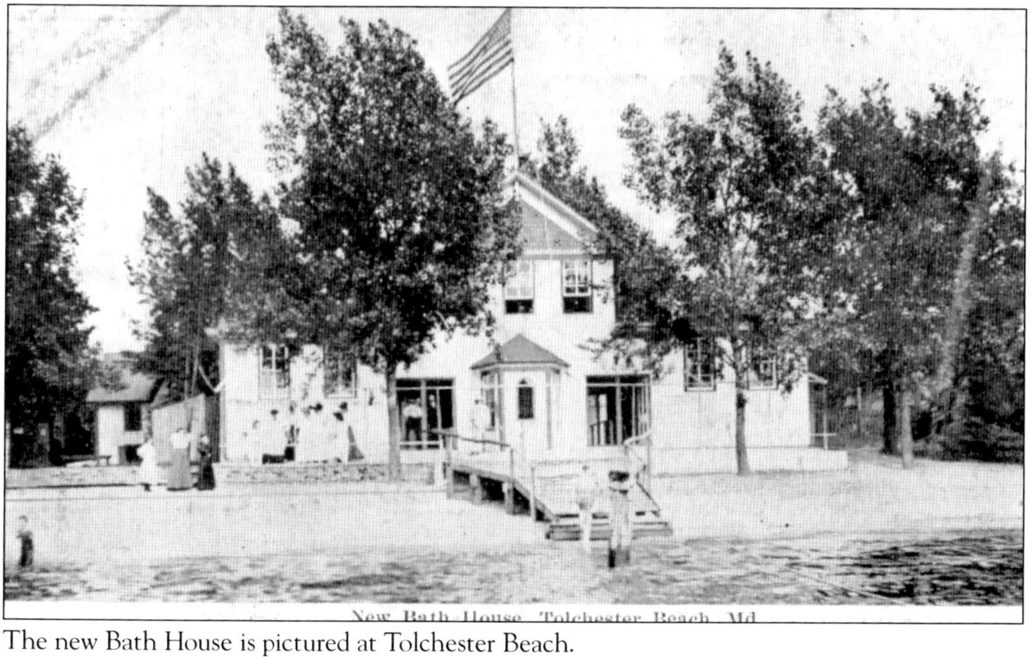

The new Bath House is pictured at Tolchester Beach.

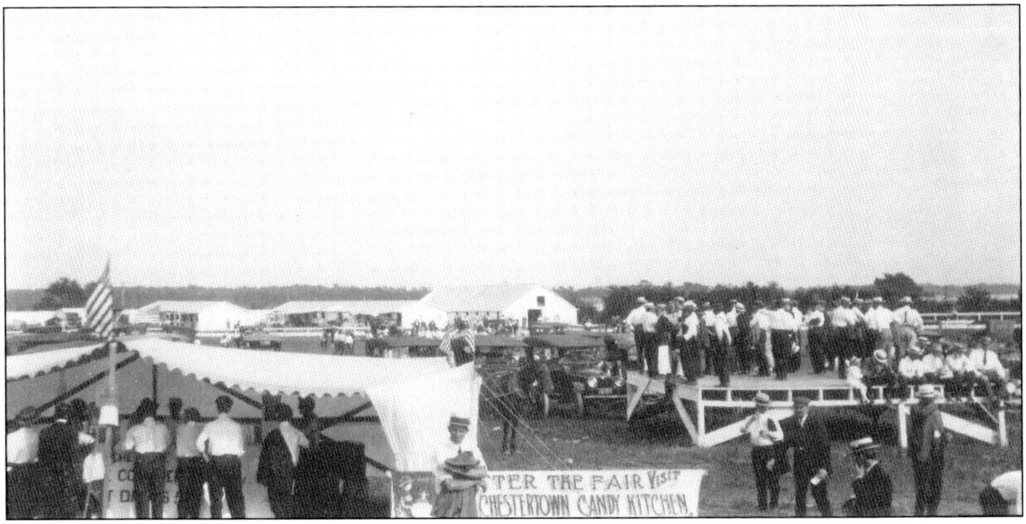

This is an early-20th-century photograph of the county fair in Kent. A plea to visit the Chestertown Candy Kitchen is in the forefront.

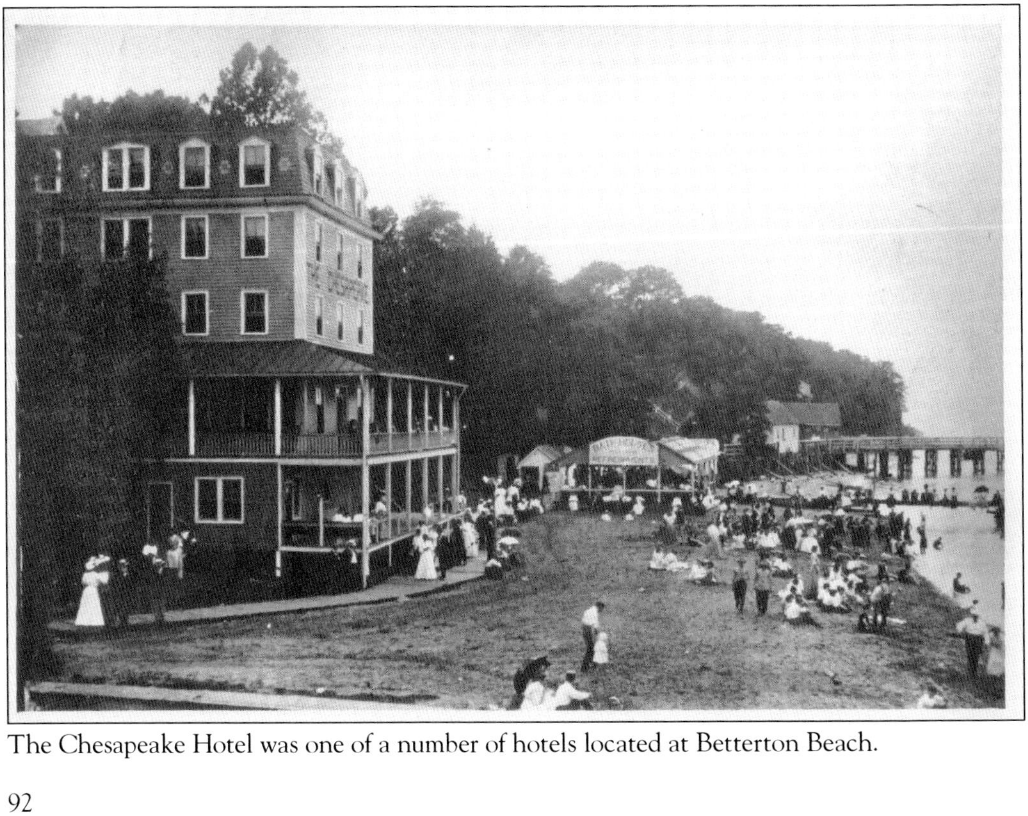

The Chesapeake Hotel was one of a number of hotels located at Betterton Beach.

Eight

ALL IN A DAY'S WORK

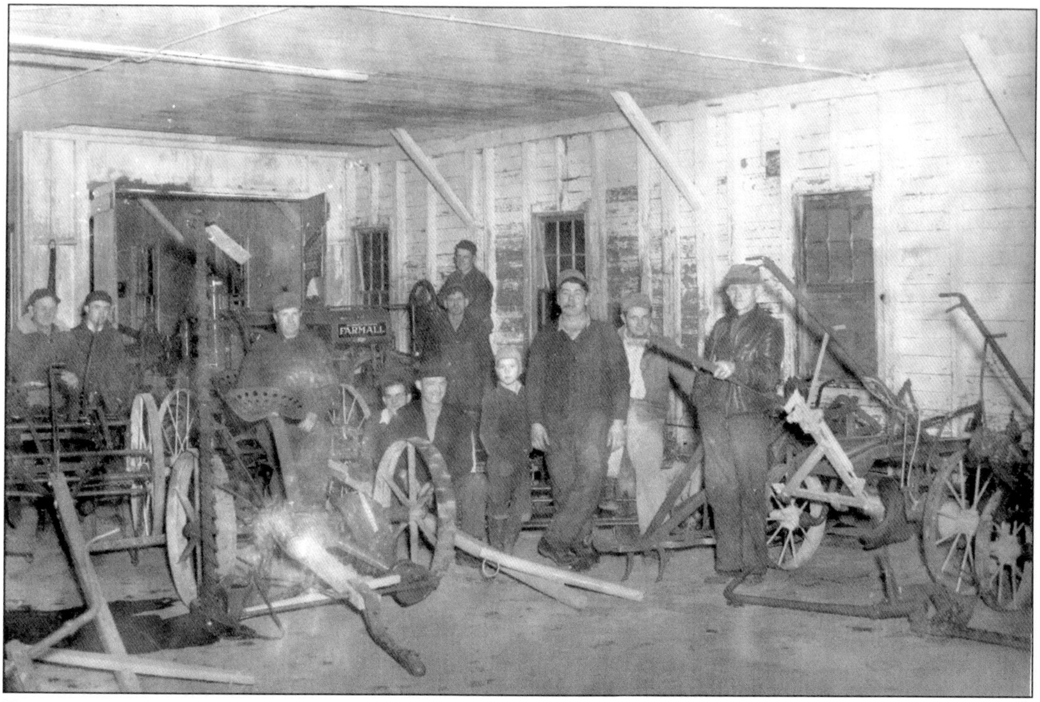

Farming was and is still big business in Kent County. Shown here is an early photograph of men and boys with farm equipment of the era.

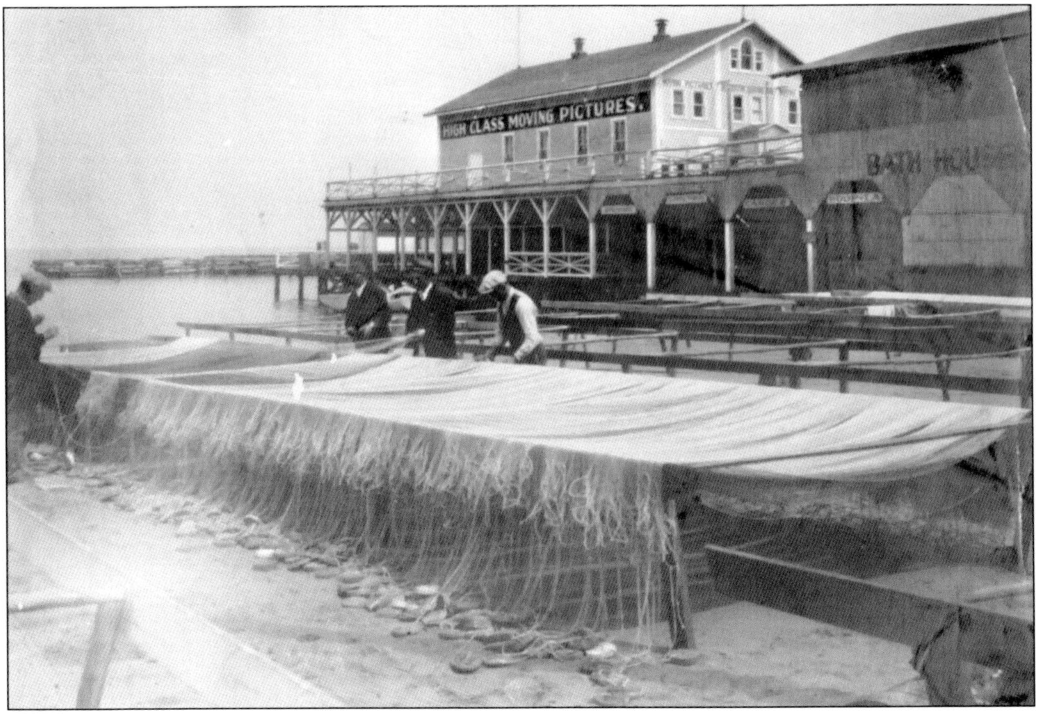

To most, Betterton was a place to play in at the turn of the 20th century. However, to some it was a place to work. Pictured here in a 1936 picture are a group of men repairing shad nets on the beach in front of the Betterton Bath House.

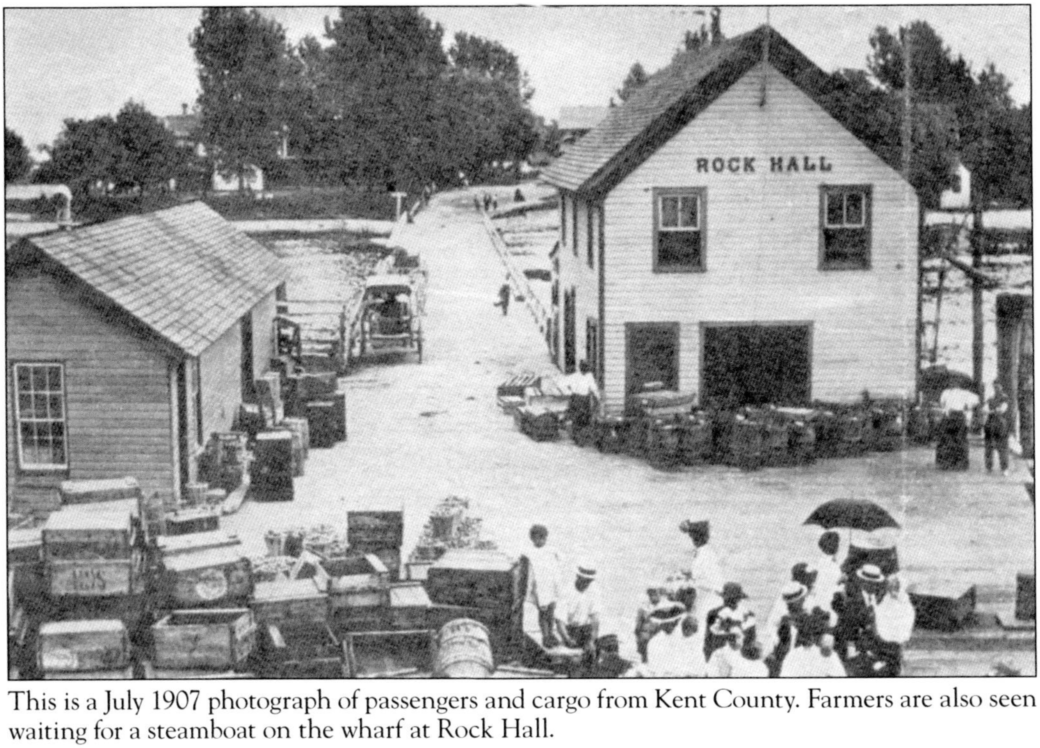

This is a July 1907 photograph of passengers and cargo from Kent County. Farmers are also seen waiting for a steamboat on the wharf at Rock Hall.

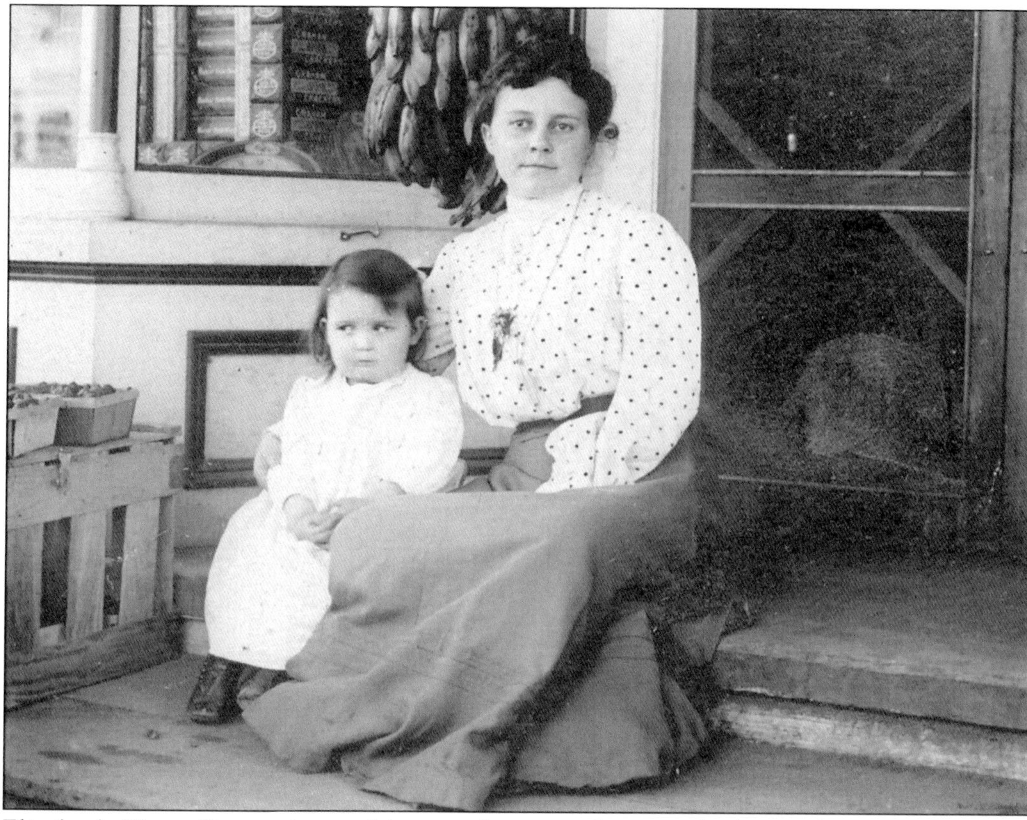

Elizabeth Sloan Bottomley and her mother are photographed outside the family store in Millington.

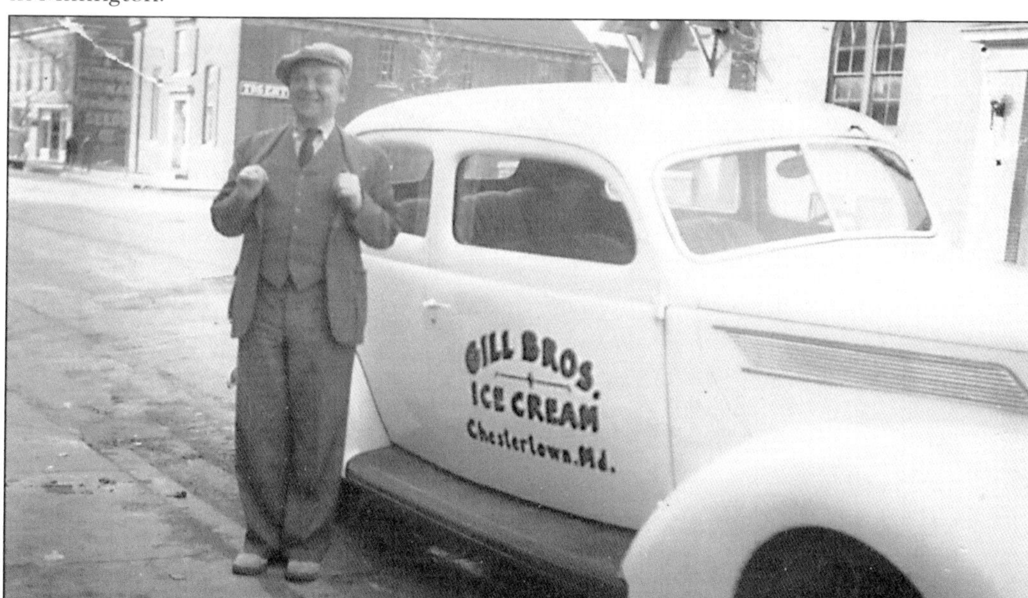

Henry Gill, of Gill Bros. Ice Cream Factory and Dairy, is shown standing on Cross Street in Chestertown. Jane's Church and Kent Printing are seen in the background.

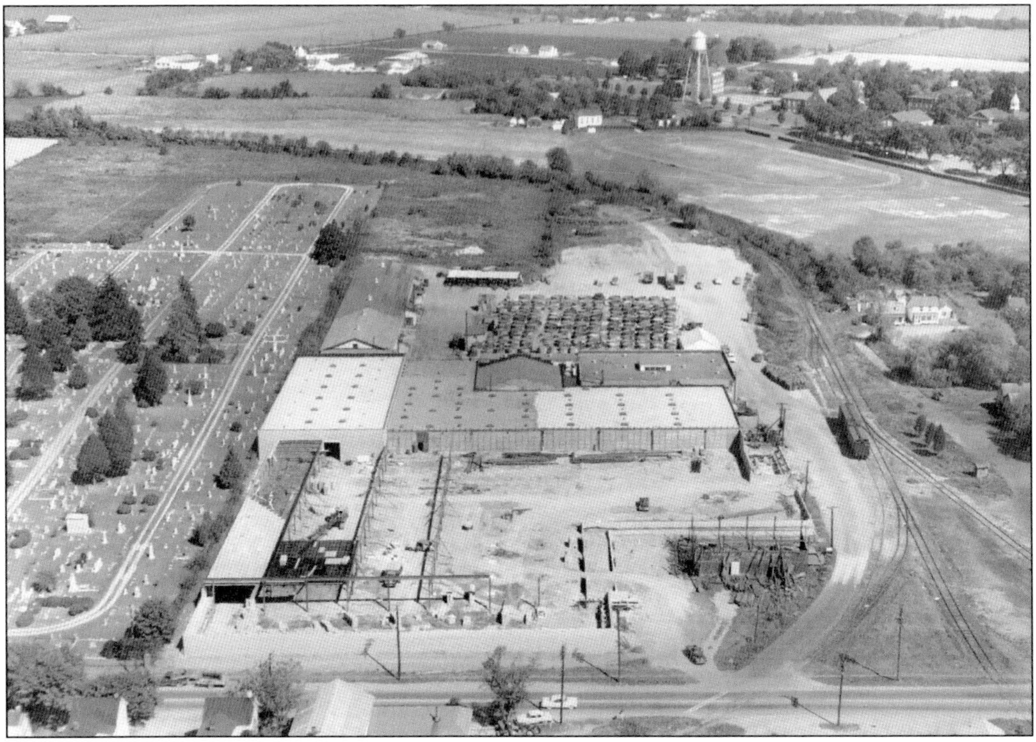

Here is a view of Chester Cemetery in Chestertown on the left. The former Vita Foods plant (now Dixon Value and Coupling) is seen on the right.

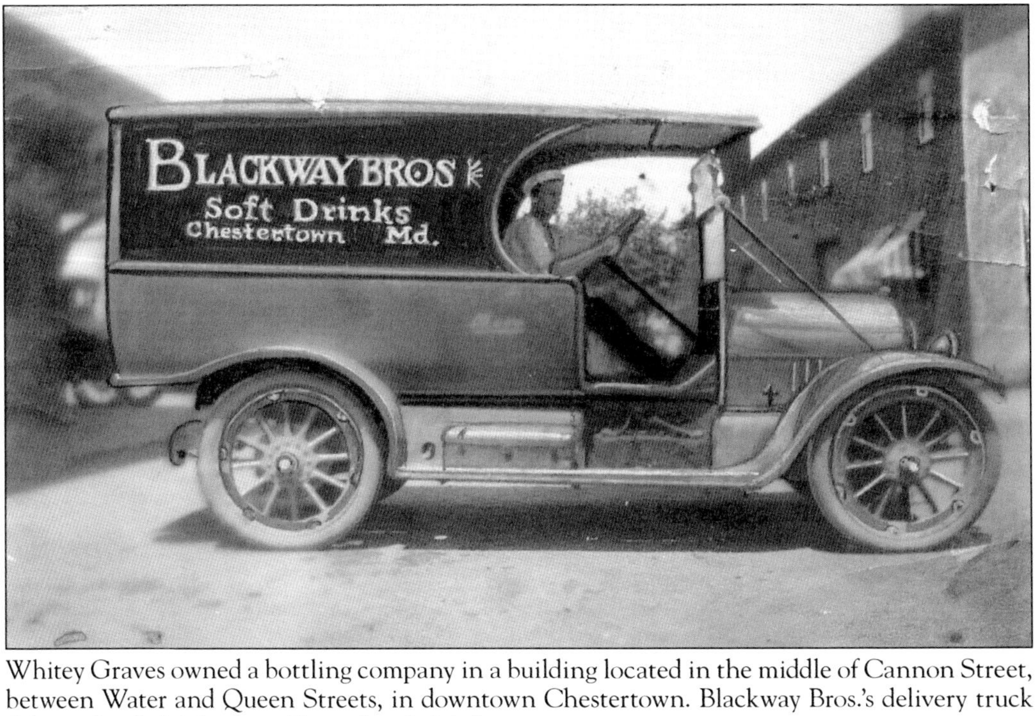

Whitey Graves owned a bottling company in a building located in the middle of Cannon Street, between Water and Queen Streets, in downtown Chestertown. Blackway Bros.'s delivery truck delivered soft drinks from Graves's soft drink company.

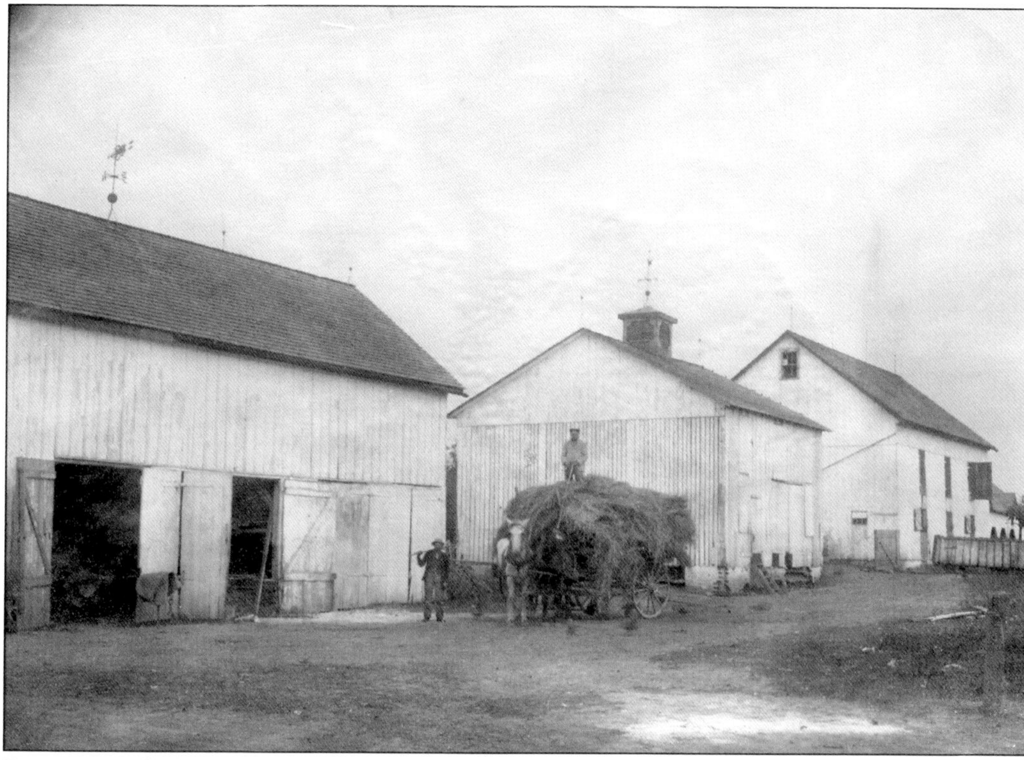

Farms are still the largest part of the geographic landscape throughout Kent County. They are also part of our cultural heritage. This early-20th-century photograph shows farmers with hay headed for the barns.

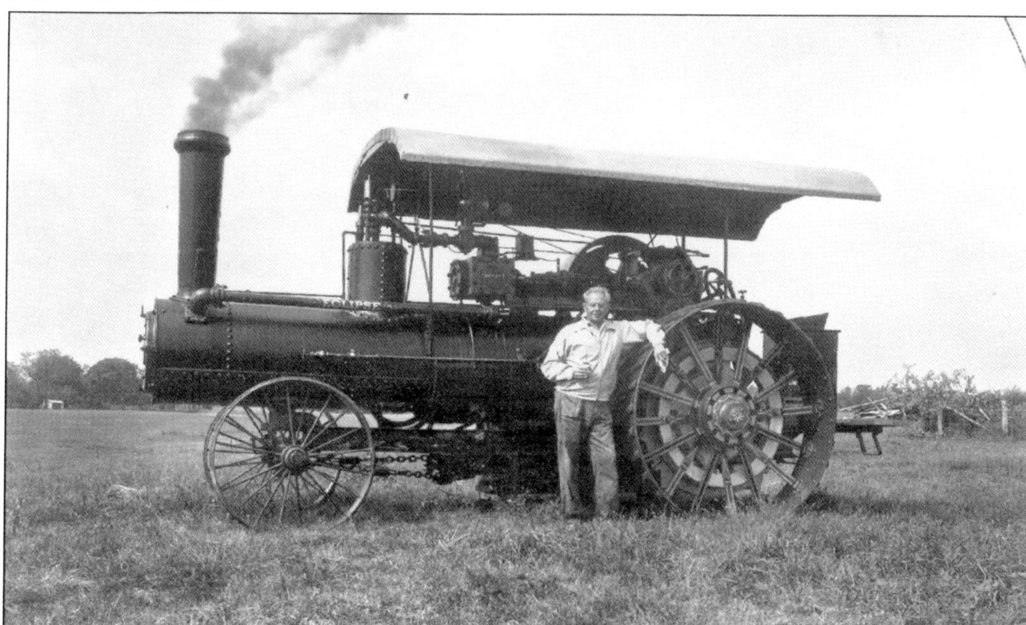

Before diesel there was steam. The above photograph shows a steam-driven tractor from an age gone by.

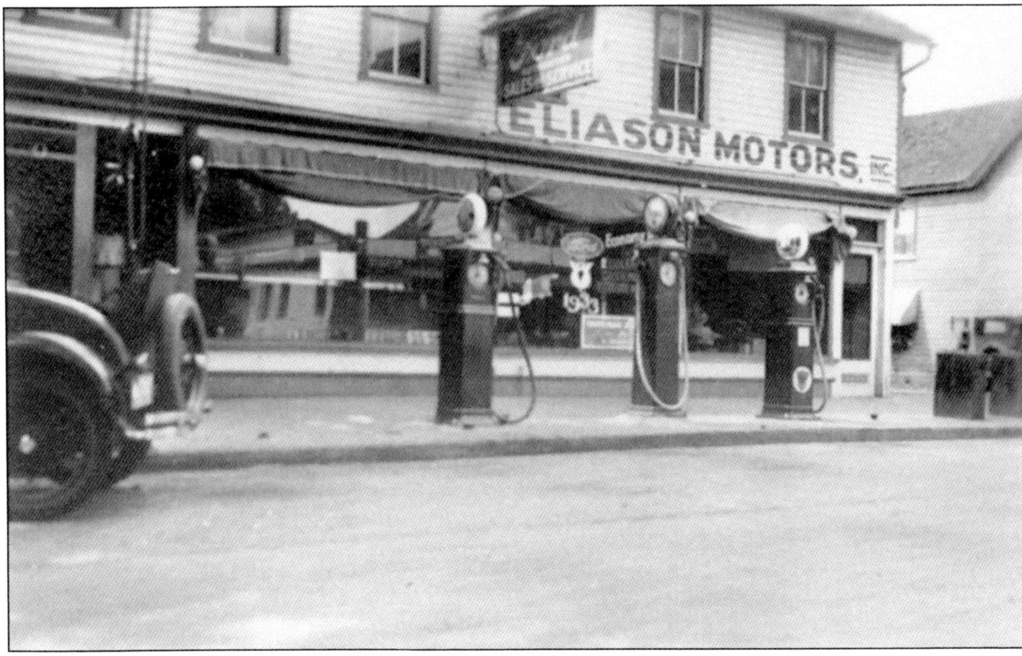

Eliason Motors, Inc., a Ford dealership, was located in Chestertown on Cross Street next to where the town hall is now. It was purchased in 1923 by Mr. Thomas W. Eliason. The building was formerly the Armstrong Hotel. The dealership was sold in 1975.

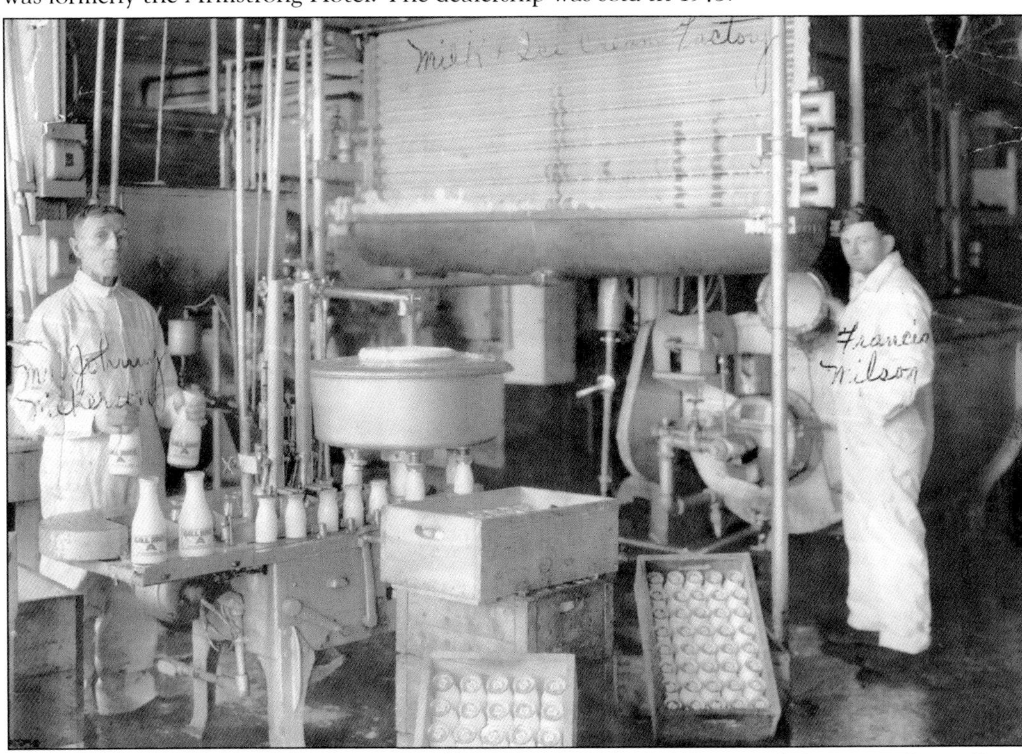

This photograph shows the inside of Gill Bros. Ice Cream Factory and Dairy on Cross Street where Twigs and Teacups is now located.

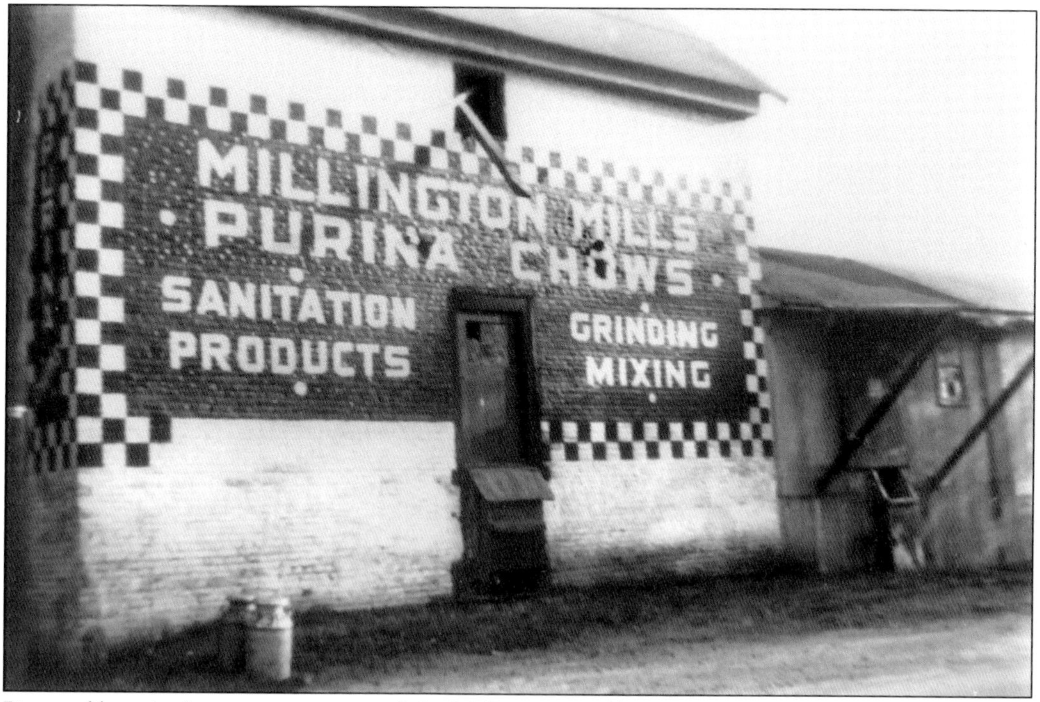

Pictured here is the remaining sign of the Millington Mill. It is said that Millington got its name from the many mills located in that area.

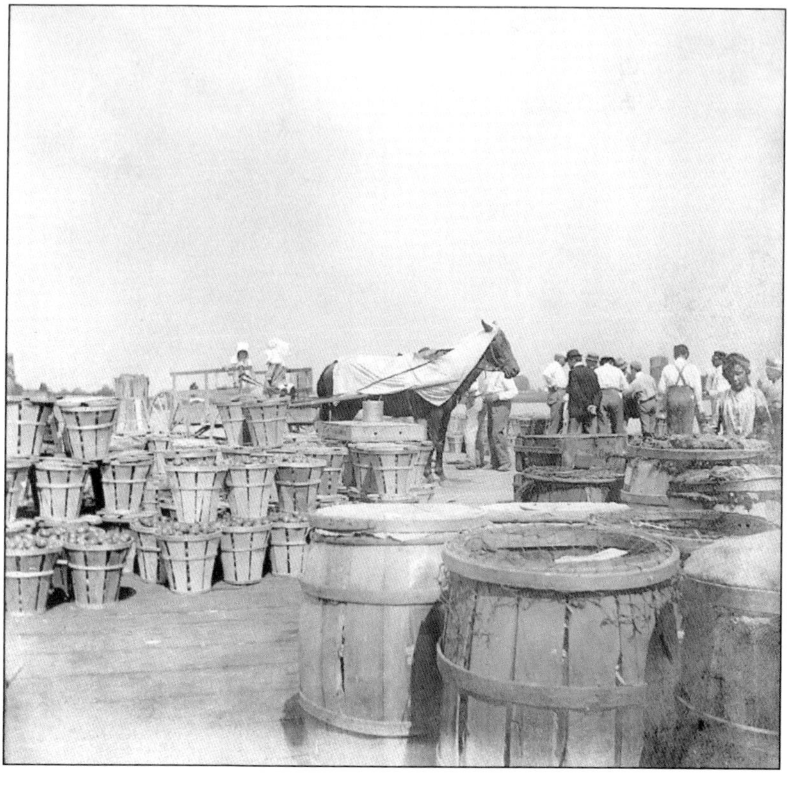

Kent County farmers depended on river and bay transportation to get their produce to the Baltimore and Philadelphia markets. Shown here in a late-19th-century photograph is produce sitting on the dock and ready for the boat.

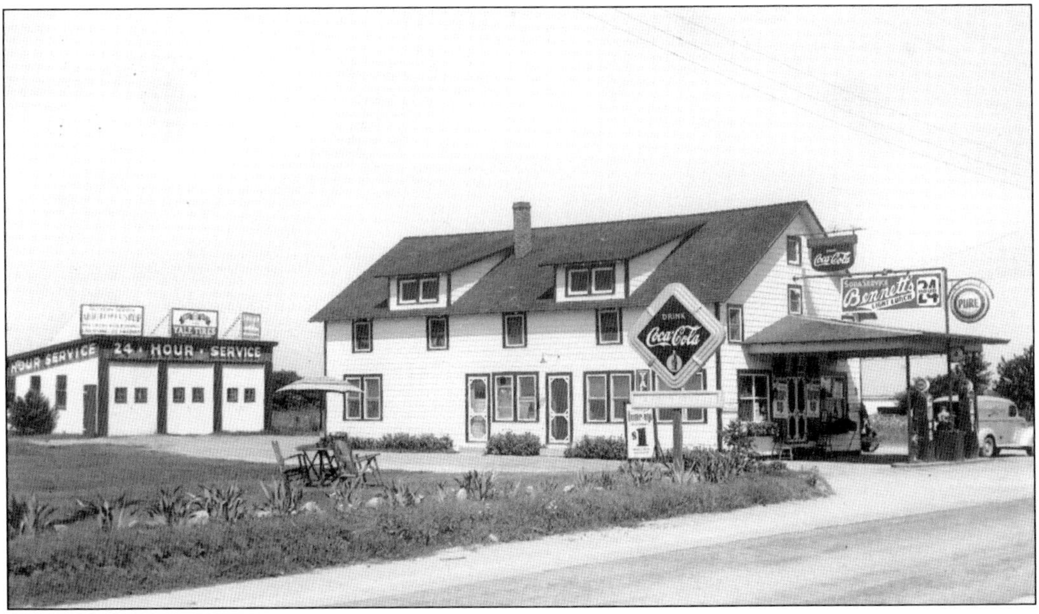

Bill Bennett's Service Station and Luncheonette on Washington Avenue in Chestertown was a popular spot for local teenagers as well as Washington College students in the late 1930s, 1940s, and 1950s. A dance floor was enlarged about 1940 where patrons danced to local bands or a juke box. In the late 1940s, when television was brand new, locals could go to Bennett's, have a bite to eat, and watch the *Ed Sullivan Show* or wrestling.

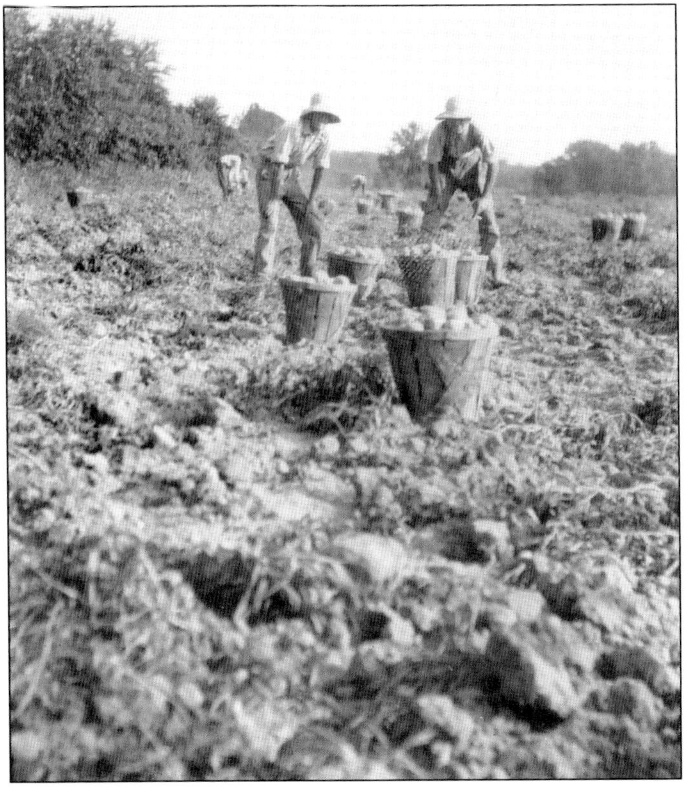

This is an early photograph of workers picking peaches. In the past, Kent County was known throughout the shore for its peaches.

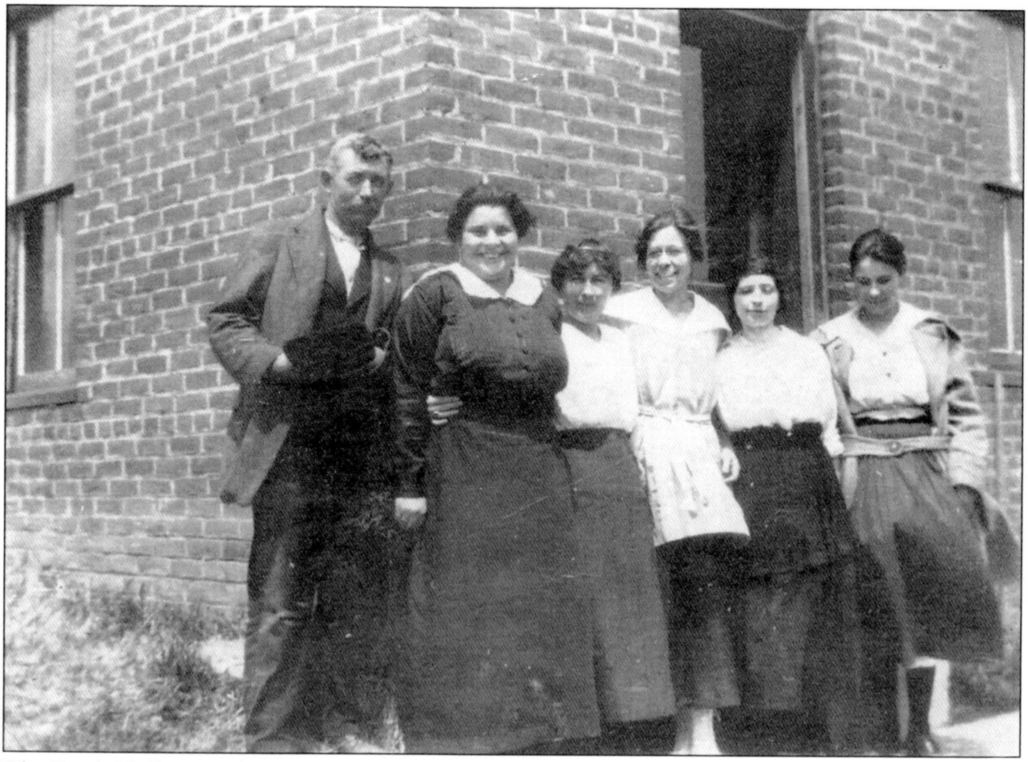

The Rock Hall Manufacturing Company sewing factory started operations around 1915 just off Main Street in Rock Hall. This photograph shows workers outside the factory.

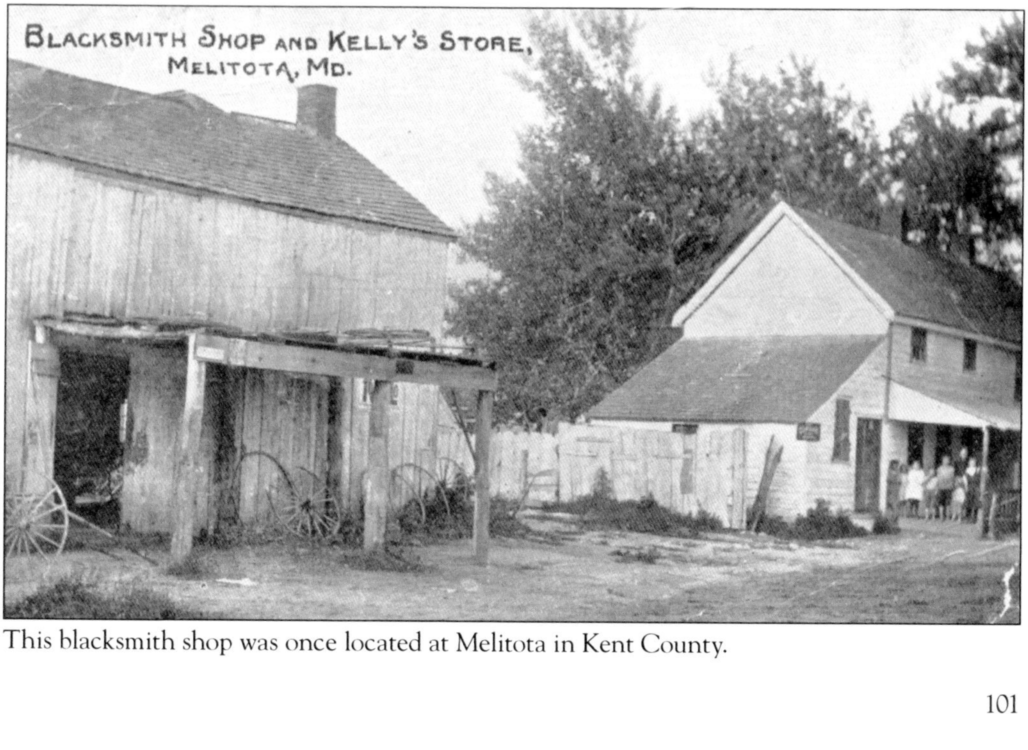

This blacksmith shop was once located at Melitota in Kent County.

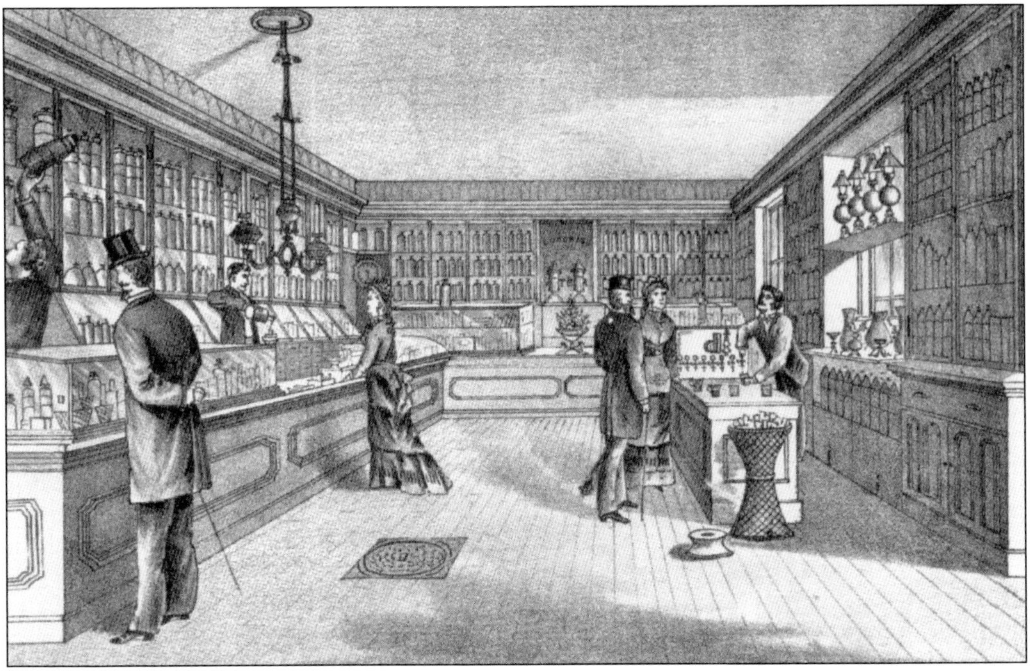

Pictured here is an image of the interior of Stam's Drug Store as it appeared in 1877. Stam's Drug Store is still a working drug store and is located at 215 High Street in downtown Chestertown.

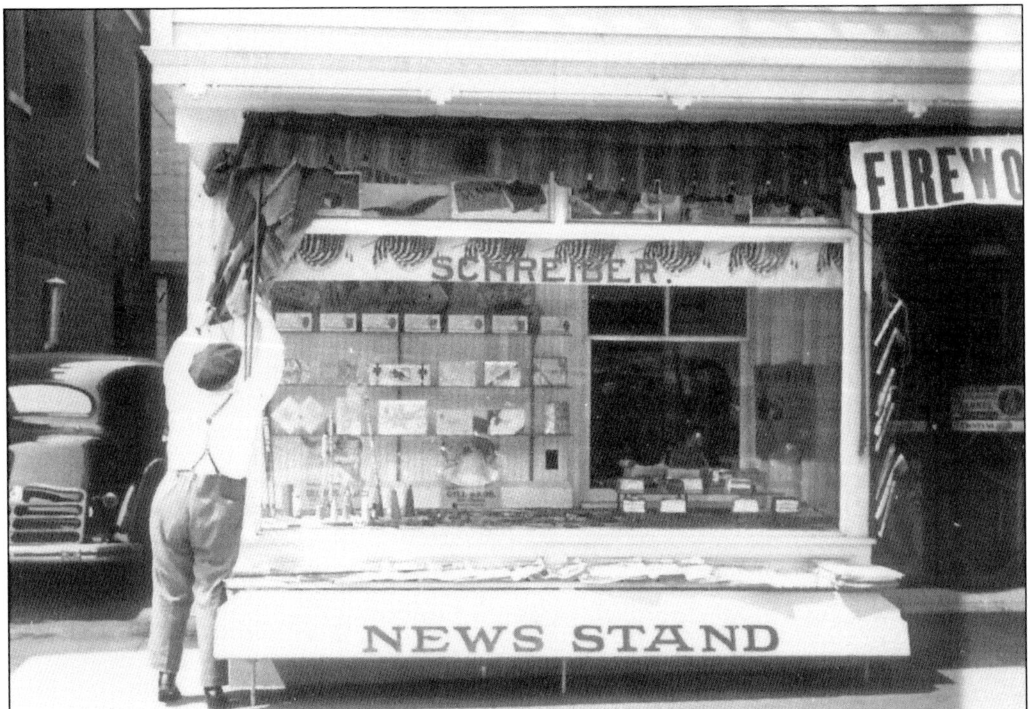

Mr. Charles C. Schreiber of Schreiber's Wholesale and Retail Confectionery is shown in front of his business on High Street in downtown Chestertown. He also sold newspapers, magazines, and fireworks.

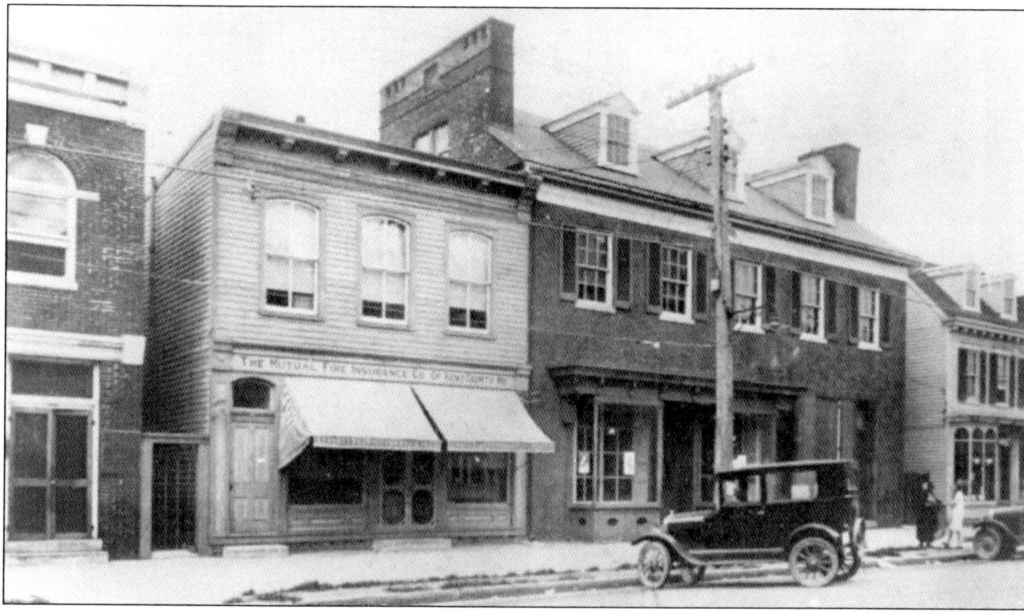

Every county business or farm needs insurance, and Kent County was not any different. Here is an early-1930s photograph of the Mutual Fire Insurance Company of Kent County.

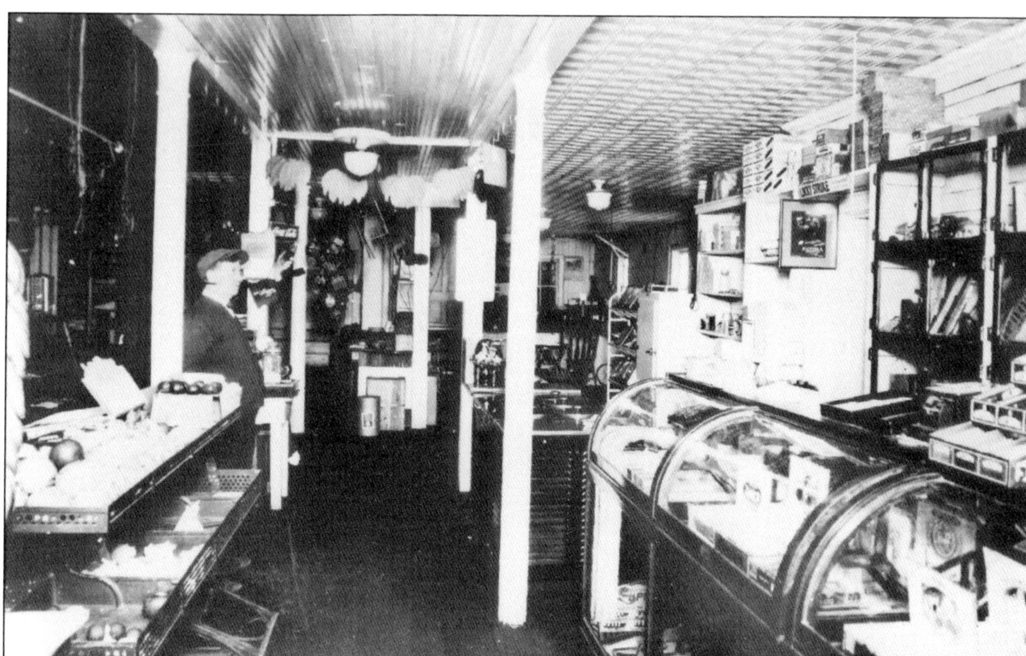

Charles C. Schrieber of Schreiber's Wholesale and Retail Confectionery stands inside his store on High Street in downtown Chestertown.

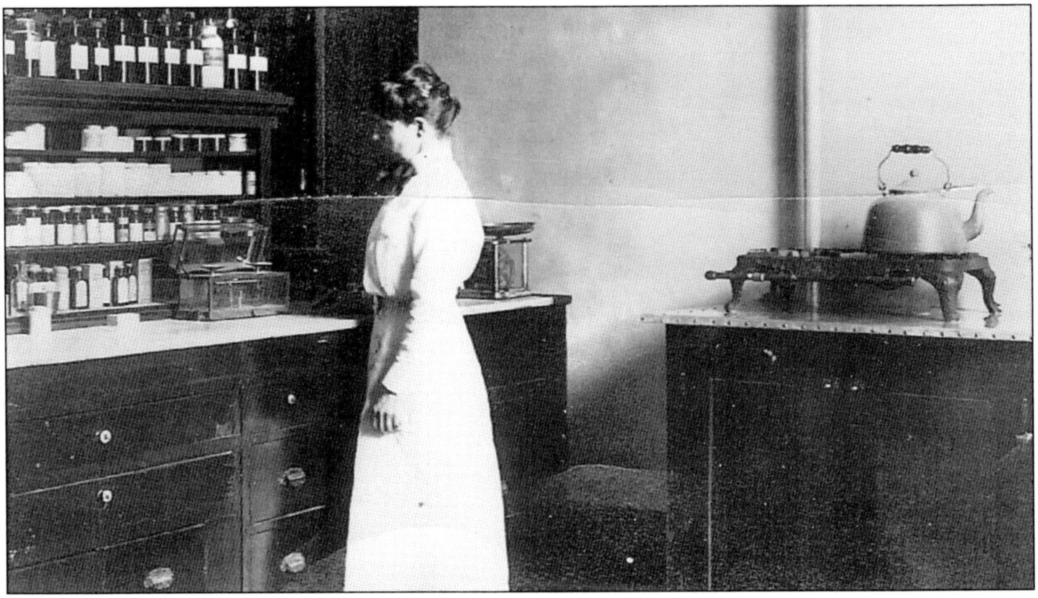

Miss Jane Craven Cooper, daughter of Samuel Ford Cooper and Ann Edytha Rasin Cooper, was the first woman pharmacist in Maryland. She worked for Dr. Stam at the old Stam Drug Store across the street from the present one. Dr. Stam sent her to the School of Pharmacy at the University of Maryland. After working at pharmacies in Baltimore, she returned home to Kent County in the mid-1940s and worked as a pharmacist until she retired in 1960 at age 86.

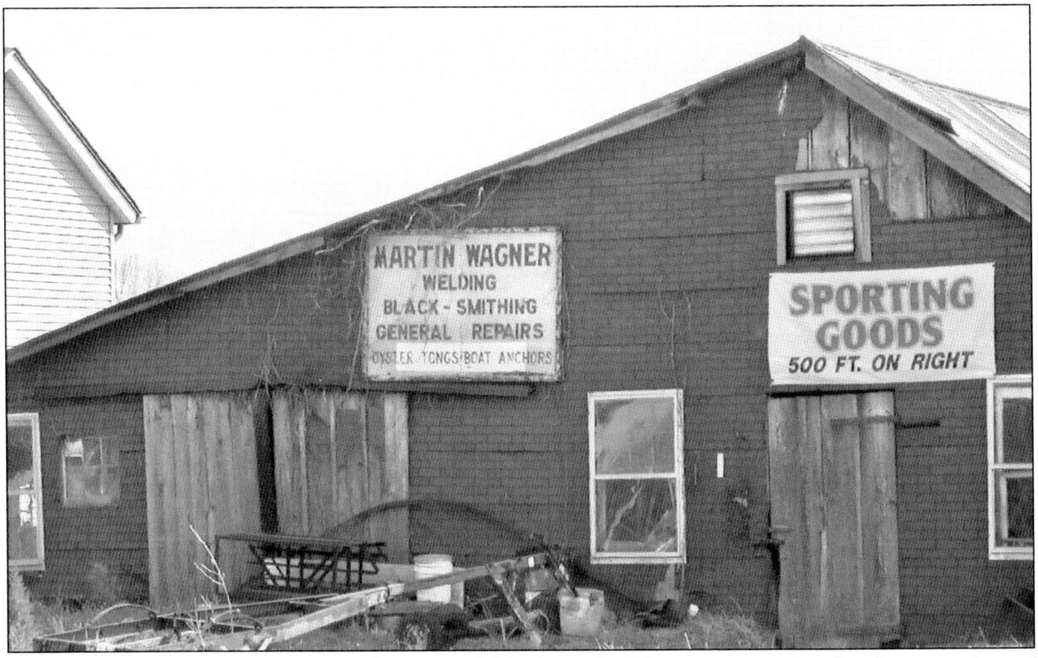

Martin Wagner was a master machinist and blacksmith. He represents the third generation of his family that worked with forge, torch, and anvil on this site. The Wagner Blacksmith and Machinery Repair Shop, just outside of Rock Hall, began serving the residents of Kent County in the early 1850s. They repaired manufactured equipment and created new products for farmers and watermen.

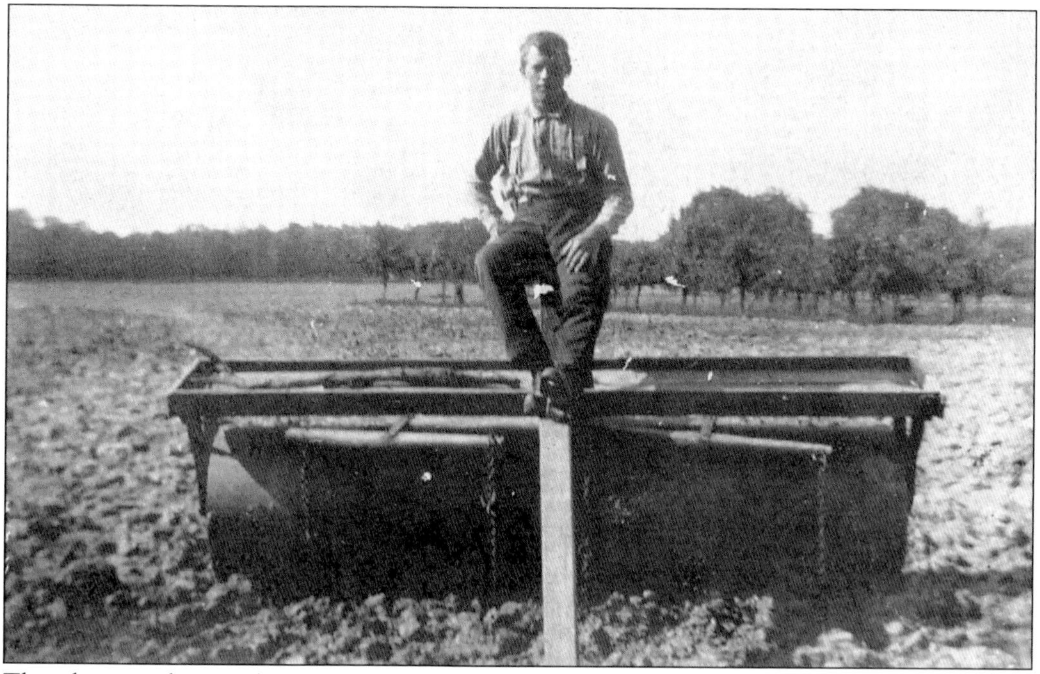

This photograph was taken around 1915. It is a picture of Walker Ball Lamb Sr. sitting on a roller at Horn Farm (now Chesapeake Farms).

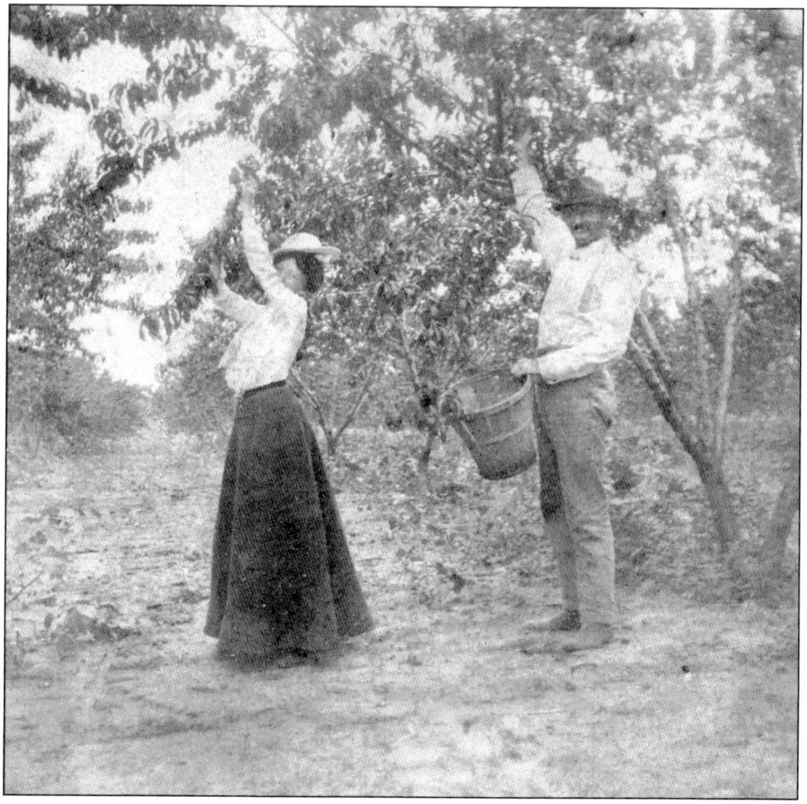

Mr. VanZant and Miss Loucille Jarvis are pictured picking peaches at Raymond Farms in Kent County in 1904.

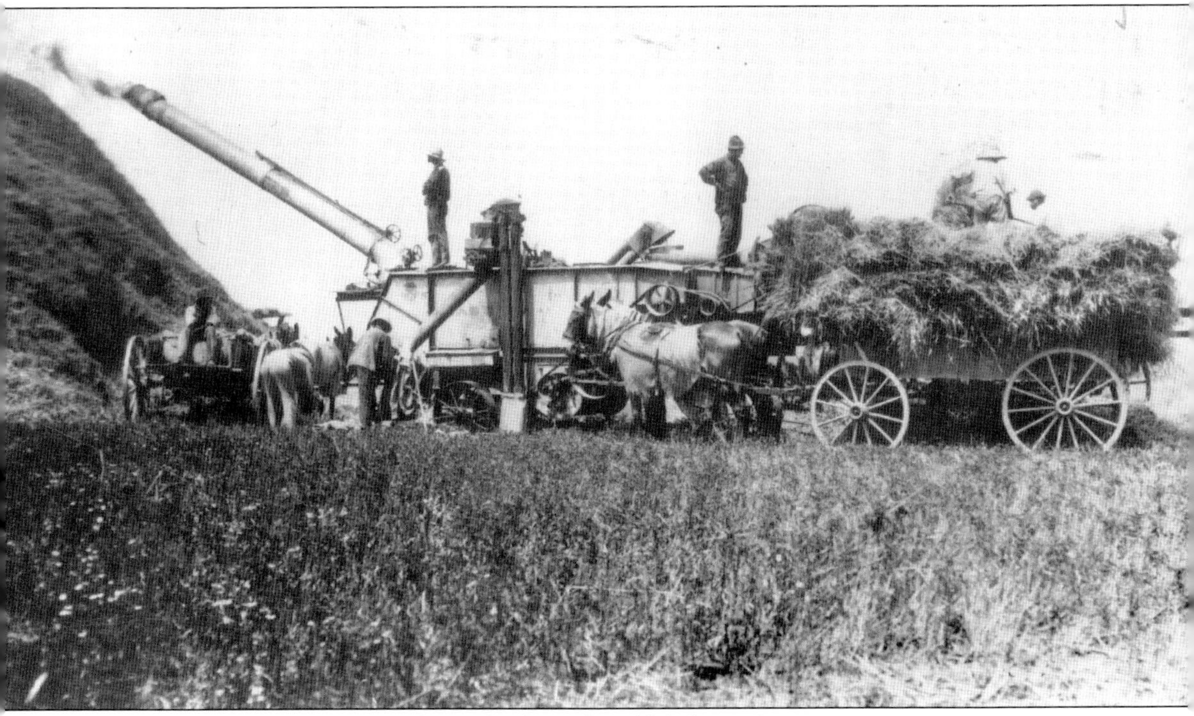

This image shows people working the farm the old-fashioned way.

Nine

Time Passes By

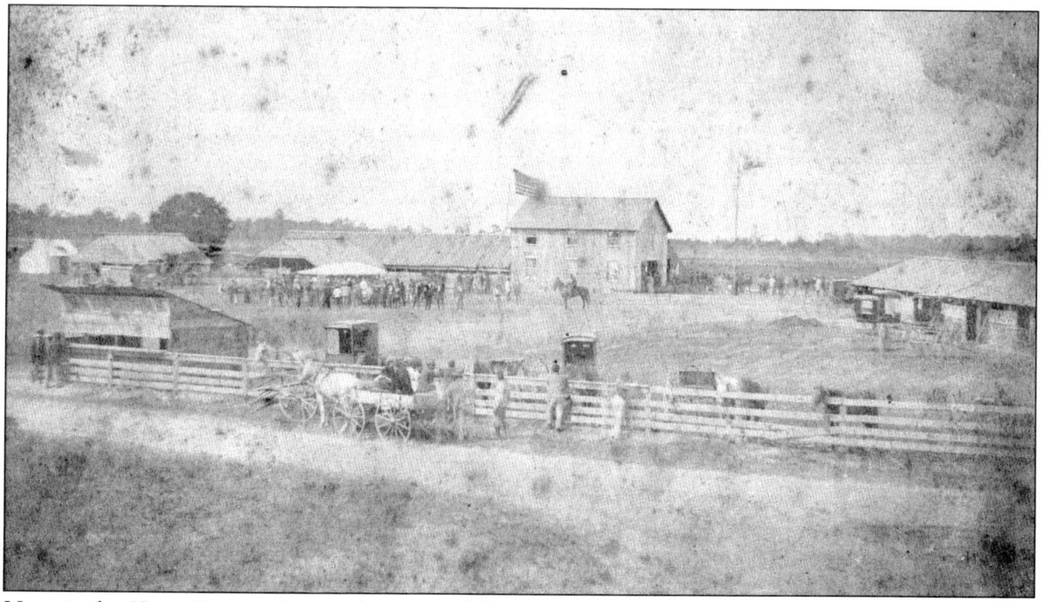

Here is the Kent County fair at the turn of the century.

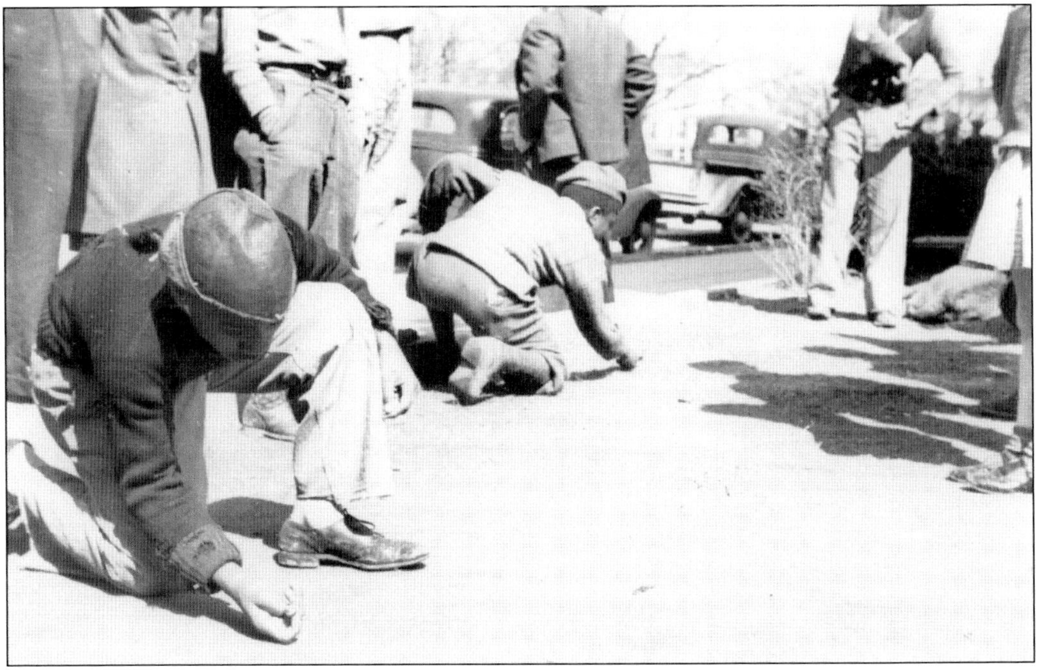

People here are passing time in Kent County with a marble game.

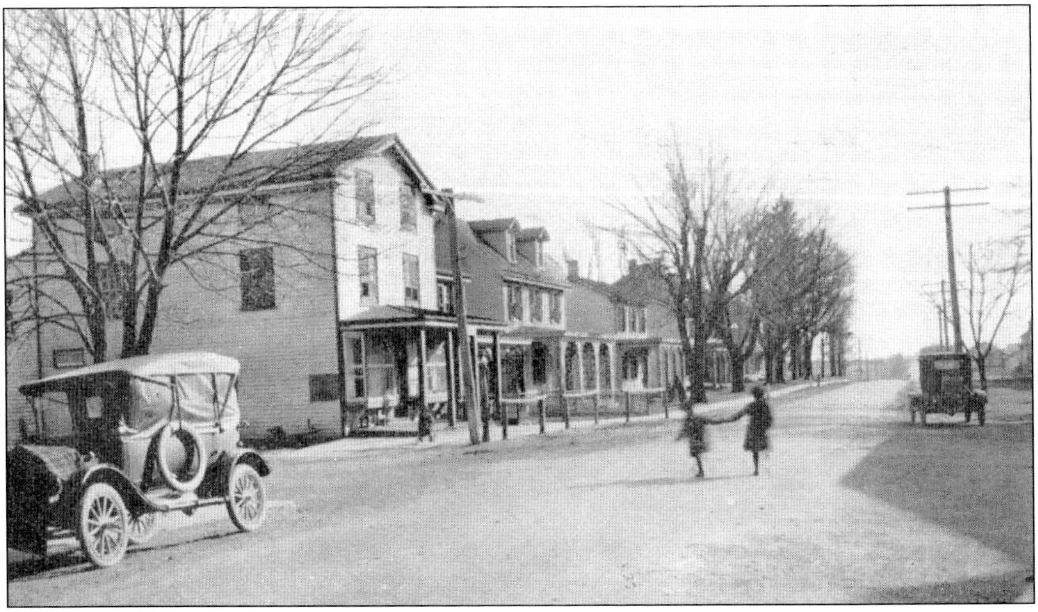

Kennedyville is a village on the Philadelphia, Baltimore, & Washington Railroad. This is a picture postcard of Main Street in Kennedyville during the early 1930s.

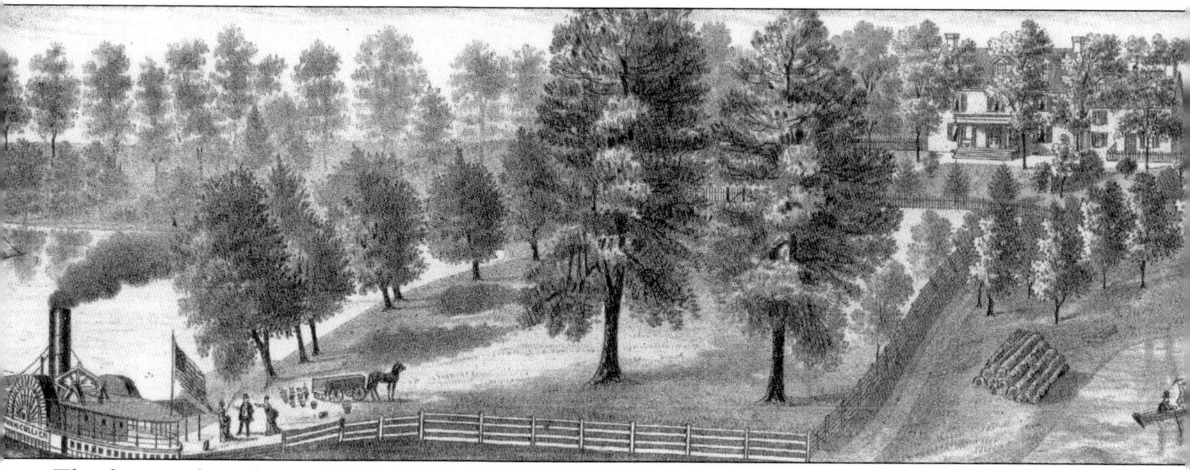
The farm and residence of Samuel Vannort is depicted in this 1877 engraving.

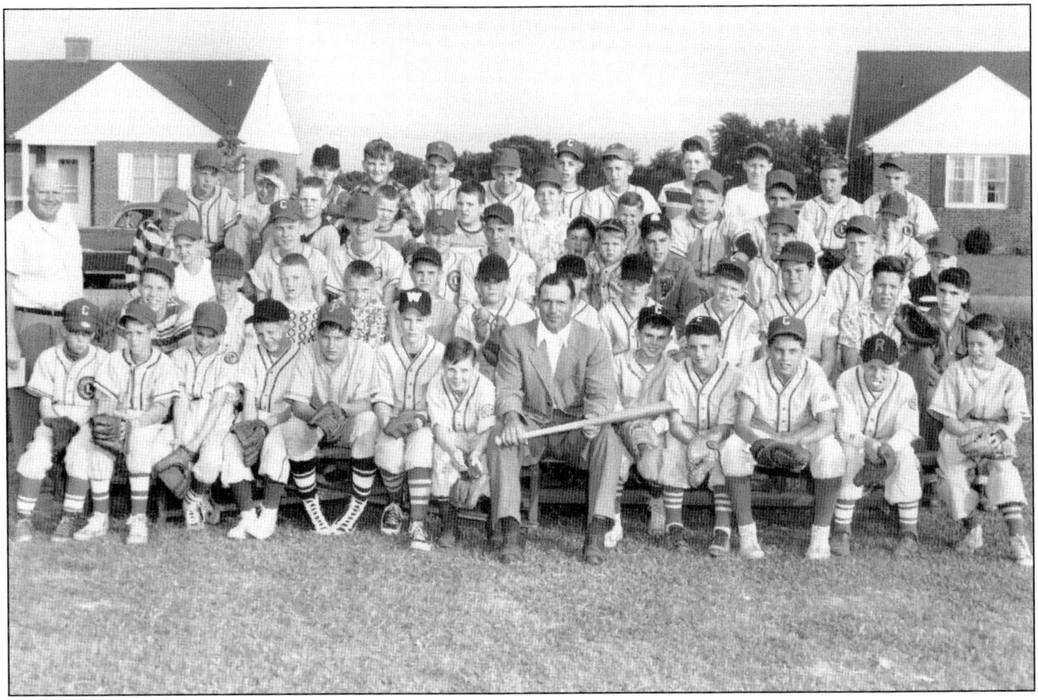

William B. (Swish) Nicholson (first row, center), a Kent County resident who played professional baseball from 1936 to 1953, is pictured with one of Kent County's little league baseball teams. Coach Ellery Ward is pictured on the far left. Among those pictured are the following: Bobby Lord, Sandy Knapp, Tommy Bramble, Ted Morris, Allen Gsell, James Bickling, Richard Jacobs, and Frankie Smith.

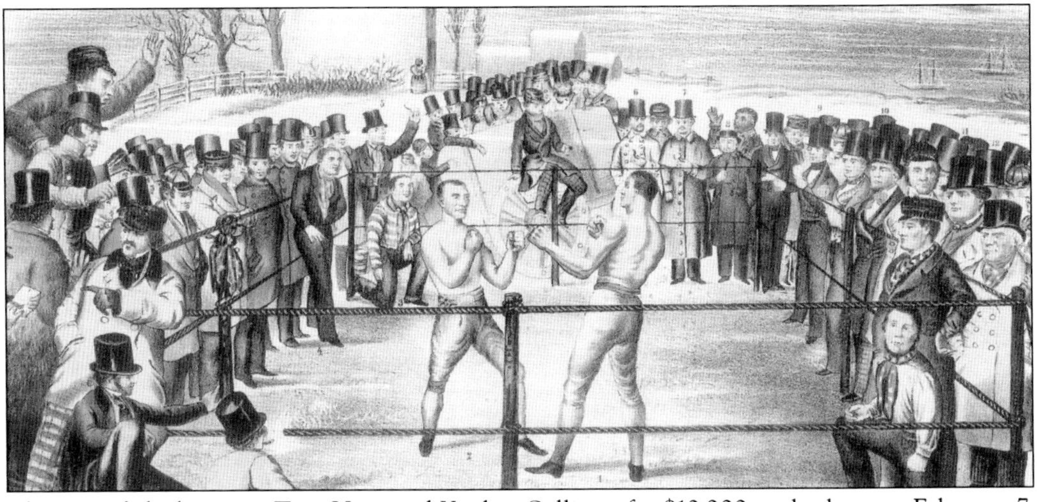

The great fight between Tom Hyer and Yankee Sullivan for $10,000 took place on February 7, 1849, at Still Pond Heights near Still Pond. Boxing was illegal at this time. A ring was improvised using stakes and topgallant halyards (sailing rope) from one of the vessels that had transported the fighters to Kent County.

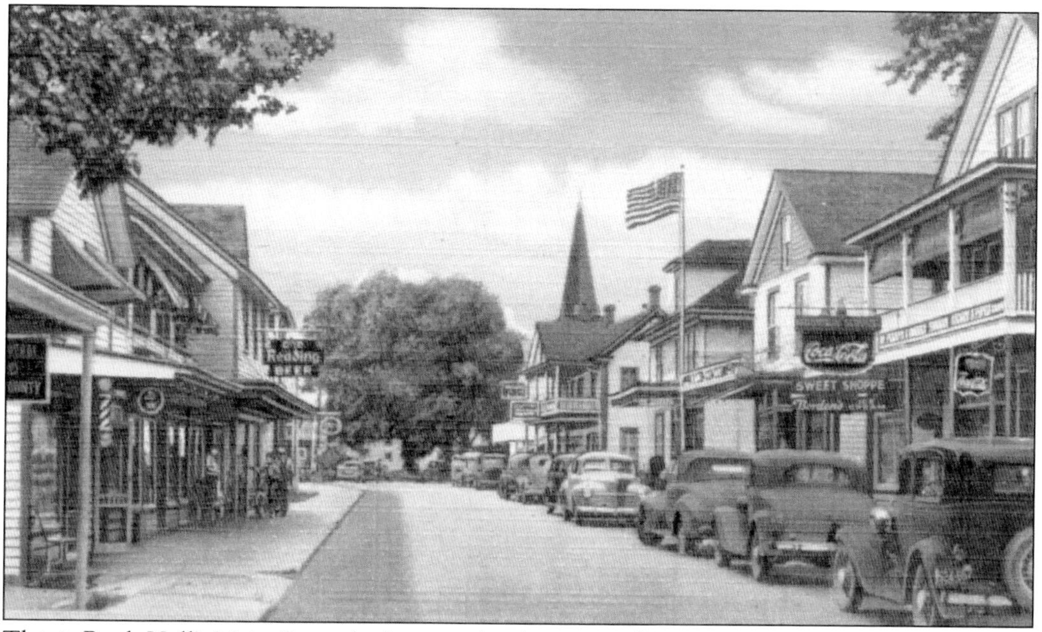

This is Rock Hall's Main Street looking in the direction of Eastern Neck Island.

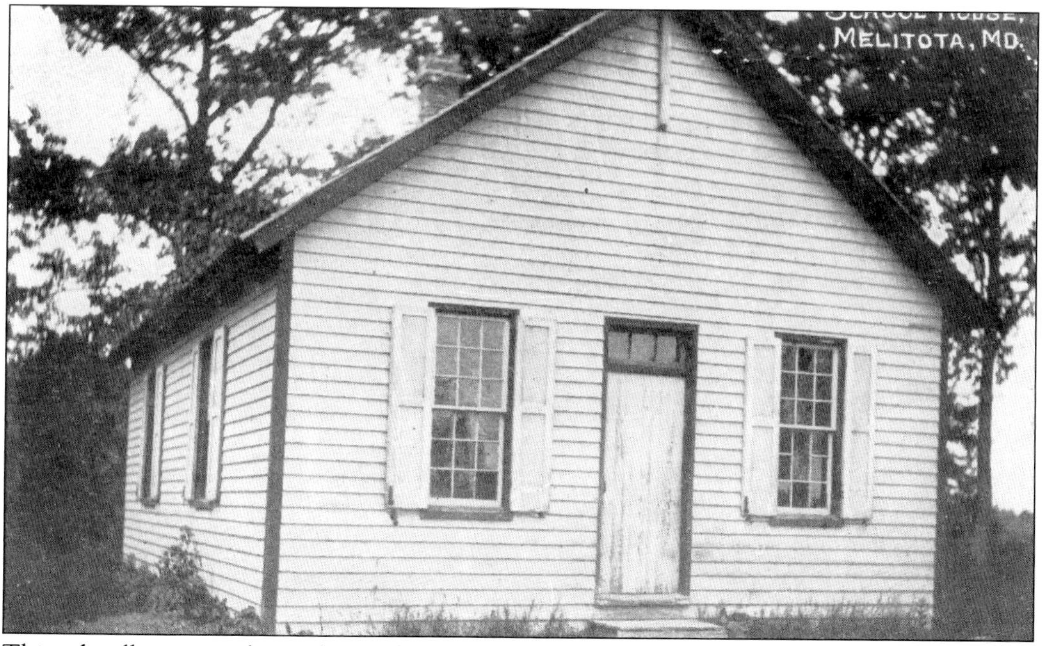

This schoolhouse was located at Melitota in Kent County.

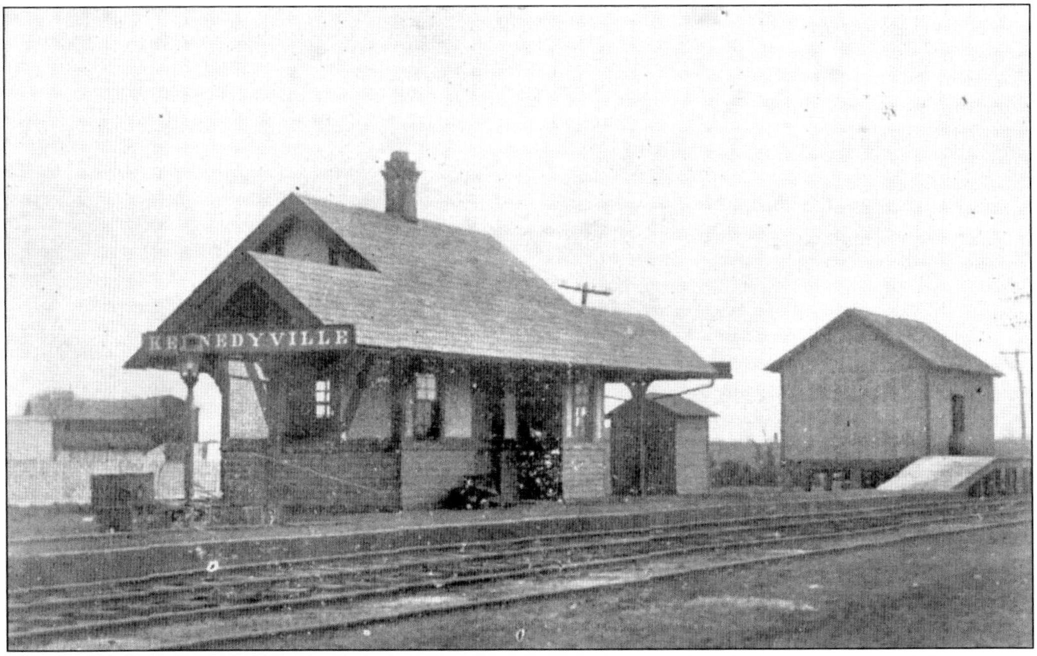

The Kennedyville Train Station building was moved to Greenbank Station near Wilmington, Delaware, in 1963. It was re-erected by volunteer members of Historic Red Clay Valley, Inc. and served as the main station and ticket window until 1993, when it was moved to Hockessin, Delaware, where it sits today.

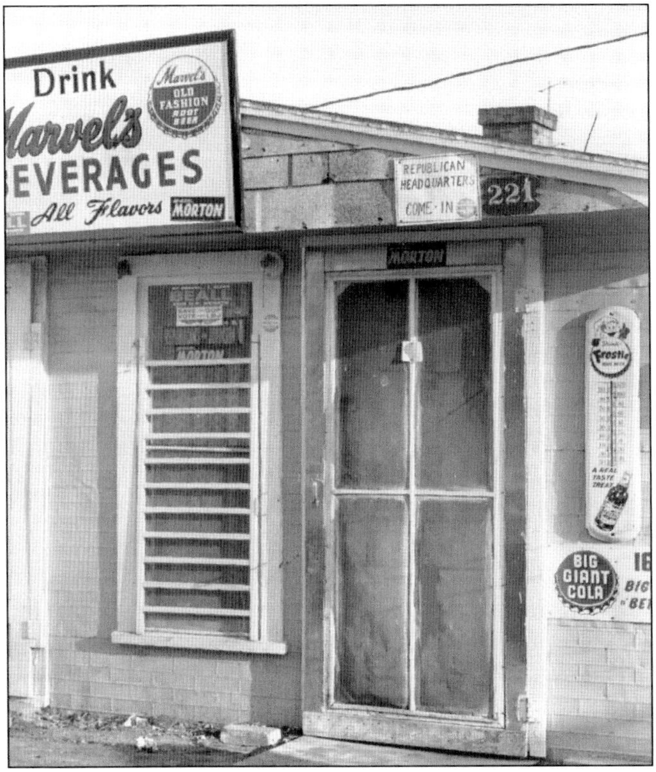

Time does change. Shown here is the Kent County Republican headquarters c. 1964.

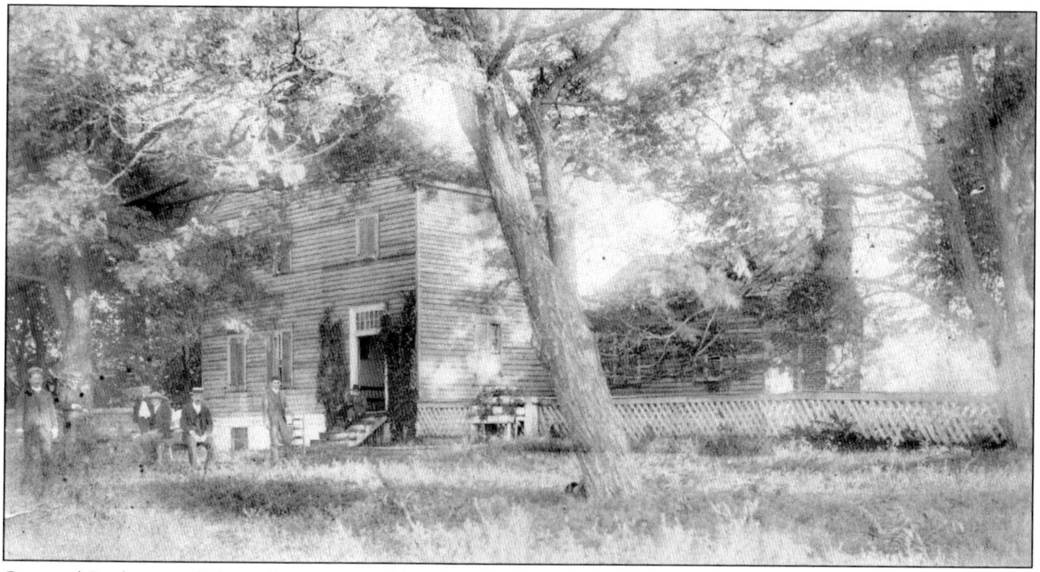

Samuel Jackson of Kent County and his five sons appear in this 1880 photograph. It appears Mr. Jackson had Southern sympathies during the War Between the States, since he named one son Samuel "Stonewall" Jackson.

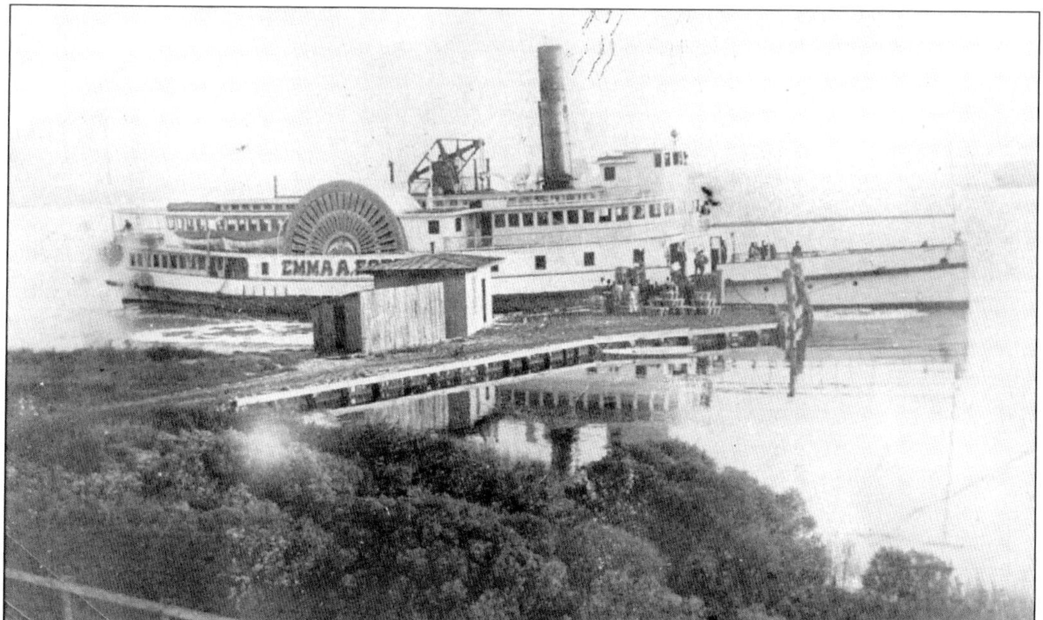

This photograph shows the steamer *Emma Giles* docked in Kent County, Maryland, at the turn of the 20th century.

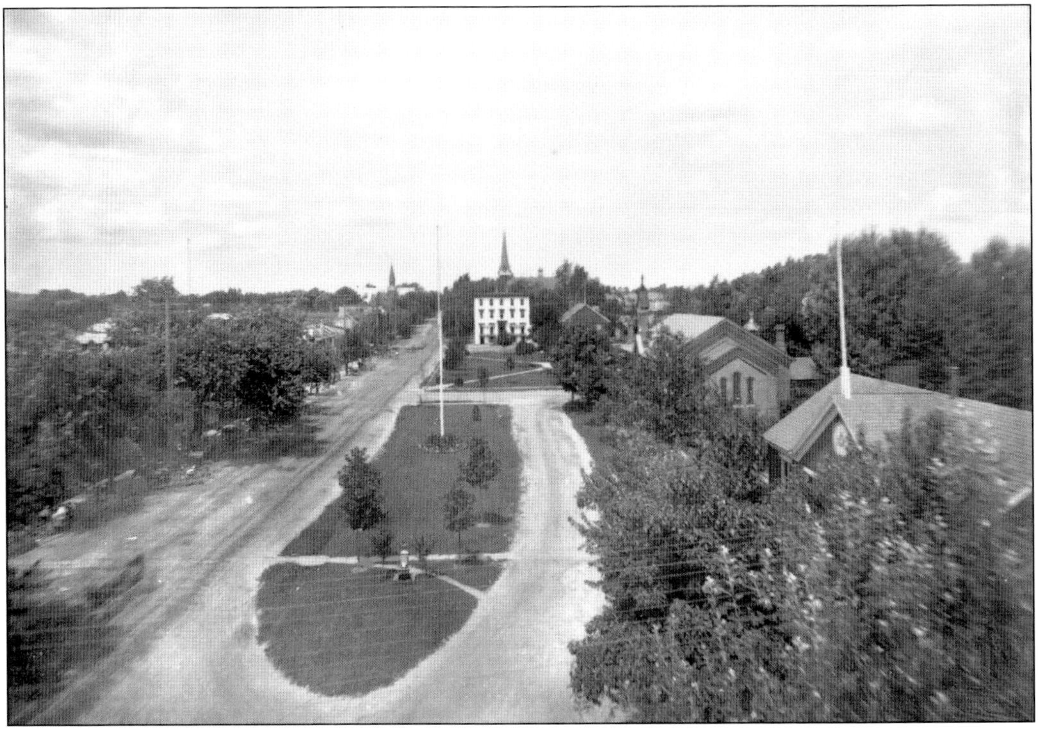

This is an aerial view of downtown Chestertown in the early 1920s.

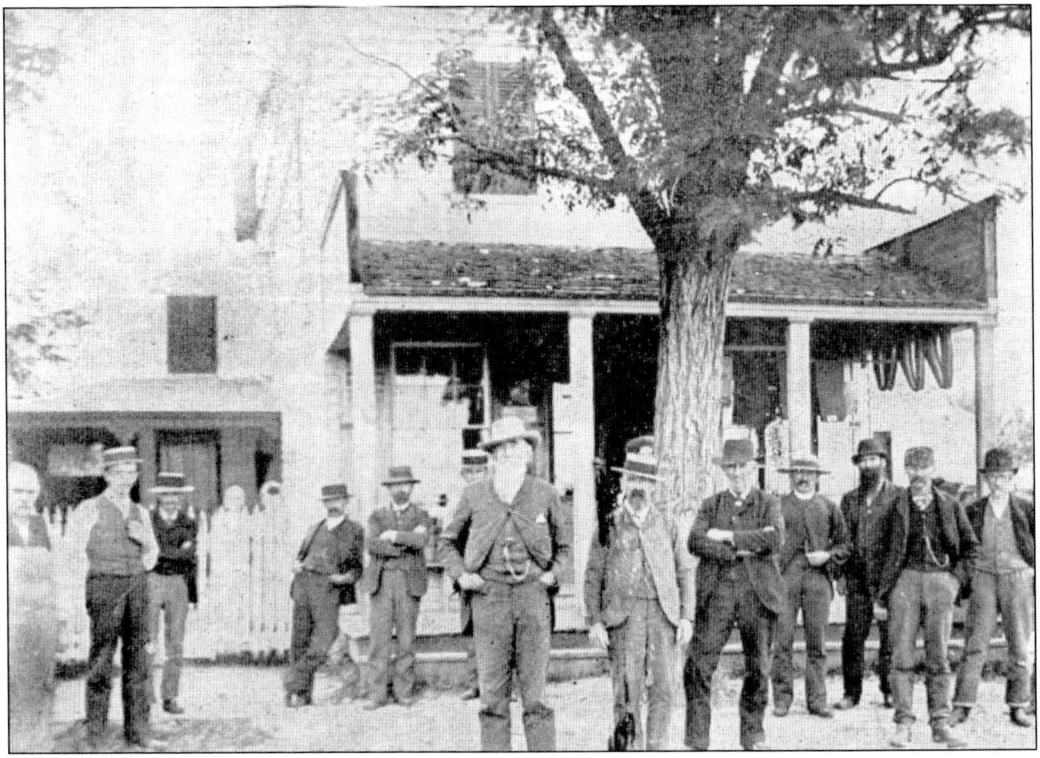

Democratic Party headquarters is pictured here at Edesville near Rock Hall.

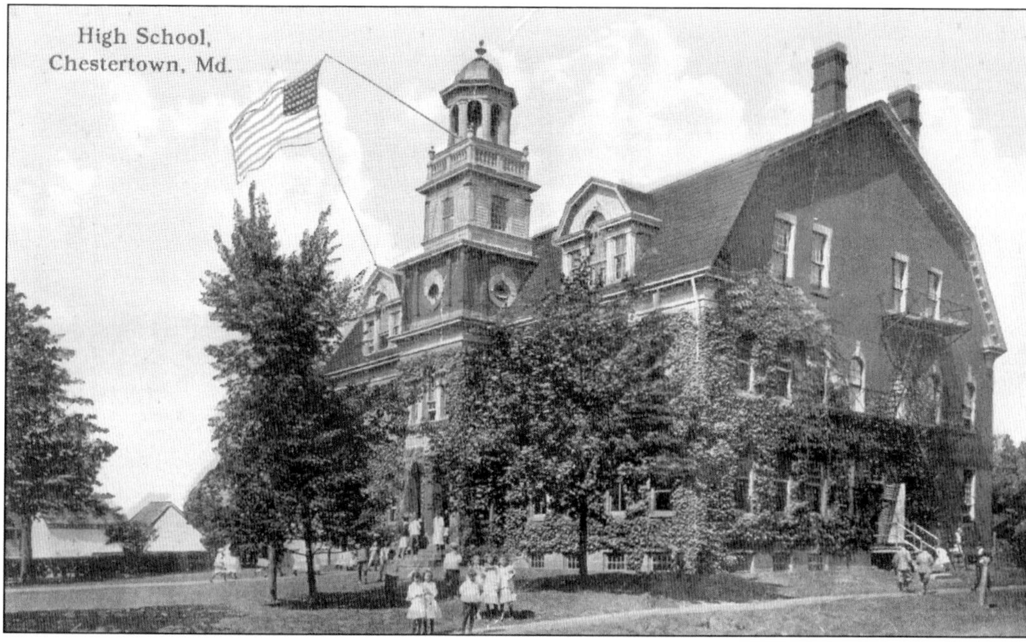

This image depicts the high school in Chestertown in the early 1900s. This building is now the home of the Kent County government offices.

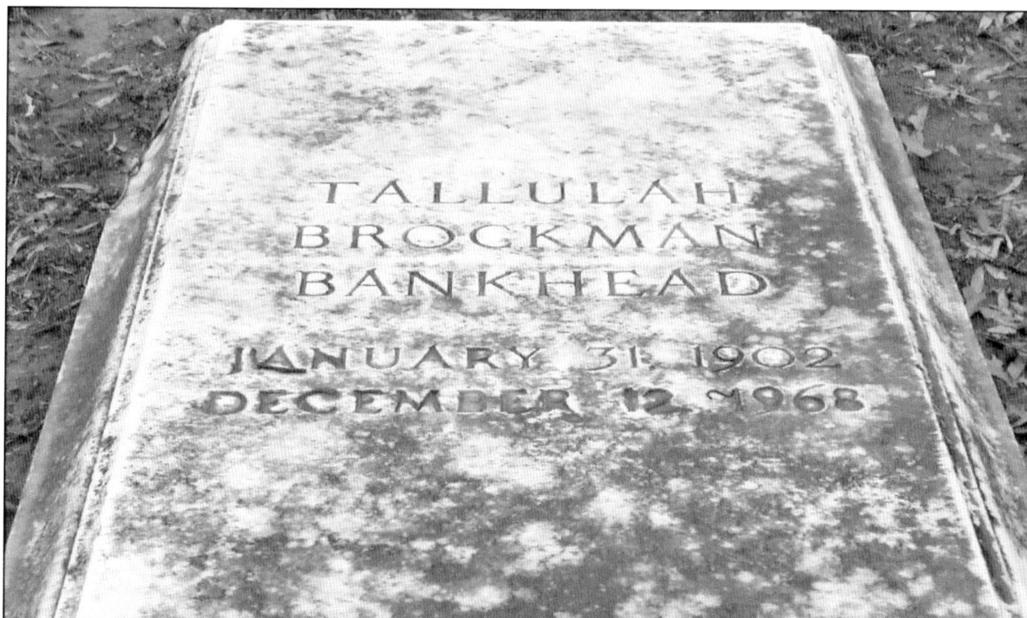

Famous actress Tallulah Brockman Bankhead is buried at Old St. Paul's Cemetery near Chestertown next to her sister, Eugenia. She was born January 31, 1902, and died December 12, 1968. Tallulah achieved stardom on stage, screen, radio, and television. Her career lasted from the 1920s through the 1960s. Her film credits include *Woman's Law, His House in Order, Tarnished Lady, My Sin, The Cheat, Thunder Below, Faithless, Make Me a Star, Devil and the Deep, Stage Door Canteen, Lifeboat, A Royal Scandal*, and *Die! Die! My Darling!* She was the most popular actress of London's famed West End, which is much like Broadway. She is also remembered for her famous "Dahling."

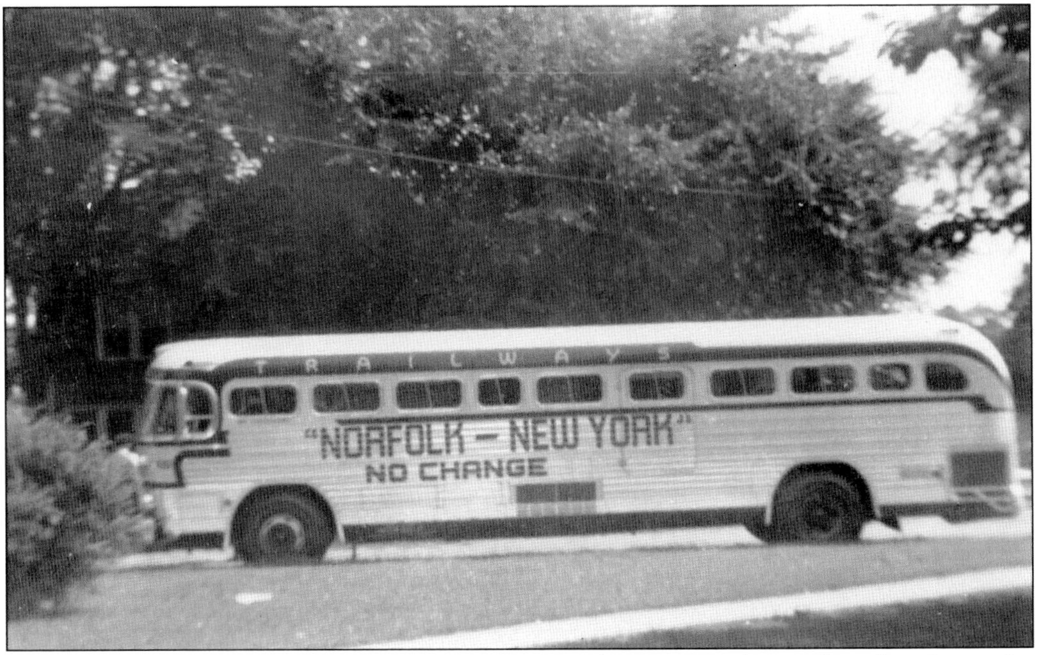

Trailways bus service was offered from Chestertown to locations to the north and to the south.

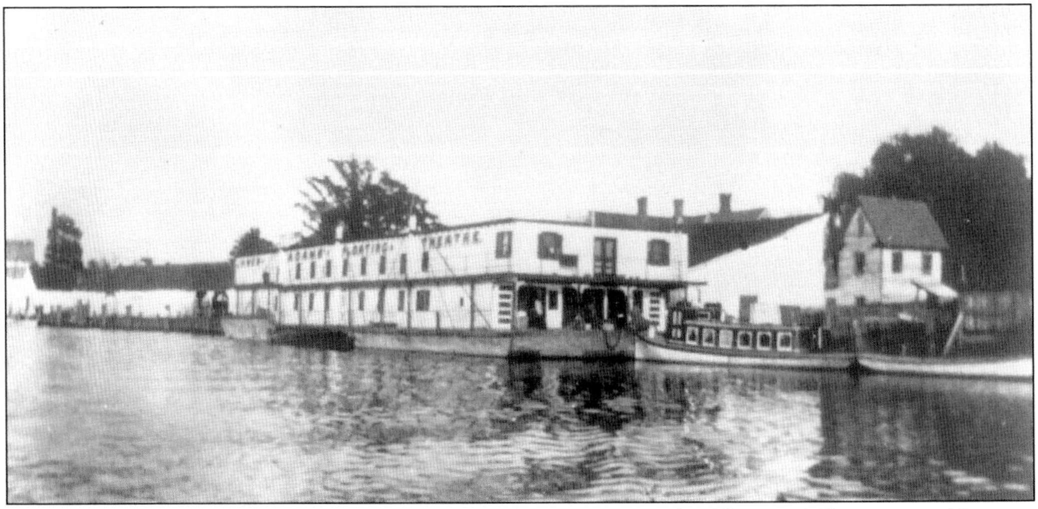
The Adams Floating Theatre docked on the Chester River. The Floating Theatre would go up river as far as Crumpton.

Pictured are those attending dedication ceremonies of the Frank M. Jarman American Legion Post Number 36 near Chestertown.

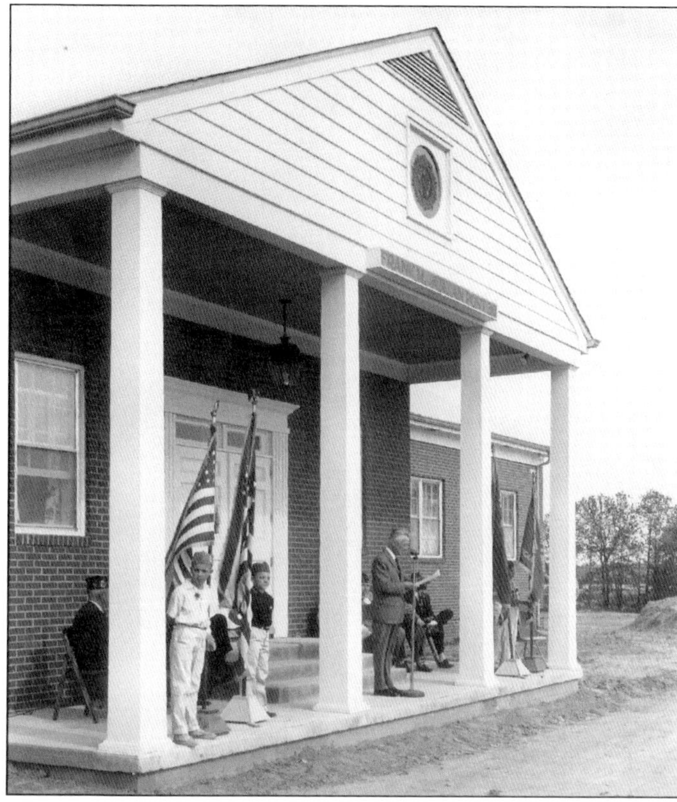

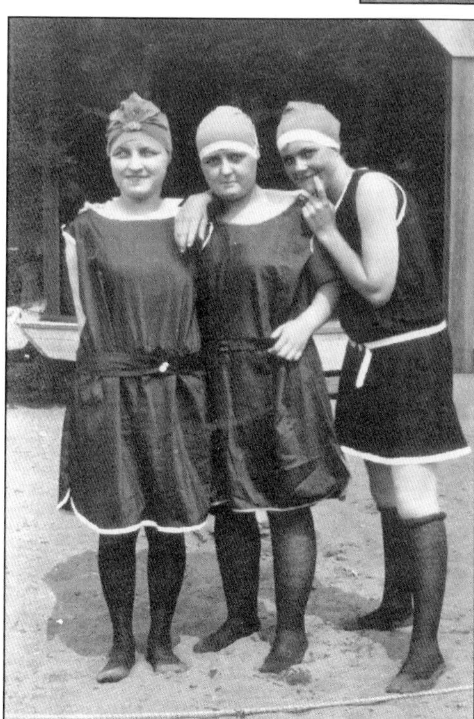

Bathing beauties at Betterton Beach stop for a minute for a quick pose in this 1923 photograph.

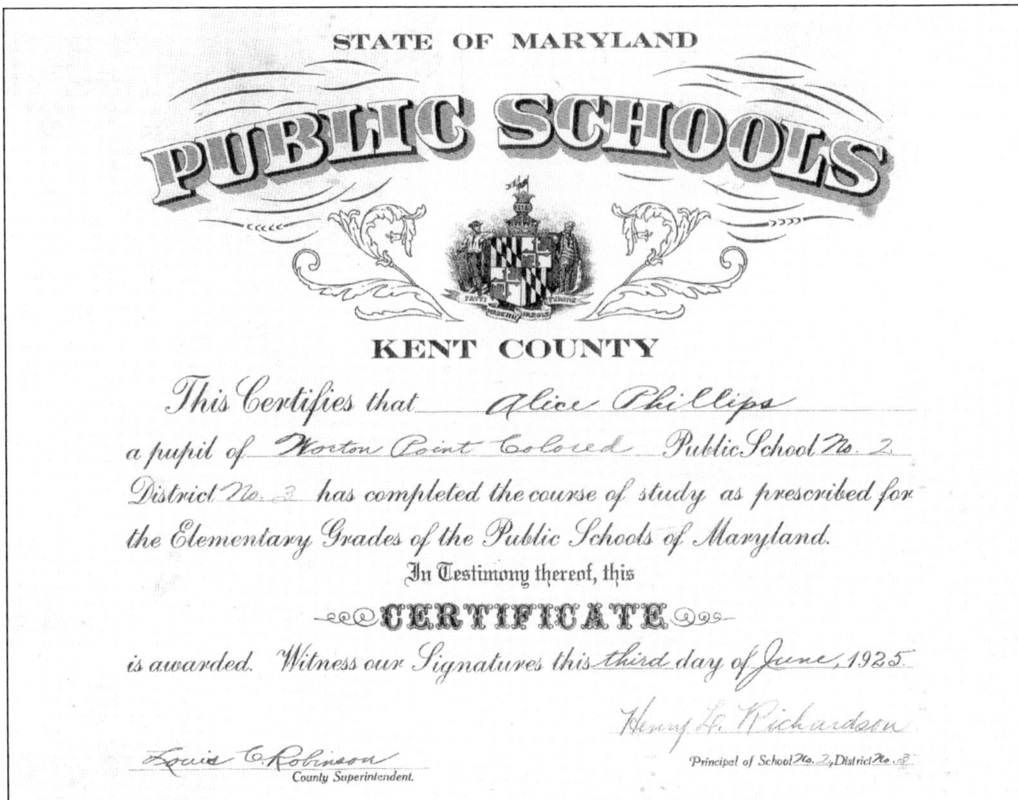

STATE OF MARYLAND

PUBLIC SCHOOLS

KENT COUNTY

This Certifies that Alice Phillips

a pupil of Worton Point Colored Public School No. 2

District No. 3 has completed the course of study as prescribed for the Elementary Grades of the Public Schools of Maryland.

In Testimony thereof, this

CERTIFICATE

is awarded. Witness our Signatures this third day of June, 1925.

Henry H. Richardson
Principal of School No. 2, District No. 3

Louis C. Robinson
County Superintendent.

Alice Phillips, a pupil of Worton Point Colored Public School No. 2, District No. 3 in Kent County, received this certificate for completing elementary school on June 23, 1925. It was signed by Louis C. Robinson, superintendent of schools for Kent County, and Henry Richardson, principal of the Worton Point Colored Public School No. 2, District No. 3.

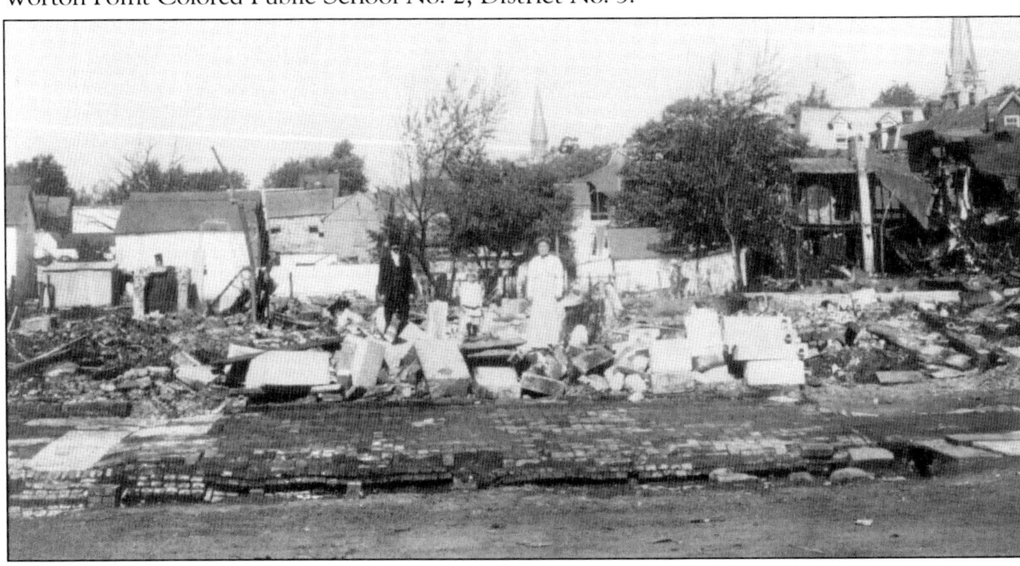

The Chestertown fire of 1910 wiped out the entire block across the street from the fire house. The Kirby family is standing where their house once stood.

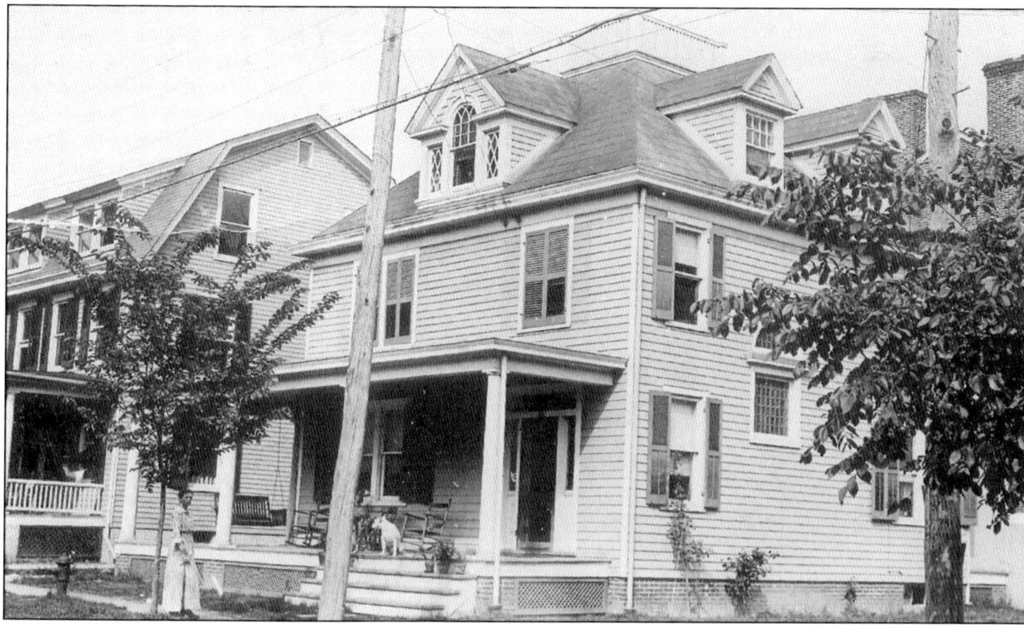

This house is located on the corner of Queen Street and Church Alley in Chestertown.

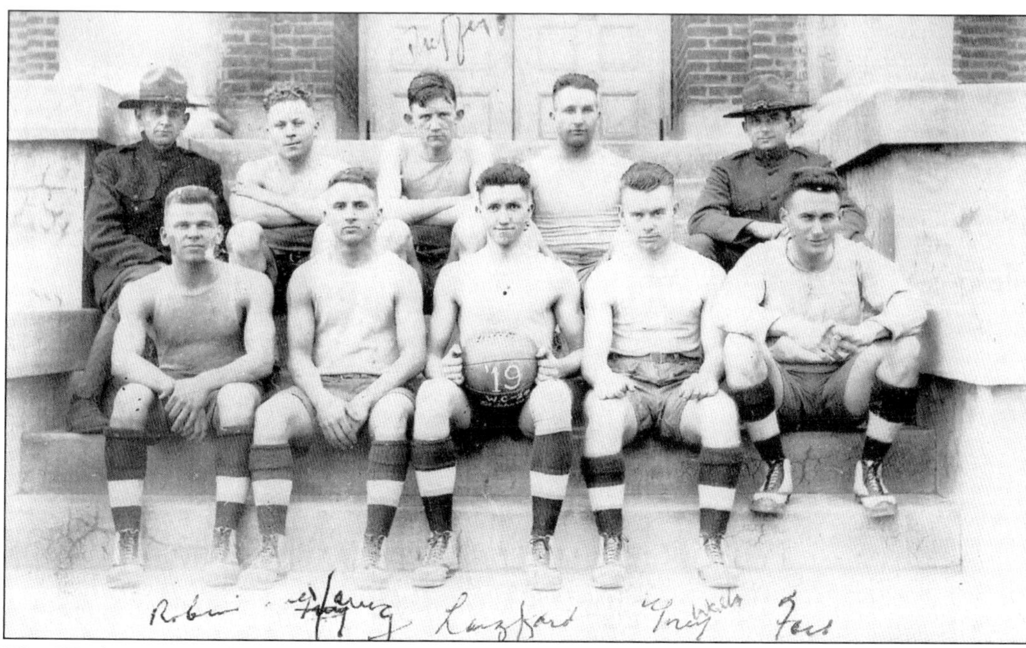

The Washington College basketball team is pictured just after the "war to end all wars" in this 1919 photograph.

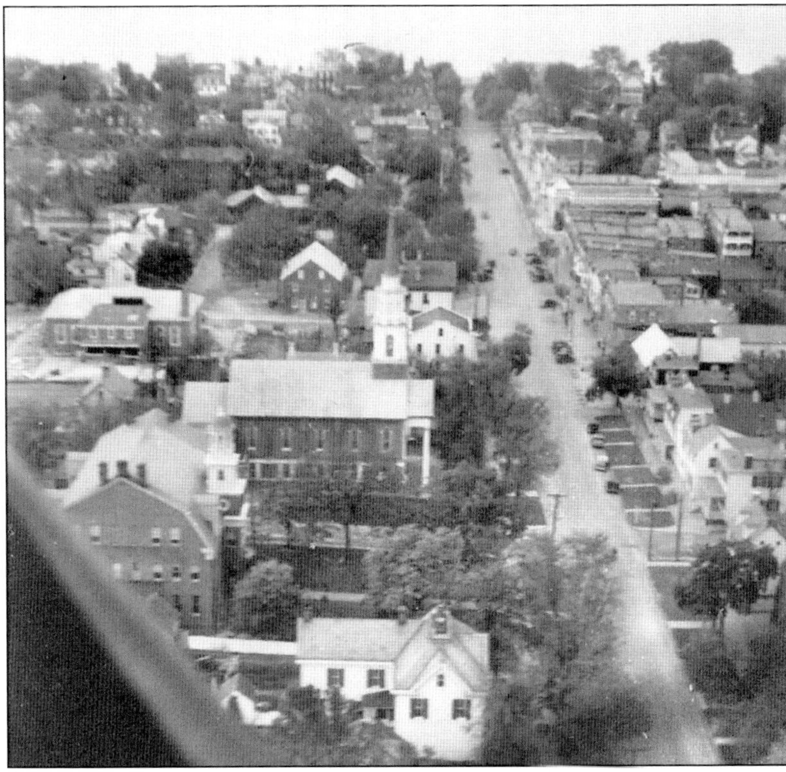

This view of High Street looking east in downtown Chestertown was taken years ago. The First Methodist Church is prominent on the left, as is the back of the current post office. The Voshell House is still in existence across from the old Market House, which is near the Nearly New Shop and owned by the hospital auxiliary.

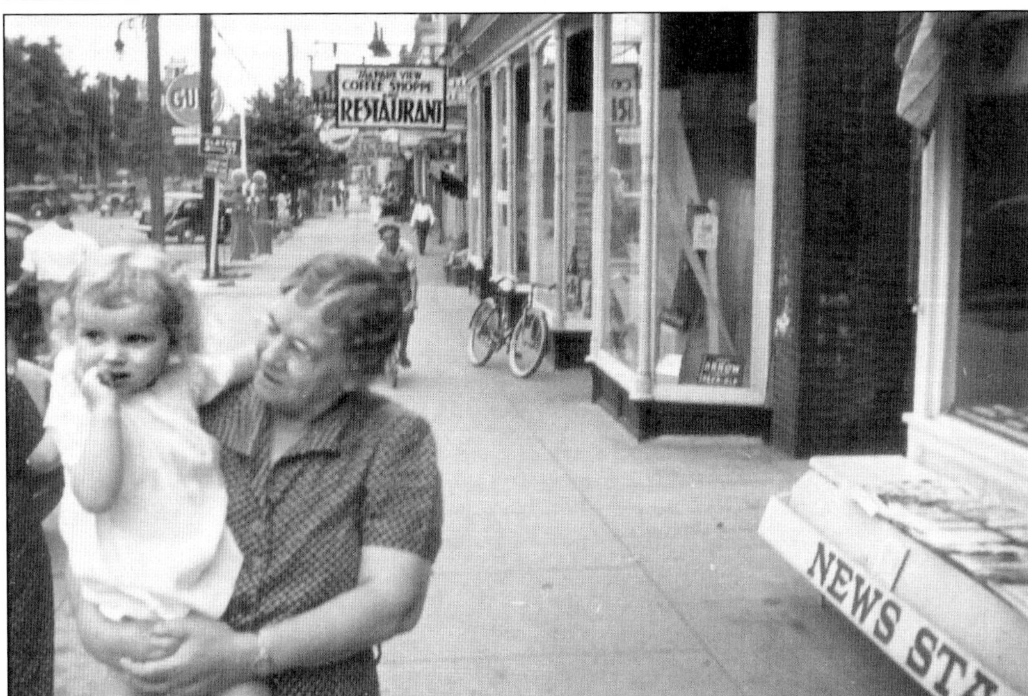

Mrs. Charles C. Schreiber of Schreiber's Wholesale and Retail Confectionery is standing in front of her business on High Street in downtown Chestertown. She is holding her granddaughter, Ann.

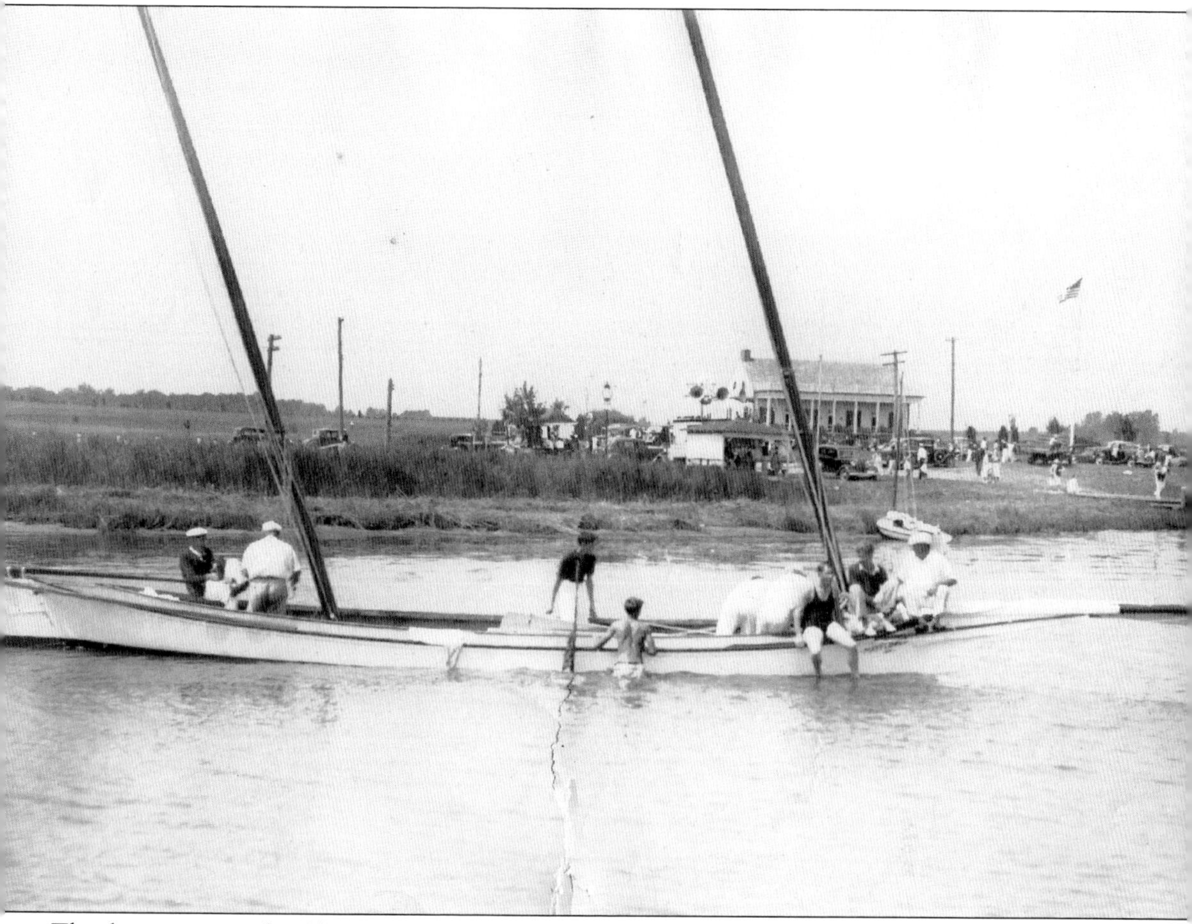

This log canoe on the Chester River is sitting in front of the Chester River Yacht and Country Club near Chestertown.

BIBLIOGRAPHY

Adams, Charles S. *Roadside Markers In Maryland*. Shepherdstown, WV: Charles S. Adams, 1997.

Bourne, Michael O. *Historic Houses of Kent County*. Chestertown, MD: The Historical Society of Kent County, Inc., 1998.

Brugger, Robert J. *Maryland, A Middle Temperament*. Baltimore: Johns Hopkins University Press, 1988.

Byron, Gilbert. *Captain John Smith Explores the Chesapeake*. Talbot County, MD: Historical Society of Talbot County, MD: 1960.

The Chestertown Story. Chestertown 250th Anniversary Program, 1956.

Danson, Edwin. *Drawing the Line: How Mason and Dixon Surveyed the Most Famous Border in America*. New York: John Wiley & Sons, Inc., 2001.

Dumschott, Fred W. *Emmanuel Episcopal Church 1772–1972*. Kent County, MD: Chester Parish, 1972.

———. *Washington College*. Chestertown, MD: Washington College, 1980.

First Parishes of the Province of Maryland. Programme of Services and Pilgrimages Commemorating the 250th Anniversary of the Establishment of the Thirty Original Parishes in the Province of Maryland in 1692 and the 150th Anniversary of the Consecration of the Right Reverend Thomas John Claggett, D.D., First Bishop to be Consecrated on American Soil. 1942.

Gannett, Henry. *A Gazetteer of Maryland and Delaware*. Baltimore: Genealogical Publishing Co., 1976.

Grier, Margot E. *Old St. Paul's Kent: Kent County, Maryland*. 1971.

Harrington, Norman. *Religion in America*. Easton, MD: Queen Anne's Press, 1980.

Horsey, Patricia Joan O. *Chestertown Maryland History 1978 through 1993, State of the Town Addresses*. Chestertown, MD: Delmarva Publications, 2004.

Horsey, Patricia O. and Kathleen B. White. *Chestertown, Maryland, An Inventory of Historic Sites*. Chestertown, MD: Town of Chestertown, 1981.

Janson-LaPalme, Robert. *Chestertown: An Architectural Guide*. Chestertown, MD: Town of Chestertown, 1985.

Kanely, Edna A. *Directory of Ministers and the Maryland Churches They Served 1634–1990*. Westminster, MD: Family Line Publications, 1991.

Kenny, Hamill. *The Placenames of Maryland, Their Origin and Meaning*. Maryland Historical Society, 1984.

Kent County Bicentennial Committee. *Kent County Guide*. Chestertown, MD, 1976.

Kent County Historic Trust Tour Brochures.

Kent County Tourism Office. *A Walking Tour of Old Chester Town*.

———. *Driving Tour of the Kent County Peninsula*.

"Lee Lawrie Statue to be Dedicated at 175th Anniversary." *The Elm*. April 3, 1957.

Papenfuse, Edward C. and Joseph M. Coale III. Maryland State Archives Atlas of *Historical Maps of Maryland 1608–1908*. Baltimore, MD: Johns Hopkins University Press, 2003.
Usilton, Fred G. *History of Kent County, Maryland 1630–1916*. Chestertown, MD: Perry Publications, 1980.
——— and William B. Usilton Jr. *Scenes in Old Kent and Chestertown*. Chestertown, MD: Perry Publications, 1982.

INDEX